ECOLOGICAL DEMOCRACY

By Roy Morrison

South End Press   Boston, MA

Cover by Beth Fortune
Text design and production by the South End Press collective
Printed in the U.S.A. on recycled paper

Library of Congress Cataloging-in-Publication Data
Morrison, Roy
Ecological Democracy/ Roy Morrison
    p. cm.
Includes index.
ISBN 0-89608-513-9 (alk. paper). —ISBN 0-89608-514-7
1. Environmentalism. 2. Social ecology. I. Title
GE195.M67   1995
363.7—dc20   95-8991
                                                   CIP

South End Press, 116 Saint Botolph Street, Boston, MA 02115
    01 00 99 98 97 96 95   1 2 3 4 5 6 7 8 9

Contents

To Jan and Sam

AUTHOR'S NOTE

FINISHING A BOOK is not simply the end of a marathon, an occasion for exhaustion, relief, and sometimes exhilaration. Book writing usually lacks the opportunity for measured strategy that the fixed nature of a predetermined course provides. Any piece of writing, no matter what its length or subject, must become, at least in part, a voyage of surprise and discovery for the writer as well as reader if it is to rise above the hackneyed and pedestrian.

Writing a book is the occasion not just for measured pace, but sudden sprints, unexpected climbs and descents. To finish the journey we must rely on the advice and kindness of both friends and strangers as well as the collegial wisdom and thoughtful efforts of those who have explored this terrain before.

I began writing this book, as I do many of my projects, at a small camp that Jan's family owns by the shores of Plunkett Lake in Hinsdale, MA in the summer of 1991. The first draft was completed shortly before the birth of our son Samuel Schaffer-Morrison on December 19, 1992. Most of the writing was done at the Davis house on Newmarket Road in Warner, NH, where we'd lived for several years.

We left the Davis house six months later. We moved into Phebe Bower's house in Webster as short-term tenants. Our friend Phebe had died suddenly that spring. Her family needed transitional tenants and we needed a refuge while our house was being built on Newmarket Road by our neighbors who are also skilled craftspeople.

While living at Phebe's, the book changed direction, both from the suggestions and guidance of editor Steve Chase and the deepening of my thinking about the nature of industrial society in transition. It became a more ambitious and, I hope, better work. In spring 1994 we moved into our new house and the book was finished in the summer of 1995 following the work by my friend Peter Solomon editing the final manuscript with compassionate skill, and by Sonia Shah of South End Press laboring with discipline and dedication to make *Ecological Democracy* a reality.

Of those who assisted me during the journey, I want to especially thank Paul Fleckenstein for his careful and thoughtful reading of early versions of much of the manuscript; my parents Helen and Leo Morrison, for their love and support; Peter Ladd for his incisive Thoreauvian vision; Bob Bower for his provocation to bring theory to practice; Doug Newton for his logger's scepticism and inventiveness; Nancy Ladd for her help as librarian and encouragement as friend; Arnie Alpert and Judy Elliot for their comments and insights; Brian Piecuch for his bravura efforts on the copying machine one desperate afternoon; Lena Canepa for her creative work caring for Sam while I wrote; Jan Schaffer for her love and friendship. Jan's my partner in life, and in raising our son Sam. Being Sam's dad is the best thing I've ever done.

The errors and shortcomings of this work, of course, are mine. Its strengths must be shared with many.

—Roy Morrison
Warner, NH
July 1995

PREFACE

THIS IS A BOOK ABOUT SOCIAL TRANSFORMATION, about building an ecological society from an industrial one. It is informed by more than economics, politics, and statistics. There is a certain optimism, a degree of adventure and risk and pleasure in my life that has inclined me toward thinking basic social change is possible. Before we launch this pursuit, I want to take a moment to explain, to cherish the flashes of possibility and freedom that are the sources of hope and of change.

I am a countryman by choice. I lived for about twenty-five years in New York City, but for more than twenty years I have made my home in northern New England. Warner, New Hampshire is hardly wilderness, but I can still walk for miles north or south from my house in woods, only occasionally crossing a road. Moose walk down Newmarket Road. There are many deer. Black bear stripped some of the apple and pear trees this year and ate a neighbor's lamb. But to the southwest, with the wind, I can hear the rumble from Interstate 89.

The Mink Hills, where I live, once hardscrabble farm, have turned back to forest: rough hills, folded over one another with shielded hemlock glades and many rocky glens, perfect shelter for animals. The swampy brook-fed hollows have marsh marigolds and moose. Porcupines, wild turkeys, woodcock seem to be everywhere. Hawks keep watch from the trees for the mice and voles. Snakes have taken up residence beneath the mulch hay in the garden; just outside the garden, for the last two springs, a baby deer has been born and lived its quiet early weeks. Owls call out fiercely in the night. Downy and pileated woodpeckers hammer on trees.

This is not wilderness, but it is alive, it is country filled with creatures living life in rough balance. Yesterday we dug 100 pounds of potatoes from the garden, laid the last of the pumpkins and squash on the stone walls to season. We made our crop when it was ready.

Building an ecological society means protecting and preserving wilderness and diversity. An ecological society rejects the industrial view of a world divided between wild and civilized, exploited and protected. An ecological society means embracing nature, re-creating our lives as conscious and sensuous human beings within a vibrant, living world. The wild is not something we have to travel to or a property to sell or to guard; the wild can touch us in the deepest heart of our cities. Building an ecological society means reviving the planet—creating wilderness corridors, greenbelts, and green spaces; turning toward the deepest values of nature, which are profoundly, powerfully human values as well.

This book is an exploration of the processes of ecological change. It addresses the often ponderous issues of economics and politics as matters of concern to ordinary people, as choices we make that shape our lives and the lives of our communities—and the lives of our children and, in grand passage, of our grandchildren's grandchildren. We live on the brink of millennial change, the change of civilizations. It is an adventure we did not seek, but it is an adventure that we cannot, and must not, ignore.

This book is about building better lives, creating and nurturing ecological communities, and transforming the world. I invite you to join with me in this adventure of building both freedom and community. It is the adventure of family, of pleasure, of rediscovering our lives. Come walk and climb and sit quietly with me.

chapter one

AN INTRODUCTION

THIS BOOK IS ABOUT FUNDAMENTAL CHANGE, about the movement from an industrial to an ecological civilization. It is a call for democracy, not better management or stronger authority. It is about making democracy itself once again a personal and community adventure in which, as Thomas Jefferson wrote in 1776, "we mutually pledge to each other our lives, our fortunes and our sacred honor."

We are amidst beginnings and endings. The Cold War is over, the threat of nuclear war has abated. A new global industrial order is taking shape. The United States of America stands as sole superpower and global political leader.

But these are also Dickensian times, times of heartbreak as well as hope. There is a pervasive unease throughout the countries that are called rich, although many of their citizens are far from that. They fear not only losing economic advantage; their malaise is also political, social, ecological, and moral. We've entered an age that is as yet nameless, referred to in terms of what it no longer is: post-communist, post-Cold War, postmodern. The capitalist triumphalism that greeted the lowering of the red flag above the Kremlin lasted months, not decades. Even as Francis Fukuyama[1] declared the end of history, history rendered a different opinion.

The Persian Gulf War, ethnic cleansing in the former Yugoslavia, and genocide in Rwanda quickly disabused us of illusions of a new Gilded Age or Pax Americana. But the problems are not confined to war or to political instability. For rich and poor, for both capitalism and socialism, business-as-usual is not sustainable. Business-as-usual means ever-escalating production, consumption, and pollution; business-as-usual means ecological catastrophe, militarism and war, inequality and famine.

The challenge we face is to transform a capitalist industrial present to an ecological future. Industrial civilization, with its inherent excesses, calls forth a welter of countervailing and potentially transforming ecological responses. This transformation depends on our actions and will be the work not of days or years, but of generations.

Our concern is with constructive change in response to industrial reality. This change must be shaped by choice in the context of democracy, choice based upon the exercise of freedom and the building of community. Our view is optimistic in recognizing that industrial reality can mean constructive change as well as chaos. But it rejects the notion of inevitable progress and historical fate. Industrial civilization may bring forth a turning toward an ecological civilization, but it will not do so without our conscious efforts.

It is possible to see, broadly speaking, three alternatives contesting for the future of industrial civilization.

First are attempts to continue and intensify what *is*, through the ever more aggressive elaboration of global management strategies. The guiding purpose of this alternative is to maintain industrial expansion until the last possible moment. This is the world of global markets and collapsing nations, of the North American Free Trade Agreement (NAFTA) and the General Agreement on Tariffs and Trade (GATT).

Second is the rise of a new authoritarianism, the embrace of a tyrannical order and the state in the vain hope of alleviating the excesses of industrial modernity. This is the world of ethnic cleansing, theocracy, and neofascism.

Third is the pursuit of an ecological and democratic path that allows individual and social choices at first to limit, and ultimately to transform, industrial civilization. This is a world of unity in diversity, of voluntary cooperation, guided by the desire to sustain and protect intertwined natural and human ecologies. This alternative will affect the way we govern, our economic relationships, our perception and understanding of the world and each other.

A Declaration of Interdependence

An ecological democracy is rooted in the understanding that freedom and community are indivisible. This understanding resolves the libertarian/communitarian antimony: it embraces both individual rights and the community structures that protect those rights. Freedom is not the unrestrained action of individuals, limited only by its negative effect on others—my freedom to move my arm ends where your nose, or your fear for your nose, begins. Rather, freedom is both positive and negative—freedom to swing and freedom from being bopped. We seek not only the negative rights of freedom from government interference, but rights of action.

Freedom must also be understood in the context of political, social, and community rights. This understanding of freedom is not unique to ecological democracy. Indeed, modern democratic political freedom arose from the combination of individual and community. Thomas Jefferson wrote in the Declaration of Independence in 1776, "We hold these truths to be self-evident, that all men are created equal, that they are endowed by their Creator with certain unalienable rights, that among these are life, liberty, and the pursuit of happiness."

The Declaration bears the contradictions of its time: Jefferson was a slave owner; only men were asked to sign the Declaration; and the pursuit of happiness was soon elided to the pursuit of private wealth. Still, the Declaration of Independence is a towering assertion of community rights and responsibilities: the independence declared was not merely that of individuals, but of communities, of the thirteen colonies that became "FREE AND INDEPENDENT STATES" (emphasis in original). The Declaration's case against the Crown is a community case, and the Declaration begins with a ringing statement of community:

> When in the course of human events it becomes necessary for one people to dissolve the political bands which have connected them with another, and to assume among the powers of the earth, the separate and equal station to which the laws of nature and nature's G-d entitle them, a decent respect to the opinions of mankind requires that they should declare the causes which impel them to the separation.

Of the Declaration's thirty-two paragraphs, twenty-nine detail the violation by the King and his government of communal, not simply individual, rights, beginning with: "He [King George] has refused his assent to laws, the most wholesome and necessary for the public good." (See Appendix for the full text of the Declaration.)

Certainly, there are tensions between the individual and group inherent in the pursuit of freedom and community. Indeed, one could say that the essential task of democracy is not for an elected elite to govern, but for limited government to justly help equilibrate tensions between the individual and group. So Jefferson offered not only a statement of individual rights, but the assertion that "governments to secure those rights are instituted by consent of the governed." As the next paragraph in the Declaration makes clear, this statement is not merely a prescription for association between individuals that foreshadows a market society of contracts; Jefferson is addressing *individuals in community:*

> That whenever any form of government becomes destructive
> of these ends, it is the right of the people to alter or abolish it,
> and to institute new government, laying its foundations on
> such principles and organizing its powers in such form, as to
> them shall seem most likely to effect their safety and happiness.

This position is a reasoned understanding of the relationship between freedom and community. It is a call to resolve common problems through community democratic action. It reflects the common wisdom of people living in an agricultural society, as well as Jefferson's eloquence. It is also a clear message for us living 220 years later in an industrial society.

Thus, ecological democracy is conservative in that it rests upon a revitalization of fundamental democratic values; it is radical in that it seeks the transformation of the industrial imperatives of production and consumption, profit and power.

Building an Ecological Democracy

In trying to engage the complex question of ecological and democratic transformation, I reject both narrow reforms and simple determinism—whether economic, biological, or philosophical. Building an ecological democracy is not a matter of finding a technological fix. True, in trying to consider this question with due regard for its intricacy, I risk not seeing the forest of social transformation for the wonder of the trees. And it is also true that for social change to take place we *do* need elegant simplicity: our task is to clarify and demystify. But simplicity does not mean embracing reductionism.

A focus on economic reform, for instance, is likely to be hobbled by the very industrial definitions and constraints that must be changed. The economic realm as we know it is, after all, the creation of industrial society; so we must move beyond the economic realm. Transforming a civilization is a matter of a grand confluence of actions and causes, a matrix of shifting and interacting influences and circumstances. It requires a departure from the economic thinking of industrialism. Ecological and democratic transformation challenges the determinism of economics by bringing forward the forces of community and democracy, which under industrialism are subordinate to the power of markets and plans.

Let us begin by introducing six basic areas that structure the nature of our exploration:

- Industrialism
- Ecological civilization
- The economic system of an ecological society
- The ecological commons
- Sustainability
- Ecological democracy

The discussion that follows is not offered as complete or defining, but as a way to help engage the crucial issues; these comments represent points of entry, not closed doors.

Industrialism

The term *industrialism* does not merely refer to a systematized form of machine production. It is a way of organizing the world and the lives of those who live in the world. Industrial civilization is a global system of economic, political, and social power; and it is everywhere characterized by two central imperatives: to maximize production and consumption, and to maximize profit and/or power. The industrial march and industrial malaise is global.

To name a civilization is to plant a flag, to claim mastery: "industrial civilization" is an assertion not just of being, but of becoming, an affirmation of dominance that attempts to mortgage the future as well as make a claim upon the past.[2] With astonishing arrogance, industrial civilization reduces all the world's substance to "resources" to feed the production machine, all the world's people to "customers" and "workers." The attempt to continue forever the growth of production and consumption is deeply contemptuous of life.

We are no longer denizens of a sensuous, living world where we wrestle to maintain a rough balance between wild and home, but customers at theme parks. Extended families implode like dwarf stars, colliding into a pinched existence as individual producers and consumers. Our industrial lives are supposed to find meaning in the shopping mall, in the consumption of televised spectacle, in the purchase of the accoutrements that constitute lifestyles. But beyond the spectacle of making and using, the real life of industrialism grinds on.

The negative consequences of industrial practices are called "externalities," as if the poisoner had not intended the death of the victim. But the degradation of the living world is not simply a preventable accident; it is the unavoidable consequence of the pursuit of the fundamental industrial imperatives. This assault goes beyond destruction of habitat and the extinction of species to every aspect of life. Our problem is more social than technical; salvation from industrialism is not about to be delivered by market forces and scientific progress. Industrialism seeks maximization, not equilibrium.

This is reflected in both capitalist and communist industrialism. Capitalism privileges the individual and profit, communism the group and power. Their dynamics differ, but the failures of one do not mitigate the failures of the other. Both pursue industrial ends through industrial means; both are guided by a common underlying ideology based on three elements: hierarchy, progress, and technique, linked to form the steel triangle of industrialism.

- *Hierarchy* is the basic industrial ordering principle. Industrial hierarchies rest not on caste or class, but on success in fulfilling industrial imperatives.

- *Progress* is industrial society's way of identifying all industrial change as good, almost without regard for consequences.

- *Technique*—that is, science, technology, bureaucracy—is the fruit of instrumental reason put at the service of industrial hierarchies. Industrial society presents technique as the nearly magical materialization of inevitable scientific forces—the H-bomb and automobile culture made flesh.

Industrialism is unsustainable not merely because it is committed to endless growth, but because of its inherent tendency toward war. Industrialism's huge surpluses are squandered to a remarkable extent on war and preparation for war; war expands and maintains elites and the hierarchical social structures they rule. This association with war exposes the emptiness of the myth of the market. War is not the result of market failure. War, as has been noted, is the health of the state, particularly of the industrial state where spending on war serves not only the recognized function of military Keynesianism (to stimulate demand through military deficit spending), but as the unparalleled expression of industrialism: the exercise of hierarchy using technology justified by a doctrine of progress, all raised to a high pitch in the wars of industrialism against the "enslaving," "backward" forces of fascism/capitalism/communism/fundamentalism.

With the growth of global markets and the weakening of the nation state, industrial civilization has entered a new phase. The nation state, long the anchor of industrialism and sponsor of expansion for both capitalism and socialism, is no longer capable of filling the demands for still more growth. The outstanding feature of this new world market is not trade, but a flow of speculative financial capital moving at light speed at the rate of $1 trillion a day.

Although we live in a post-Cold War, post-communist world, our world has not become more peaceful, but is full of grave instability. The nation state, driven by industrial imperatives, tries to move beyond its historical role and rise to a grander agglomeration of power, even as it faces the damage unleashed by centuries of heedless industrial practice. As we shall see, one response to the centrifugal forces afflicting the world has been the rise of authoritarianism, a desperate attempt to war against the culture of modernity.

Ecological Civilization

An ecological civilization is based on diverse lifeways sustaining linked natural and social ecologies. Such a civilization has two fundamental attributes. First, it looks at human life in terms of a dynamic and sustainable equilibrium within a flourishing living world: humanity is not at war with nature, but exists within nature. Second, an ecological civilization means basic change in the way we live: it depends upon our ability to make new social choices. It will not be established by an act of Congress, created by the management of industrial enterprise, or imposed by authoritarianism; it is not based on regulation, green consumerism, or shopping for a better world.

Building such a civilization will involve a change that could be as significant as the transformation from an agricultural to an industrial civilization. Change, of course, is inevitable. Industrial societies are preeminent vehicles for a continuous process of what Joseph Schumpeter called, referring to capitalism, "creative destruction."[3] The question we face is not whether to change, but the nature of the changes sweeping over our world.

An ecological civilization is not a prescription for order, but a description of the arrangement of disparate societies, of the exquisitely complex web of their relationships with one another and with the biosphere. The creation and building of ecological societies is a task for each of us, starting today, starting here. We can no longer treat nature and culture as independent realms. Basic change in our relationship to the living world depends absolutely upon basic change in our relationship to others, that is, upon social or human ecology. Our concern is not to control nature and each other, but to live in harmony with nature and each other.

An ecological civilization means time for our families, for love, for art, for pleasure, for rambling in the wilderness, and for the diversity of cities as friendly, healthy, and dynamic places to live. An ecological civilization is predicated upon the ability of civil society to create a wide range of voluntary social forms that allow democratic choices to creatively limit and transform industrialism. This means the revitalization of community through a process of social and economic empowerment. Civil society, in this sense, stands outside the ruling hierarchies of the state and the corporation. Civil society represents the realm of community institutions and social movements; it is the source of the ecological commons, the social space of an ecological civilization.

An ecological civilization is built upon three interdependent pillars: democracy, balance, and harmony.

Democracy means free choice, based upon the ability to make clear decisions about the issues that affect our lives. Classically, democracy means one person-one vote, but it can also mean consensus. An ecological society is a free society, but this is freedom in the context of responsibility and self-management. Democracy in an ecological society is meaningless without strong family and community ties, as well as individual rights.

Balance in an ecological society rests upon the pursuit and maintenance of freedom and community: enduring freedom requires community; true community demands freedom; this is the social concomitant of the basic ecological principle of unity in diversity. The sense of community extends from the social to the living world. Balance also means justice: an ecological society cannot exist in a world of the wealthy few and the impoverished many. Justice does not mean absolute equality, but sufficient resources and the ability to live freely in healthy communities for all.

Harmony does not mean the absence of struggle or conflict, but the ongoing pursuit of a dynamic equilibrium between and among individuals and the groups and associations that shape an ecological society. Harmony rests upon the ability to articulate and understand needs, and to search for points of agreement. In an ecological society, harmony also means striving to include the voices and values of the living world.

In an ecological society, some areas of our lives will expand, others will contract. For example, we will spend more time in family and community relationships, and fewer hours in mandatory work. We will use far more renewable resource technologies, and far less fossil fuels and nuclear power.

The global reach of industrialism makes it necessary to think of a global ecological civilization. We live and work in particular societies, but we cannot hope to build durable ecological islands surrounded by the poisoned world of industrialism. We must not only think globally and act locally. Sometimes we must act globally as well.

The Economic System and An Ecological Society

The economic and social life of an ecological civilization is shaped and organized by an ecological or "green" market and planning system. Such a system is not designed in advance—it is lived. It reflects the social choices made to transform the conduct of industrialism by changing corporate and statist economies to a community-centered economics. An ecological economic system develops, as we shall see, contemporaneously with the ecological commons.

"Community-centered economics" means our jobs have a real connection to our communities and their well-being. This is an economy of small businesses, cooperatives, community-based non-profit groups, and local government organizations. Business, banking, educational, and social institutions are owned and controlled in the community. Confederations and associations of community enterprises,   institutions, and local government make and implement community plans. On state, regional, national, and international levels, confederations shape appropriate plans to condition and guide the conduct of an ecological market system.

We look to democratic, community-based planning because neither the market nor state planning has proven able to govern industrial civilization. Market exchange—no matter how free—has not protected and strengthened the social and natural ecologies. Similarly, comprehensive planning has been accompanied by the growth of centralized bureaucracies that pursue the industrial goals of the ruling hierarchy. The proof of the failure of markets and planning is the reality of ecological and social misery. This reality suggests the need for a balance of market and planning to guide the transition to an ecological society.

This idea is nothing new: both capitalist and socialist industrialism, behind the ideologies, are in fact mixed market and planning systems. But in an ecological society, new democratic social choices and ecological ethics guide and condition market exchange and planning. These choices are based not on some mythical consumer need, but on real community sovereignty; they are choices that touch all aspects of our lives, not only decisions about what things are made, and how things are made and used.

In its details, then, an ecological or "green" economy involves community-based, voluntary market exchange, combined with decentralized, democratic political mediation and planning that flows from the grassroots. Market and planning mechanisms cannot be separated from each other, or from the political system. It is a self-serving industrial conceit to believe that decisions about monetary and fiscal policy, for example, are technical economic matters. A market without democratic planning is brain-dead. Planning without free exchange creates hierarchies and undermines democracy and community.

A community-centered economics challenges the fundamental assumptions of an industrial political economy. It not only challenges the industrial dogma that the economic realm can be separated from the political realm, and that political democracy can exist without economic democracy; it also argues that the human needs of the majority must not be kept subservient to the economic needs of the minority. Industrialism—capitalist or socialist—holds that the choice of market or planning determines the nature of society: capitalist industrial society promotes the market, socialist industrial society the plan. These beliefs are fairy tales—especially in their unquestioning acceptance of the need to pursue industrial ends; in staying blind to the manifest misery of the many; in identifying industrial means and ends with the desirable form of economic, political, and social organization.

Our exploration of community economics in Chapter Seven will focus on three existing social systems in market economies: the Mondragon cooperative system in the Basque region of Spain, Co-op Atlantic in Canada's easternmost provinces, and the Seikatsu Cooperative Club of Japan. These groups offer evocative examples of emergent systems capable of making new social choices to limit and transform industrial society. Their importance is not merely in their economic dynamism—they represent ecological democracy in action. They do not represent the limits of possibility, nor are they necessarily models; they are heartening examples of what is possible *now*.

The Ecological Commons

The growth of an ecological society is predicated upon a new locus for social action and social meaning: the ecological commons is the necessary community response to industrial excess, the arena in which ecological principle can become practice.

An ecological commons is a social space or realm of activity. It is the product of formal and informal agreements and social choices made by individuals and their communities to shape, guide, limit, and transform industrialism. The ecological commons protects the social and natural ecologies, and facilitates the creation and growth of the social matrix of an ecological society.

In a sense, this idea is an extension of the traditional notion of a commons as a shared physical space, such as the grazing commons (e.g., Boston Commons), or the common air we breathe or the water we drink. The ecological commons embraces what is significant about the traditional commons—not simply its physical reality or its resources, but the social relations that support its well-being. The ecological commons must be understood as not only an economic, but also a community-centered social and political entity.

Industrialism looks at individual things and their disposition. An ecological commons looks at relationships and their elaboration. An ecological commons may be created from and associated with a particular geographical region, or it may be entirely or largely immaterial—for example, in electronic cyberspace. Its community may be a neighborhood, town, region, nation, continent, or the entire planet. Ecological commons can be nested within one another, overlap, exist in parallel, or exist in more or less splendid isolation. (A social commons need not be ecological: the capitalist market is decidedly a non-ecological commons.)

The ecological commons represents a new intermediate form of social organization, located between the community and larger entities. It is a logical response to both the centrifugal and atomizing forces dividing communities and breaking down nations, and to the centripetal and integrative forces pushed by global management and supranational entities. It corresponds to the unity in diversity that characterizes the ecology of healthy living systems; it expresses freedom and community in contrast to the oppressive hierarchies of industrial progress. Industrialism orders and counts; the ecological commons liberates and catalyzes change.

An ecological commons is rooted not in any particular form of ownership, but bound by a balance between our right to use the commons and our responsibility to maintain it as individuals and communities. The commons is built on agreements and participation, not on the notions of state monopoly of force and exclusivity of citizenship. In this way, the ecological commons represents a peace system to replace the war system that characterizes the industrial state.

For example, a rural commons would attempt to balance farming and logging activities by managing them on a sustainable basis. This balancing could mean building long-term values by organic agriculture that is both nonpoisonous and less expensive than petrochemical farming. Farmers might also develop direct relations with city customers in a community supported agriculture plan, where customers provide the farmers with working capital and, in return, receive the produce. Agricultural efforts might also include food-processing and transport co-ops. Similarly, forestry would not just involve sustainable, selective cutting and rotation, but would also include protection of wild area corridors, and development of cooperative venues for milling and manufacture.

The creation of this community commons is predicated upon community-based, as opposed to transnational-corporate or national government, control. The legal and technical means to turn corporations into community-based enterprises are largely in existence, such as the use of Employee Stock Ownership Programs (ESOPs) in the United States. Through payroll deductions, ESOPs allow employees to become owners, and owners to receive favorable tax treatment. When democratically structured, ESOPs are a powerful tool for building community.

Governance of a system based on relationships between and among commons would reflect the gradual expansion of civil society and the gradual devolution of nation states, as well as the revivification of cities, neighborhoods, and regions (bio-regions and others). Over time, a revitalized civil society would challenge and supplant the centralized instrumentalities of industrial power, as the growth of a civil society once challenged the hegemony of feudal hierarchs and, more recently, the communist *nomenklatura*.

An ecological civilization implies a radical democratization of existing government structures.* The basic integrity and self-management of each commons would call for participatory and democratic structures at all levels from town to state to nation and beyond, guided by an ecological ethics. An ecological ethics is rooted in the common respect for common survival. Such a system is the antidote to the counterfeit "global interests"—aptly described by Vandana Shiva as the "globalized local"[4]—used to justify the further aggrandizement of the industrial state and the corporation. Thus, the imposition of giant hydrodams, nuclear and coal-fired power plants, road building, industrialized agriculture and aquaculture, and the full panoply of industrial infrastructure are described by promoters as being economically, socially, and environmentally beneficial.

A Sustainable Society

An ecological society is a sustainable society. Such a society considers growth and change in the context of the need to nurture the inextricably linked human and natural ecologies. To speak of this goal is to express a broad guiding principle, not to offer a

---

*The increase in social complexity reflected by the elaboration of the ecological commons marks the reversal of global industrialization as an ordering and homogenizing force. The strains on that order are clearly reflected in the rise of identity politics, and in the devolution of nations and empires, but it is equally clear that such forces do not necessarily lead—as the agonies of Bosnia sadly demonstrate—to an ecological end. The result of such tendencies is a matter for social practice. The swift collapse of the former Soviet Union briefly reflected, in the terms of nonviolent theorist Gene Sharp,[5] a sudden, enormous, and decisive withdrawal of consent from industrialism's most brittle and unitary system. This cannot be called an enduring victory for industrial capitalism: industrial socialism merely collapsed first. We await the fall of the other, and much heavier, shoe.

universal mandate. Sustainability means making political, social, and ethical choices. An ecological democracy would likely not choose to sustain, for example, the HIV virus or Nazism.

"Sustained growth" is a cruel falsehood if it just means increasing production and consumption: on a finite planet, ultimately, such growth is a physical impossibility. Talking about growth with no context is meaningless: growth can be good or bad or irrelevant; it must be judged in terms of its effects on people and nature, not in terms of the cash value of goods and services. Increased spending on nuclear weapons and increased spending on preventive health care services both contribute to the Gross National Product (GNP), but only one is of any value in a society concerned with human welfare.

For the industrial establishment, "sustainable" refers primarily to the ability to use a particular resource for an unspecified period. But real sustainability is a broad social question: "resources," as Wolfgang Sachs and his cohorts point out,[6] are the creation of industrial ideology, a concept that rationalizes exploitation.

Arguing with industrialists on their own terms about the wisdom of sustainability resembles the well-reasoned polemic in *Foreign Affairs* in the early 1980s, when Carl Sagan and others sought to convince the nuclear-war-fighting establishment that it would be prudent to reduce nuclear arsenals below the total megatonnage that could trigger nuclear winter. Similarly, when British economist Michael Jacobs holds that "sustainability is an *ethical* concept,"[7] he bases his argument for equity on the very industrial notion that "future generations should be left the opportunity to experience a level of environmental consumption equal to that of the present generation."

However ingenious these arguments may be, true sustainability means basic change. Changes at the margin and reforms, modest or radical, are useful, but a sustainable society must break the automatic identification of quantitative growth with social and economic good. A sustainable society is concerned with quality of life, not just with a balance sheet where life is cheap or valueless; the ecological commons raises questions of quality aside from the brute fixation upon quantity without regard to effect or equity. Industrialism, on the other hand, is supremely confident that quantity will translate into qualitative benefit for all—witness the ceaseless prattle about GNP as a reliable representation of economic and social well-being.

A truly sustainable society has enormous implications for both the industrialized and the industrializing world. In a sustainable world, no one can continue to burn fossil fuels and dump toxic wastes as citizens of the United States, Western Europe, and Japan do today. The world cannot support a country like the United States, with 6 percent of the world's population consuming 30 percent of the world's industrial resources. Moreover, the growth in resource use cannot keep pace with population growth. World population is expected to reach six billion in the year 2000; use of steel at current European per capita levels would require a 140-fold increase in steel production.[8] In other words, the destructive appetites of the industrialized states must be transformed into ecological lifeways, and the path of change pursued by poor nations must depart from the model of advanced industrial states. For the future of all life, nations must escape the trap of industrialism.

Sustainability, then, means that both rich and poor societies must make the social choices needed to create new relationships. The rich can no longer "mine" the poor as a convenient source of raw materials, food, cheap labor, high profits, and huge interest payments. An ecological path is based on partnership and a mutual interest in a sustainable future. This partnership means transforming both the industrial system and the hierarchies that order and maintain it; it means the emergence of new and revivified social forms. This is the challenge and promise of an ecological civilization.

At the moment, supporters of unregulated industrial growth are inclined to simply declare the achievement of sustainability by fiat. In the United States, industrial interests have launched a broad-based assault upon the framework of existing environmental regulation as both unnecessary obstacles and government violations of property rights. Market-driven industrialism, because it monetizes almost everything and stimulates technical innovation, is said to inherently move toward equilibrium and sustainability. Anti-environmental science "proves" ecological concerns are misplaced and overstated. Journalists, such as Gregg Easterbrook, argue the age of pollution is ending, supported by such evidence as the significant relative decline of Los Angeles smog levels, the air becoming less officially poisonous.[9]

Meanwhile, sober scientists, such as E. O. Wilson, founder of sociobiology, and decidedly not a liberal, warn of the unparalleled industrially caused mass extinctions now underway. "Clearly, we are in the midst of one of the great extinction spasms of geological history," Wilson states in *The Diversity of Life*.[10]

Such industrial assaults are reflected, for example, in the global decline of amphibian species. This is a result of a complex mix of industrial effects. These include habitat destruction, air and water pollution (acid rain and snow, fungicides, insecticides, industrial chemical toxins, including estrogen-like compounds) with which amphibians are unfortunately most intimately in contact, and increased ultraviolet-B radiation. As a consequence of ozone destruction, heightened surface UV-B radiation kills the eggs of sensitive amphibian species and increases the vulnerability of others to disease. Vanishing amphibians represent not just a parochial concern for a class of vertebrates, but a reflection of both environmental insult and the destruction of the integrity of complex ecosystems and food chains where amphibians are both hunters and food supply. They are the canaries in the mine.[11]

Ecological Democracy

Democracy is integral to the nature of an ecological civilization. To speak of ecological democracy is to juxtapose two powerful
ideas. Democracy's record ranges from the very imperfect Athenian system of 2,500 years ago to the still quite imperfect United
States democracy, now two centuries old, and to the dozens of
fragile new systems across the world that may represent democracy's new beginning.

These new beginnings come with the assertion of civil society
as a creative venue for change, as with Solidarity in Poland. This
civil society is a realm outside the norms of bureaucratic state and
corporation. The ecological justice movement, grassroots environmental groups, community-based Green parties, cooperatives, unions, workers' and farmers' associations, artisan and professional
groups, community housing groups, health care alliances, educational systems, appropriate technologists, socially active spiritual
movements, artists, writers, filmmakers, videographers, rappers,
folk and rock musicians—all of these groups and individuals
visibly enliven the dynamism of civil society.

Democracy means rule of the people (or at least some of
them). This was true for the slave-based agricultural and trading
city-states of ancient Greek democracy, and it holds for today's
democratic industrial capitalist nation states: the people, or at
least some of them, rule. There are no perfect people and no
perfect democracies, but democracy can be moved toward the
realm of freedom and community.

Ecology's provenance is much less exalted and less clear. It
is a German scientific coinage, ökologie, named by Ernest Haeckel
in 1870, derived from the Greek oikos or house, plus logia or saying.
Originally, it referred narrowly to the study of the relationship
between organisms and their environment—the study not of individuals but of communities. Ecology's current power as signifier
contrasts with its humble beginnings. Haeckel had an ear for

words, but his social views inclined to *Volkish* and racialist positions. Indeed, one line of ecological thought and practice embraces protection and purification of a romanticized people and their land—a blood and soil view that reached murderous pitch as applied by the Nazis, and continues today as anti-immigrant sentiments from otherwise admirable ecologists, such as the late Edward Abbey.

I put ecology's worst foot forward deliberately. A green flag—like a red flag or a red, white, and blue flag or any flag—can be easily spattered with the blood of innocents. Ecology is no more or less able to be compromised than other human social conceptions. Democracy too can lead from *liberté, egalité, fraternité* to the Terror; democracy can be perverted—the apartheid South African state practiced "democracy" for over forty years. Neither democracy nor ecology is a mantra that, when merely repeated, will end the need to make hard moral, social, political, economic, and environmental choices. Rather, ecological democracy facilitates and encourages making those choices in ways that creatively and constructively involve all the voices of the community.

Ecological democracy is more than the means to balance industrial humanity's conduct with the living world—although that is a first order task. It is more than a path for better management of industrial civilization. It is a way to build an ecological civilization. Such an effort means revitalizing democracy to meet the challenges and opportunities posed by the growth of industrial civilization.

What's Ahead?

This book is divided into three main sections. Part One: Industrial Reality examines the nature and character of industrialism as a social system. It explores the latest stage of industrial civilization and its implications given the conflicting imperatives for expansion and limitation, and discusses some consequences of industrialism and its difficulties.

Part Two: Undemocratic Alternatives examines the nature of global management and prospects for its evolution, then looks at the rise of new redemptive authoritarian orders contesting for industrialism's future.

Part Three: Ecological Democracy further explores democratic and ecological developments and considers three existing cooperative social systems as examples, then examines the dynamics of an ecological commons, and finally considers a number of transformative venues for moving from industrial to ecological civilization.

chapter two

INDUSTRIALISM AS MACHINE AND MYTH

THIS CHAPTER EXAMINES INDUSTRIALISM—not simply capitalism—as the basic organizing principle of our civilization. Industrialism is a system for maximizing production and consumption, but it is also something more: industrialism is a civilization.

Industrial reality is the current human context for most of us. This is not to say that industrial reality is a reflection of underlying human nature. True, it is rooted in our past, but it is also evolving: aspects of industrial reality possess the potential for change. And we must face industrialism's cold mechanical stare until it breaks into a visage of possibility; unless we see what industrialism is, we will be unable to gain an appreciation of the emergent forces that suggest what our civilization may become.

To begin, we need to consider industrialism's basic claims, the assumptions that condition industrial society and mold the industrial mind. But we cannot succeed if we use a reductionist industrial methodology, expect to disassemble industrial civilization, catalog and examine the pieces, then reassemble it into an ecological society. Neither can we privilege or ignore particular aspects of industrial reality, for instance the economic or social realms, as a way to escape from the assumptions and limitations of those disciplines. We must see industrialism with ecological eyes; we must remember the tragic error of Marxism in power, i.e., that it embraced industrial means in an attempt to achieve liberatory ends.

It is time to come to terms with the extraordinary nature of industrial civilization. Those who work for fundamental social change can no longer afford to confuse industrialism with capitalism. I am not forgetting Frederick Douglass' painful wisdom that power concedes nothing without a struggle. I am attempting to understand both the nature of that power and the nature of our struggle.*

Whole libraries are filled with analyses of capitalism and socialism while industrialism itself, in comparison, has been largely ignored. Industrialism and capitalism developed in overlapping ways, but they are not the same things. Twisted skeins of commerce, science, religion, and power combined to transform a feudal world into an apparently seamless amalgam of capitalism and industrialism. But capitalism exists without industrialism—commercial capitalism appeared before industrial capitalism—and industrialism has demonstrated that it can function without capitalism—although capitalism has demonstrated that it

---

* Industrialism is chosen as the best description of the underlying reality of the world system. I use "system" without the connotation of cybernetic mechanism; the more neutral term would be arrangement, a word, however, often best left for French farce and British diplomacy.

"works," i.e., can maximize production and consumption, better than authoritarian socialism.

Industrialism's Victory

Industrialism is relatively unexamined because it is the common practice of an industrializing world. Industrialism and its values have become the basis for normal behavior and common sense. The struggle to defend what English social historian E. P. Thompson calls the old "moral economy" against the encroachments of industrialism, which began in the 18th century, gradually changed into a struggle for justice and freedom within an industrial world. In the 19th century, the new working class and its allies increasingly accepted the idea that a perfected industrialism could deliver it from the clear and present agonies of capitalism. Industrialism was to be the servant of humanity, despite William Blake's horror at the "dark satanic mills" and Ralph Waldo Emerson's warning that "things are in the saddle and are riding mankind."

Industrialism was certainly shaped by the appetites of an emerging capitalist class and nation state. Capitalism seized upon and shaped the application of industrial technique in service to a new hierarchical and progressive order. But the underlying ideology is that of industry, not of capital, and this coheres into the steel triangle of hierarchy, progress, and technique mentioned in Chapter One (see Figure 2-1 below).

The industrial state traffics in power, not simply money, and wields this power with a blind commitment to growth. Power is at the center of the industrial state—in general, the social forces that inform capitalism and industrialism cannot be reduced to the pursuit of private profit. Capitalist industrialism is a power system; so, too, is socialist industrialism. By abolishing capitalists and profit, industrial socialism did not abolish hierarchical order, the exaltation of progress, or the embrace of technique.

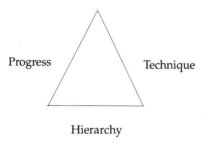

Figure 2-1. The Steel Triangle of Industrialism

Progress   Technique

Hierarchy

Progress is the code word that defines exploitation and destruction as beneficial. Hierarchy is the ordering principle of inequality that channels love and aspiration into obedience, and defines this obedience as good. Technique captures human creativity and reason into the service of progress and hierarchy, and defines this captivity as the search for truth and the *summum bonum.*

While industrialism is informed and shaped by social choices and social forces, it is also the "product" of its own internal logic—the reductive, separating logic of the machine and the computer; the logic of domination, of difference, of exclusion; the logic of yes/no, either/or, inside/outside, self/other. Industrialism subsumes familiar defining dichotomies of market/planning, capitalism/socialism, reason/emotion, man/woman, human being/other.

Industrialism is a machine civilization both held together and riven by its own logic. Indeed, following French anthropologist Claude Lévi-Strauss, we can view industrialism as the grand elaboration of oppositional thought—of the raw and the cooked, as it were—placed at the service of hierarchy, technique, and progress. Industrialism is a civilization gone mad by following its own logic.

This legacy of oppositional thought looms large even for many in the ecology movement. "Humanity," "humanism," and "anthropocentrism" have become epithets. Some ecologists set an abstract humanity apart from and against nature. Industrialism and its values have, in the minds of some of its staunchest opponents, become synonymous with humanity itself.

In "advanced" industrialized nations, it has become fashionable to speak of a "postindustrial society" and an "Information Age." No doubt, industrial society is less and less a matter of smokestacks, and more and more a microprocessor-mediated social order. And the typical worker will now more likely find work in an office or service facility than in a factory. But these changes are not departures from industrial society. They are signs of its development and evolution.

If we believe that industrialism will calmly metamorphose into a high-tech computer utopia, we are making an error similar to that of the 19th-century followers of Robert Owen in England, who believed that demonstrating the manifestly superior industrial reforms he pioneered would be sufficient to cause their general adoption. This error is not merely a matter of vain human hope, but a belief system that claims deliverance can be found with successful technique—in the name of progress and supported by logic, scientific experiment, and truth. According to this belief, the application of enlightened industrial methods will lead inexorably to material and moral benefit.*

---

* Such inclinations are roughly similar to the confidence shown by many within the safe energy movement (I include myself) that just demonstrating the technical, economic, social, and political benefits of solar and renewable resource technologies would lead to their general adoption. In the real world, of course, we must take into account the countervailing interests of the global energy industry. Its commitment to fossil fuel and nuclear power is anchored by several hundreds of billions of dollars of investment capital, trillions of dollars worth of energy reserves, and tens of billions of dollars of annual income. This financial stake is expressed through geopolitical realities that flow from the concentration of investments and resources.

What Is Industrialism?

Industrialism eludes simple definition. It's easier to define its attributes than its essence; easier to describe its character than delineate its limits. Industrialism as technique is more than just the adoption of the factory system based upon mass production and facilitated by the division of labor, standardized and inter-changeable parts, and specialized technologies. Industrialism as social practice is more than just the imposition of wage labor upon artisans, tradespeople, laborers, and farmers. The develop-ment of industrialism was a complex process of social invention and innovation.

Industrialism is thus a comprehensive system of social rela-tions shaped by industrial reality; a psychology that makes repres-sion a virtue and defines accommodation to the intolerable as normal; an ideology based on the interlocking principles of hierar-chy-progress-technique; and a complex myth that defines our values, and shapes our feelings and behavior.

Industrialism is all these things and more. Industrialism is within and without, it is both machine and method. It encourages not just acceptance of the stresses and inanities of the day, but positive identification with its machine values as common sense. The triumph of industrialism is to make individuals not just ser-vants of the machine, but part of the machine.

Industrialism as civilization rests ultimately upon the com-plexity of the deep social structures that have evolved over millen-nia. Social reality is a continuously evolving process, the sum of our individual and collective experience that shapes us and is transmitted to successive generations.

The industrial world, our world, confronts us with a series of startling paradoxes. This world supposedly proceeds on the basis of rationality and scientific logic, yet everywhere we are surrounded by ecological catastrophe, by the madness of war or the threat of war that can swiftly destroy human civilization.

Never has a civilization produced so many things and had the capacity to produce so many more, yet never have there been so many desperately poor and impoverished.

In spite of this, we yearn, too often, for more things that define life in industrial terms. The educated, the dispossessed, the global teenager, the former Soviet citizen who erected little shrines from McDonald's boxes, the vacant-eyed wanderers in shopping malls: all pay obesience to the imperatives of industrialism. What is striking about industrialism is the global reach of the common irrationality that we embrace and that embraces us.

Industrialism in the abstract works to maximize production and consumption, but historically the system in action has not been driven simply by lust for things or for capital (which can be understood as potential things) or even, in the most elemental form, for the accumulation of power itself. Again and again, industrialism accumulates huge surpluses at a frightful, irrational cost, and then squanders them in a frightful, irrational way. This irrationality cannot be reduced to the exploitation of labor, the extraction of surplus value, and the logic of accumulation as described by Karl Marx; nor can it be reduced to a matter of simple greed at the expense of the living world, nor to the control of power as described by Michel Foucault. Each explains a part, but no one alone can explain the system's irrationality. Other critiques—for example, that industrialism is an expression of patriarchy or of racism or of hierarchy in general—have their virtues, but these too only describe a part of the industrial leviathan. To argue that industrial domains are interdependent and interrelated is not to suggest that all the system's aspects are equivalent.*

---

* For example, the economic aspect is indeed very important, but this importance does not mean that the economic realm defines the rest of the social superstructure. As the communist experience has demonstrated, we embrace one-dimensional definitions of efficiency and equality at our peril. As for poststructuralism, deconstruction, *et al.*, the

Industrialism as Machine

Our living reality is organized as if it were a creation of industrial reason, as if it were a machine. It is certainly not a simple machine—not a lever, a pulley, an inclined plane, a wheel, a wedge, or a combination of these. Industrialism is more than the sum of the mechanical devices that spew forth from our factories; more than the factories themselves plus the built environment of cities, roads, and factory farms and fisheries; more than the entire technostructure; even more than this stupendous agglomeration of things plus the social structures that order its conduct. Industrialism includes ourselves: we are a part of this great machine, and not merely as servants or supposed masters. Industrialism is our way of life, a machine of such scope that the unindustrialized vestiges of the living world are now strange and exotic, to be confined in parks and reserves for their own protection.

This machine has many components. It has a biological component of people, domesticated animals and plants, and those still-wild beings defined as "resources" to be "harvested." The machine's informational component includes personal knowledge, all the world's writings, electronic media, and now life's genetic code. Its material component includes the planet itself—the machine classifies all material existence (air, water, earth) as inputs to satisfy its appetites, or to serve as a dump for its wastes.

This industrial megamachine, then, is an evolving global system of interacting hierarchical orders—which include material

---

linguistic turn usually offers little for the practice of social reconstruction beyond semiotic prestidigitation. The once-radical theorist, French writer Jean Baudrillard, for example, has moved from an incisive critique of Marxism as industrial ideology (in The Mirror of Production) to a postmodern absorption with the endlessly unfolding industrial spectacle.[1]

and informational domains—that seek integration in both political and economic realms (see Chapter Three). To understand its ambitions, we can look at its precursor in the ancient labor-powered megamachine whose extraordinary physical accomplishments were achieved through the pain of enslaved workers placed at the service of divine pharaohs, kings, and emperors. This megamachine was employed to serve the grandiose longings of the pharaoh's master builders and to assist in the conduct of war. The ancient megamachine was artfully described by Lewis Mumford in his germinal 1966 work, *The Myth of the Machine: Technics and Human Development.*

> Kingship deliberately sought by means of the megamachine to bring the powers and glories of Heaven within human reach. And it was so far successful that the immense achievements of this archetypal unit for long surpassed, in technical proficiency and output, the important but modest contributions made by all other contemporary machines.
>
> Whether organized for labor or for war this new collective mechanism imposed general regimentation, coerced and punished, and it limited tangible rewards largely to the dominant minority which created and controlled the megamachine. Along with this, it reduced the idea of communal autonomy and personal initiative. Each component below the level of command was only part of a human, condemned to work at only part of a job and live only part of a life. Adam Smith's analysis of the division of labor taking place in the eighteenth century toward a more dehumanized system, with greater productive efficiency, illuminates equally the earliest "industrial revolution."[2]

The industrial megamachine has surpassed the power, and probably even the ambition, of the pharaohs in both size and complexity. However, although the industrial megamachine is resolutely hierarchical, it cannot be understood as the perfection of domination and order. The collapse of Stalinist industrialism, the most rigid and comprehensive of unitary hierarchies, reflects the fact that human freedom and aspiration are integral to the functioning of industrialism. This need creates tensions, hence instability and the continuing possibility that those in the system will change its nature. Industrialism will not be undermined by the barbarians at the gates, but by the awakened within.

Industrialism as Invention

As a child in the 1950s and 1960s, I learned the history of industrialism as a story of inventions, a litany of accomplishments, all significant milestones of limitless progress in which I, as a young technotwit, was to play a part. Our allegiance to scientific progress was seamlessly integrated with the great contest against communism as we crouched under our desks or silently lined the hallways in preparation for nuclear war.

I now realize that this early indoctrination was misleading. Industrialism is the creation of modernity, but modernity itself did not spring forth with the opening of the first silk factory in 1756 near Lyon in France; or with the invention of the spinning jenny by the poor cotton spinner James Hargreaves in 1757; or with the steam engine patented by James Watt in 1769 and first used commercially (but unsuccessfully) in 1776 (the year Adam Smith's *The Wealth of Nations* was published); or with Oliver Evan's construction of a mechanized, continuous production grain mill in 1785; or with the development of the overhead rail assembly line in the late 1860s probably first in Cincinnati slaughterhouses.[3] Industrialism and modernity are less an expression of *invention* than of the social processes driving and guiding technological innovation. Industrialism is characterized by an endless succession of technological horizons—glimpsed, rising, then suddenly disappearing.[4]

Thus, industrialism involves substituting machine power for muscle and mental power, but industrialism is not simply defined by technology. A technological society need not be industrial: industrialism chooses and shapes the nature of the technologies it employs. For example, the development of thermonuclear weapons capable of obliterating human civilization many times over represents an ensemble of social choices, not an inevitable consequence of technology.

Of course, the applications of a particular technology have profound influence on the nature of industrial society. For a grand and obvious example, take the internal combustion engine and the automobile. A more subtle instance is the invention of the telephone, which made skyscrapers practical for business. But the idea of technological determinism, that is, of technology removed from the social matrix, has merit only in that allows experts to speak with perfect hindsight, as if everything was intentionally invented for its present uses.

The most common and deeply resonant metaphor for our world remains the machine—whether the clockwork device of the 16th century, the steam engine of the 19th century, the computer of the 20th century, or the megamachine as social description. However, industrialism clearly represents something more than Jacques Ellul's classic definition of a machine as pure technique.[5] The trajectory of industrialism includes the machine made flesh.*

This is obvious in the corvée and slave labor gangs that provided the motive power for the imperial megamachine, and is once again becoming clear with the focus on biotechnology and patented organisms. These technologies produce "intelligent" machines and a sort of developing human-machine hybridization, life as resource for marketable information obtained from breaking, parsing, and recombining the genetic code.

---

*   Industrialism is suffused with a profane materialism whose scope is, of course, figurative as well as literal. The ceaseless parade of industrial objects—powerful, respected, and feared—is both evidence of industrialism's secular magic, and the prison cell of our imagination and spirit sealed by our own emotions. Magic is now lodged in our machines not in human insight and transcendence. Dazzled by objects, the wonder slips from our senses.

But the real glory still surrounds human self-consciousness. This is the once common terrain now ceded by civilization to the mystic. Such transcendence is manifest, for example, in kabbalistic terms, in the miraculous transformation mediated by language of the primal Hebrew *davar* ("thing") to *davar* ("word"). As theologian and mystic Arthur Green writes, "*It is this apprehension of the One become word in the human mind that we call revelation—G-d becomes word as we become human.*" [emphasis in original][6]

Industrialism and Reason

The middle passage between ancient and postmodern mega-machine is the subjugation of life to a lonely reason. The 18th century was understandably intoxicated by reason. Immanuel Kant writes in "What is Enlightenment?":

> This enlightenment requires nothing but *freedom*—and the most innocent of all that may be called "freedom": freedom to make public use of one's reason in all matters. . . . By "public use of one's reason" I mean that use which a man, as *scholar*, makes of it before the reading public.[emphasis in original][7]

And Antoine-Nicholas de Condorcet in his "Sketch for a Historical Picture of the Progress of the Human Mind," written during the French Revolution, affirmed his faith in science and the perpetual progress of humanity:

> We shall find in the experience of the past, in the observation of the progress that the sciences and civilization have already made, in the analysis of the progress of the human mind and of the development of faculties, the strongest reasons for believing that nature has set no limit to the realization of our hopes.[8]

Industrial science is the sometimes sour fruit of reason. Modernity presupposes that the exercise of reason—even "instrumental" reason, i.e., applying technique to the goals of industrialism—is at once powerful and liberating, and hence progressive. This "liberation" of classic industrialism absorbs our lives as participants in the machine; it is the liberation Charlie Chaplin mocked in *Modern Times*. That assembly line has now become the computer network monitoring operator keystrokes, the electronic supervisor constantly and relentlessly measuring output.* Reason as a living force wilts if it is starved of the ambiguity that is reality's inescapable human context, the ceaseless play of experience and relation. Isolated reason is, in Franz Kafka's chilling image, a hunger artist—not without power, but self-limiting and self-destructive. Industrialism attempts to change reason to method, to accommodate reason to the requirements of power.

The Enlightenment shouted "reason" from the rooftops—reason as Tom Paine's *Common Sense*, as Jefferson's self-evident truths (for Jefferson, reason affirms that we the people, members of the democratic polity, recognize liberatory truth). But for industrial modernity, reason has devolved into technique: reason's dialogue has been ceded to method, stamped with the imprimatur of science—physical science, economic science, social science. And from reason to method and science we leap to technology and bureaucracy, the objects and structures of industrial power. We still speak of scientific reason when we largely mean the application of technique.

Industrialism as Myth

Industrialism has created, and is supported by, a mythic edifice as grand and elaborate as the technostructure it helps to guide. This is starkly visible in the fables of "private" and "public" realms. For the impoverished imagination of our time, with its

---

* This critique is not meant to condemn reason or the ideals of the Enlightenment; it is a cautionary tale, however, about the exercise of reason adrift from social and moral moorings, of the dangers of identifying dramatic change with real improvement.

increasingly homogeneous political parties, complexities of social life and social policy are reduced to a simple continuum whose antipodes are private life and public life.

The private realm does not so much describe the personal in conflict with an invasive public as it serves as a mythic representation of the social reality of capitalist industrial humanity. A countervailing myth of the public realm, developed and refined for socialist industrialism, acts in many ways as a mirror, picturing a world essentially similar to that of the capitalist private world but reversed. Both myths help individuals accommodate to the designs of industrial power, persuade them to serve the industrial state, and justify the actions of the industrial system as necessary and reasonable. Both evolve as capitalist or socialist industrialism evolves.

Consider, for example, the myth of the private realm in the United States, the most private and capitalist of advanced industrial states. Features attributed to the private are expressed as a bundle of rights and qualities, a social cloak that justifies industrialism and hides its real nature. The attributes that define the private realm include:

- Freedom for the individual and for the market, as manifest through democratic government (but not "economic" democracy within the firm or encroaching upon the firm).

- Rationality that places a value, when possible in monetary and utilitarian terms, upon all things, and attempts to reduce complex wholes to readily comprehensible components.

- Property rights that are inherent and sacred, and allow, indeed exalt, unlimited discretion to use, exploit, dispose of, or destroy property in all its manifestations.

- Rights of ownership and successorship in perpetuity that uphold the right to profit from the past, present, and future work of others.

- Efficiency expressed through the hypermobility of capital and the processes that establish, build up, and demolish enterprises and communities and land without interference—social, communal, or governmental.

- Patriotism, expressed by exalting the state as the guarantor of the freedom of the private, with the symbolic identification of blood, flag, and country.

- The right to armed self-defense not only of property and person, but the right, indeed the obligation, to dispossess and to kill those outside the group to obtain and to keep wealth and prerogatives.

- Family, community, and religion expressed through individual private striving and ritualized public display, its legitimacy based not on custom or tradition, but on a mythological Rousseauean social contract.

- The ability to create and re-create personal identity through individual actions and acts of consumption that define and reflect commercial archetypes called "lifestyles."

- The right to pursue happiness by accumulating and consuming material goods and personal services.

- Strength, integrity, independence, and individuality of "the person"—this person is, in the abstract, male, or suffused with masculine and patriarchal values.

- The power to deal with others through formal or informal contractual agreements and through self-assertion expressed intellectually, verbally, and/or violently.

- No limits upon the self-aggrandizement and accomplishments of the individual, who is in ceaseless competition with other individuals.

· The ability to accumulate endlessly without calling forth reactive violence by other individuals. (Wealth evokes, as Adam Smith suggested, sympathetic admiration. It is the poor who are hated, not the rich.)

Traditionally, a myth serves not only as a story—a way to represent and explain—but as a gate to meaning and, above all, to transcendence. But the myths of industrialism serve not as guidance, but as obfuscation. Industrialism is so complex, so volatile, its purpose so destructive and inhuman, that a cloak must be placed over human judgment or enough individuals would withdraw their cooperation to endanger the continued operation of the industrial order. This refusal to cooperate is precisely what happened in the Soviet Union and Eastern Europe between 1989 and 1991—events that offer a classic example of both the vulnerability of the supposedly impregnable industrial state and of the power of nonviolent grassroots actions.[9]

Thus, these myths help mash contradictory circumstances into the homogenized gruel of industrial truisms. They encourage us to see, for example, destruction as the heroic conquest of nature; to celebrate raping the land as self-reliance; to understand genocide as destiny. *

Moreover, the myth of the private realm cuts us off from participation in public activities. In the myth of the private, the

---

* However, as industrial reality becomes increasingly unbearable, these myths lose their power to deceive. Unable to interpret the social realities of our world, according to these myths we turn to the banal pleasantries of propaganda. Propaganda is denial of what we see—it soothes us when what we observe grossly violates the myth. Thus, members of the jury that acquitted a white policeman of the videotaped beating of an African-American could say with conviction that people hadn't seen what happened *before* the beating began. (He wiggled his ass; he resisted arrest; he deserved what he got.) Propaganda is the clean Gulf War of smart bombs bursting without the stink of thousands of corpses, shattered cities, starving children. Propaganda is photographs of fish swimming around drilling platforms. Propaganda takes life out of time, out of history.[10]

public plays the role of the despised, feared other. The public realm is denied the attributes of the social—of community, family, caring (attributes the public sphere could logically possess)—and largely reduced to the bureaucratic structures of government (but not to those of private or corporate power). Everything arbitrary and dictatorial, inefficient, corrupt, sluggish, cowardly, and doomed is in the realm of the public.

Therefore, in the myth—which is offered as truth—freedom is gained largely at the expense of community. Community is fleeting and transitory, often in conflict with the essential values of the private realm. Community is perceived not as a refuge, but as a threat, since the approach to community lies within the public sphere. Community is demonized (except in patriotic or competitive manifestations); "family values" are praised—not as a reference to happy and secure families in a community, but as code for symbolic allegiance to patriarchal nuclear families, combined with nostalgia for an idealized past undermined by capitalist industrialism.

The myth of the private realm helps accustom the well-housed and well-fed to the sight of homeless people sleeping on the streets outside their guarded homes, picking through their garbage for food. The myth eases the pain of this reality; it defines disintegration as "normal" and discourages effective social action—which must be community action, not just the personal charity permitted by the private sphere. In short, the myth of the private realm helps create a complex of cruelty and division that accelerates the disintegration of a nation plagued with violence between friends and strangers, in the home and in public spaces. The "Other America" has become everyone's America.

Social disintegration and agony in advanced industrialized states is based upon wealth, not poverty; it is a necessary result of the limitless pursuit of unmitigated private gain and aggrandizement. Intractable social problems are not an aberration, but the creation of the private realm and the pursuit of profit. Modest amelioration can come from tempering private appetites with public action, but healing the wounds of industrialism means fundamental change. The antidote for the myth of the private realm is not the myth of the public realm; the antidote for the myth of the public realm is not the myth of the private realm.

Industrialism and Psychology

When myth collides with industrial modernity it is transmuted into a psychology that attempts to explain "reality" by exploring subjective truth. Psychology traditionally rushes in to screen personal agonies from their social genesis—to buttress our ability to continue not to see, not to understand, and not to challenge what is before our eyes. Industrial psychology applies the instrumentalities of science to transform myth into a timeless and value-free explanation of human behavior and development. The psychological myths of industrialism follow two complementary paths: those of Sigmund Freud, who "discovered" the unconscious much as Columbus "discovered" America; and those of B. F. Skinner, who dispensed with mind, and focused on a mechanism reduced to learning and behavior—industrial inputs and outputs.*

Freud's iconoclastic exploration of eros and unconscious devolved into a projection of his social world, that of high Victorian industrialism, onto the human psyche. Through Freud's eyes—eyes accustomed to Vienna's gaiety and gloom—life is not a journey toward greater empathy and integration with the living world; it is a process of separation and a struggle for individual self-assertion. Near the end of his career, Freud wrote an extraor-

---

*Skinner's psychology took an exquisite reductionist tack, experimentally often dispensing with people and instead using rats to generalize about conditioning and reinforcement: rats' behavior became human analog.

dinarily sad passage that defines much of the industrial world-view: "Our present ego-feeling is, therefore, only a shrunken residue of a much more inclusive—indeed, an all-embracing—feeling which corresponded to a more inclusive bond between the ego and the world around it."[11]

Freud was correct, in the terms of industrial civilization, when he set the individual against the community and *Eros*, the life force, against *Thanatos*, the death instinct. Industrial civilization is indeed predicated upon repressing human life force—indeed, all life—for the sake of industrial values. This separation is the architecture of our particular civilization. But as we shall see, an ecological society represents the return of pleasure, and its psychologies are based upon the essential link between freedom and community.

The psychology of repression fails not because industrialism lacks the ability to demean, crush, and control it; it fails because industrial expansion requires not merely acquiescence, but creative self-expression and participation. To allow the exercise of freedom and yet not to allow freedom itself—that is the conundrum of industrialism. No wonder the civilization that represents the triumph of logic, of billiard ball cause-and-effect, must offer psychologies of repression to explain human conduct—psychologies that split conscious from unconscious, mind from body, one from the many, and that are rooted in the manipulation of shifting means and ends, not in the exalted science of cause-and-effect.[12] These divisions, like those between private and public, between freedom and community, are debilitating and ultimately false.

Industrial civilization deserves our attention, not as a new academic subspecialty, but as a venue for change. An ecological democracy, if it is to be built, will not magically arise fully formed, but will emerge from industrialism's afflicted reality—its complexity and contradictions, imperatives and paradoxes, and above all, its essential instability.

chapter three

GLOBAL MARKETS AND COLLAPSING NATIONS

A NEW INDUSTRIAL ERA HAS BEGUN, the era of global integration, of global markets and collapsing nations. Our civilization is afflicted with a sort of vertigo: a set of interrelated but discordant factors, drawn together in negative synergy, have called into question the once-calm verities of industrialism and its elites. Industrialism (not merely capitalism) is caught in a maze of its own creation; its traditional basis and well-ordered structures are being challenged by new and destabilizing realities. Our challenge is to understand the welter of forces driving global change.

The nation state, once the anchor for industrialism, is no longer fully adequate to satisfy imperatives for expansion and domination. Instead, we have global, transnational, and now supranational corporations—and an atomized world population. Industrialists offer the global market as a new universal, the giant corporation as the meaningful particular. But a global market ordered by supranational corporations is an industrial ideal without political structure; a poor basis for stability and peace. Although the capitalist market system or socialist industrial order were also ideals without political structure, the modern nation state gave them political coherence. Despite the West's triumphant smugness following the collapse of communism, chaos is today the fundamental characteristic of the world system. The Cold War served to divide and organize the industrial world; the end of this era reflects, in part, both the imperatives for globalization and the crisis of classical industrialism and its nation states.

Globalization does not mean general prosperity. While there is talk of "integration" and a "world market," in reality an ever widening gulf separates industrialized from unindustrialized, consuming class from subsistence class, rich from impoverished. Despite the celebration over a new millionaire created every minute in Southeast Asia, entire continents and great nations are in the grip of poverty and debt. In many places, the sentiment is that everything has been tried and everything has failed. In the industrialized North, the desperate call is for a job, any job, even if this pursuit of employment leads to self-destruction.

Industrialism, with its geometric growth of resource use and pollution, is obviously materially and socially unsustainable. The costs of production and consumption begin to exceed any benefits. This need to limit poisonous practices has made financial speculation, the sale of services, and traffic in information more profitable than the traditional manufacture of objects. At the same time, instability and the weakening of nations potentiate expansion of multilateral attempts to coordinate development though new political and economic protocols—yet policymakers and their critics continue to think largely in national terms.

In the broad sense, industrialism's simultaneous embrace of acceleration and limits has brought it to an existential crisis. In this chapter, we will first consider the nation state as the contested terrain of globalization and the broad question of evolving industrial relationships. Then we will examine the strengths and weaknesses of the transnational corporation and international trade, before looking at social choices in light of globalization. Our transformative strategies, our pursuit of freedom and community will take place in the context of globalization and the nation state. Their dynamics are presented not as unchangeable givens, but as the arena within which our work must occur.

The Nation State

The essential needs of industrialism now transcend national sovereignties, but there is no replacement for the nation state in sight that can reliably protect and sponsor industrial civilization—that is, its corporations, bureaucracies, and hierarchies. So we have confusion. Industrialism is not yet able to simply shed the skin of the nation state.

Thus, the modern nation state, which arose in the 19th century and proved essential for the development of industrialism and capitalism, must now be understood as an obstacle to globalization. For a long time, the interests of the nation state more or less coincided with the industrialists' need to supplant—if necessary, to crush—local and community power. But in the new industrial universe being formed between transnational corporations and multinational power groupings, the nation now represents a particular to be overcome, or at least fully domesticated. At the same time, the notion of national sovereignty is still essential to maintain the industrial order.*

The nation state protects the industrial social order by providing an orderly basis of custom, law, and coercion; and it per-

---

* The empire building of the United States and the Soviet Union was frozen in the bloc system by a combination of economic dominance and military threat. The end of the Cold War exposed the fundamental instability of a global system constrained by United States/Soviet competition. It left weakened nations, but it also released pent-up devolutionary energies—as well as removing barriers to global integration.

forms the essential function of organizing people for production and consumption. The state (capitalist or socialist) assumes the role of providing for public welfare, education, and infrastructure—tasks generally not assumed by industrial organizations. The state also socializes the costs of providing terrain and attitudes sympathetic to industry.

For private corporations, these benefits go beyond just freedom from direct costs. For example, corporations in some countries receive freedom from indirect costs, such as those of the anomalously privatized health care system in the United States, costs that can adversely affect U.S. businesses facing foreign competitors whose nations have socialized health care and health costs. Moreover, the nation state can, and often does, adopt policies directly beneficial to industry—policies to protect domestic industry from competition, to protect the state's national way of life (e.g., restricting agricultural imports for farmers), to maintain national control of so-called strategic resources (the Persian Gulf War of 1991 for control of oil is a spectacular example).

Conflicting Imperatives of the Nation State

The state today is torn between two countervailing imperatives: first, a demand for competition and loosening national restrictions on growth; second, a need for cooperation and limits on destructive industrial conduct (see Figure 3-1 below). Both effectively call for weakening the nation state.* Policymakers must

---

* Since the collapse of communism removed the threat, even in theory, of an industrialism engaged in aggressive redistribution of wealth—i.e., any distribution beyond what exists in the established social democracies—industrialists present growth as the only possible answer to social problems. In other words, any deepening of economic and social miseries is taken as *prima facie* evidence of inadequate industrial performance, and as a reason to question the value of the nation state as an organizing principle.

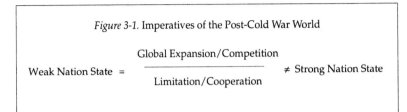

Figure 3-1. Imperatives of the Post-Cold War World

$$\text{Weak Nation State} = \frac{\text{Global Expansion}/\text{Competition}}{\text{Limitation}/\text{Cooperation}} \neq \text{Strong Nation State}$$

somehow balance two conflicting imperatives whose common center is the weakening of the very national power they aspire to guide. This is a controlling conundrum of our times—the chaotic strange attractor of globalization. It explains why leaders of industrial nations have difficulty agreeing on much beyond the need to stop nuclear weapons proliferation.

Political "realism"—maximizing national power and self-interest, expanding spheres of influence—is no longer a reliable guide to policy. Traditional statecraft (meaning Machiavellian calculation by leaders in order to advance national and personal ambitions) is no longer the highest art. In the industrial world, self-interest can no longer be identified with endlessly advancing any particular national interest. Nor can globalization be understood as an evolving neocolonialist structure. As the national sacrifices demanded by GATT and NAFTA suggest, national self-interest is increasingly subjugated in the interest of a rather murky and ill-defined industrial whole.

A Ross Perot or a Pat Buchanan has no difficulty understanding the threat to national sovereignty posed by these global interests, but even a Henry Kissinger has difficulty offering clear pronouncements on globalized national self-interest. Effective power is now related to the weakening of national sovereignty and the ability to limit environmental degradation. However, neither globalization nor environmental limits provide a comparative advantage to any one nation. In the short run, at least, the cost of cleanup, lost business, and lost capacity (not to mention social costs) exceeds the immediate direct benefits.

Nor can globalization be reduced to a plan of venal transnational corporations. Rather, industrialism as a system is imposing its logic upon the basic political, economic, cultural, and social organization of human diversity. Within this logic, the transnational corporation is an important means, but it is not a cause.

The Universal and the Particular

For industrialism, the relationship of the part to the whole is largely reduced to the facilitation of continued growth. This deeply held imperative is not only shared by investors, but even by those concerned with the increase of structural unemployment in industrialized nations and the destitution of billions living in nations peripheral to the industrial creation of wealth.

In the globalization process, industrialism must continue to break down barriers—declare ever larger free trade zones and common markets, eliminate tariffs and cultural barriers, subject more and more of our world to pollution, monetize more of family and community life, destroy more of the textured aspects of life in the interests of the universal and homogenized. The "common good" of industrialism is a world ever more rationalized for constantly growing output and consumption of products.

Tensions between the particular and the universal, like those between expansion and limitation, drive the processes of global integration. In broad terms, the industrial characterization of the universal and the particular is shown in the figure below. In other words, industrialism, for the most part, identifies the particular with obstacles to rationalization; the universal, on the other hand, represents change and therefore is of higher value. The universal also grants rights and offers protections in exchange for fealty.

An exclusive either/or logic governs the relationship between the universal and the particular: one must be privileged and

Figure 3-2. Industrial Dynamics

Logic: Either/Or

Universal = Liberation/Progress

Particular = Tradition/Past

the other subjugated. Industrial relationships are those of dominance, with the many ordered by the hierarchical organization of
power. This same logic generates otherness, scapegoats, a culture
of genocide: it poisons both the universal and the particular.*

Hierarchical succession exists both within and between industrial forms. For classic industrialism, succession was based on
a progression from individual to firm to nation—with each nation
embedded in a universe of nation states. The ordering theme was
that of nationalism. In the era of global integration, this succession
is reordered: from individual to nation to a firm, embedded in the
weak structure of a global market (see Figure 3-3 below).

Industrial evolution thus involves the creation of successive
"universals" and their destruction when they can no longer meet
the needs of expansion and progress. Globalization has not, as
yet, found a level of corporate patriotism and power that would
replace that of the nation state. While industrialism has clearly
anointed the transnational corporations as meaningful actors, a
political void remains at the center of globalization.

---

* Politically, the logic of hierarchy and federation means ceding basic communal rights
to broader instrumentalities of power. This surrender is the fine print of the social
contract—a logical extension of the idea of an order of creation from the humblest
creature, culminating in humans as masters, and of a ladder of power and grace
extending from common women and men to an aristocracy (defined first by heredity
and entitlement, then by commercial and industrial wealth).

Figure 3-3. Succession of Industrial Hierarchies

Nation States	Global Market
Nation	Firm
Firm	Nation
Individual	Individual
Classic Industrialism	**Globalization**
(Nationalism)	(Transnationalism)

It is inherently problematic to depend upon nation states to preside over their own loss of power and authority. The current globalizing strategy appointing technocratic boards to manage "free trade" agreements, such as GATT and NAFTA, and to eliminate so-called nontariff barriers to trade (that is, democratically approved national laws) in the interests of transnational corporations has its limits. The successful pursuit of industrial goals requires participation and collaboration; it requires at least the face of democracy. Industrial growth cannot be sustained by administrative fiat.

Capitalist supporters, such as Ludwig van Mises and James Buchanan, have no difficulty presenting the global market as the true universal, a domain of choice and community, with the solitary individual as particular. In these terms, a global force, making markets everywhere and out of everything, is offered as universal solvent for the social realm, the local reality, the community, the particular.

This market is not comprised of many smaller markets, but is one unitary, hierarchical order that brooks no real particular, no real civil society—"real" in the sense of a community able to effectively withdraw or change its participation, and to influence the nature of the whole. The global market, in its way, is the capitalist analogue of the unitary hierarchy that was the Soviet state.

But while there is a joyful hyperbole from ideologues and corporate executives declaring the global market as the new universal, reality is not so simple. The political and economic complexity of globalization, the devolution of the nation state, and the creation of other political/economic entities permit opportunities for positive, transformative venues quite different from capitalist utopian dreams or cyberpunk dystopian nightmares.

The Transnational Corporation

The transnational corporation is the leading edge of global industrial integration. It is a new sort of entity, operated by an elite managerial group and empowered through the global electronic network of finance. While ostensibly owned by shareholders, the transnational corporation is, in general, less subject to their wishes, or those of the major customer nations, than to the exigencies of an increasingly integrated world business cycle.

This world system is not simply organized to serve the interests of capital. Rather, transnational enterprise structure reflects the need for industrial organizations that exist everywhere and yet are specific to nowhere except the undifferentiated "industrial world." The transnational corporation must be understood as the instrument for globalization, not merely as an enormous agglomeration of productive capacity, or thousands of factories and hundreds of thousands of workers (like, for example, IBM with $65 billion in 1992 sales and 345,000 workers—before a tidal wave of layoffs in 1993).

Changes in the way society designates these corporations are instructive: from the multinationals (in many nations) of the 1950s and 1960s, to the transnationals (across nations) of the 1970s and 1980s, to the supranationals (above the nation) of the 1990s. This language reflects not simply new organizational forms, but growing freedom from limitation on international operations by any single nation state, and often freedom from effective control of domestic activities. As the term *supranational* suggests, the corporation is actively and effectively contesting the prerogatives of national sovereignty. But corporations still clearly operate within the context of multiple national sovereignties.

A 1991 study by the Conference Board (a voice for corporate America) indicated that of the 100 largest economic units on earth, fifty-three were states, while forty-seven were transnational corporations.[1] An income comparison is quite sobering: annual income for the twenty-five largest industrial corporations was over $1.713 trillion (1988).[2] Total 1991 GNP for forty economies with low ($635 or less) per capita income was only $1.097 trillion. In other words, over three billion people had less than two-thirds the annual 1988 income of the twenty-five largest corporations (twelve associated with Japan, nine with the United States, two with Germany, one with The Netherlands, and one with Great Britain).[3]

The Transnational Corporation and Globalization

The relationship between the transnational corporation and the nation state is problematic. As the latest refinement of capitalism, one predicated upon a separation between owners and managers, the transnational and sometimes supranational corporation plays multiple roles. First, it is the traditional vehicle for maximization of profits—a habit about which both neoclassical and marxist political economists have had much to say. Second, the corporation has become more than the vehicle for economic activity—not quite consciously acting as the latest and brightest embodiment of the prospects of industrialism itself.

Much current discourse focuses upon this second role, and the fault lines between nations and supranationals, while underemphasizing conflicts internal to the corporations. Yet there is an inherent tension between the new supranational corporation and the interests of stockholders, both short- and long-term. Stockholders may be concerned about their financial well-being above all else; but this concern does not necessarily lead them to identify with the corporation as a replacement for the nation state: their loyalties cannot be said to lie with enterprises in which their interest may be transitory, or only one among many interests (including interest in competing firms engaged in providing similar goods or services). Corporations issue stock certificates, not birth certificates. As we shall see, the transnational corporation itself can be transformed into an entity based on worker control, community responsibility, and management participation—a process that resolves not only tensions between owners and managers, but the more fundamental conflicts between both owner and worker, and also between corporation and community.

An individual may certainly be loyal to a class, but here, too, the issues are much more highly nuanced than is suggested by simple schematic definitions separating the world into an owning (and ruling) and a working class. One reason modern capitalist industrial society has endured is because of its ability to generate multiple hierarchies and divided loyalties both within formal political structures and within civil society. As recent history has demonstrated, unitary hierarchies can become dramatically unstable, whether or not they are armed with nuclear weapons.

The class structure of global integration is thus characterized by shifting loyalties and affinities. This shifting is both an artifact of the acceleration of economic activity and a sign of the weakening of traditional political relationships. It is also part of the mystification of the industrial system, and an incitement to further production and consumption, what Guy Debord and the Situationists called "The Society of the Spectacle."

Transnational Corporations and Financial Speculation

The fragmentary nature of the global system is reflected most graphically in the astonishing growth of international financial speculation. The industrial corporation makes or buys and sells things, and trades internationally—at least between one national subsidiary and another (this internal activity accounts for about 40 percent of international merchandise trade, according to the World Bank). But this trade in goods is now dwarfed by a tidal wave of about $1 trillion *per day* of speculative financial transactions; some forty to fifty times the volume of international merchandise trade. This development reflects not corporate power, but the skepticism of holders of huge assets about the wisdom of investments in production and consumption.

Of course it is difficult to know how much of the enormous turnover in international financial speculation indicates repeated trading of a much smaller amount, particularly since there are so few controls on the movement of capital. It is clear that speculative fever destroyed the European Exchange Rate Mechanism (ERM) twice in as many years: first in 1992, when speculators overwhelmed the once-mighty Bank of England, betting that the pound was overvalued against the German mark and would drop below the level permitted under the ERM; and again in 1993, when speculators forced the transformation of the entire ERM into a system of loosely floating exchange rates.

The daily global speculative capital casino attracts the "smart money" of those like George Soros, whose quick (and huge) profit-taking reflects a disinclination to invest in transnationals over the long term. This dematerialization of investment into financial instruments that allow investors to change a position almost instantly mirrors, in some ways, the "virtual corporation" where manufacturing, distribution, and marketing organizations join to form transitory corporate entities for specific projects, then disap-

pear six months or a year later, when the product becomes obso-
lescent. Such arrangements are facilitated by the shifting nature of
communications and advanced command, control, communications, and intelligence technologies initially developed to meet the
needs of the nuclear military.

The globalized world is thus best understood as a system
with important but relatively unstable islands of capital seeking
short-term profits, always ready to shed employees and "unprofitable" divisions. As the global system grows more intrusive and
encompassing, it potentiates an increased number of hierarchical
organizations. These organizations knit together to form an increasingly corporate-shaped civil society: an amalgam of business,
social, and political entities associated in complex ways with government on every level.

The Transnational Corporation and the Nation State

That the largest corporate entities, with operations in 100 or
more nations, are exemplars for industrial globalization does not
mean they are exempt from the influence of civil society and
government structures. Indeed, global corporations are highly
transitory within national contexts, and each nation in which a
transnational operates will generally require the establishment of
a locally chartered corporate entity that acts like a domestic and
not a foreign corporation, even though the law may permit it to be
100 percent owned by the parent transnational.[4]

Most corporate charters can be revoked for failing to serve
the public good, for illegal activity, for action outside the limits of
the charter, or for failure to file corporate reports—although such
revocation has been rare in recent decades for major corporations
in the United States. Through an organization called Charter Inc.,
Richard Grossman and Frank Adams are educating grassroots
groups on charter revocation campaigns to be used against abusive
corporate power. In addition, corporations of every sort are pur-

chased and merged, go bankrupt, are reorganized, etc. Corporations, giant or tiny, are subject to the vagaries of the capitalist market and the power of nation states: corporations can be taxed, nationalized, forced into joint ownership arrangements with nation states. Unlike the sovereign state, a corporation has no necessary association with a given territory and its peoples; corporations are configurations of business assets and, despite considerable prattle about corporate culture, they bear little resemblance to the amalgam of history and belief that supports a state. Corporations can and do die. Their passing, in general, amounts to far less than the rise and fall of nation states.

The imperatives of globalization encourage the flexible and transitory nature of the transnational corporation, which is often divided into complementary divisions acting as relatively independent entrepreneurial organizations within the parameters set by corporate strategy. Although transnationals are driven to weaken the nation state, they do not seek to replace it, for the same reason that capitalism had little interest in maintaining chattel slavery: it costs less to hire a worker than to provide for all of a person's needs.

Thus, globalization cannot, at this point, be understood as a neoimperialist effort led by the corporation to cast aside the bonds of nationhood in the interest of profit. Although the transnational corporation has enormous economic power and political influence, it has fundamental weaknesses as a basic organizational form for industrial civilization.

Still, the ultimate power of the transnationals is the collective power of the industrial system. This power can be manifested by capital strikes (that is, withholding capital or disinvestment) or boycotts—thus Francois Mitterand's French socialist government quickly found itself forced to change its ambitious agenda in response to capital flight—and can be supported by the military and political power of nation states.

Transnational Dynamics

The watchwords for the evolving transnational corporation are "flexible specialization," the use of sophisticated computer technology in design, manufacture, inventory control, and personnel management. The transnational corporation must operate in a dazzling array of different markets, creating and satisfying demand for an ever-evolving cornucopia of products. For example, 600 car models are available in the United States alone.

The corporation must become more "efficient," that is, increase sales per employee and reduce costs. This imperative means not only dismissing production workers, whose numbers have already been cut in many areas through automation, but shedding layers of middle managers and other organizational figures whose services are no longer required. Thus Johnson & Johnson, with $34 billion in sales, uses just 1.5 percent of its 82,700 workers as a headquarters staff to coordinate the operation of 166 decentralized health care-related businesses.[5] It is striking that *Business Week*, a reliable provider of aggressive managerial wisdom, notes, "Big means complex, and complexity results in inefficiencies, bureaucratic bloat and strangled communication....To avoid the fate of the old Soviet Union, corporate America is undergoing its own perestroika, splitting its assets into smaller, more efficient, more independent businesses."[6]

It is also striking that the largest corporations are adopting organizational frameworks that reflect, to an extent, the decentralist ideas of E. M. Schumacher and the practices of the successful Mondragon cooperatives in the Basque region of Spain, which generally limit individual co-ops to 500 owner members. This decentralization both limits internal bureaucracy and maintains the organization's entrepreneurial effectiveness. However, while Schumacher's ideas and Mondragon's practices indicate commitment to a community-based, human scale, transnational corporations adapt these forms unencumbered by real democracy and without true nonhierarchical structures.

For example, Floris A. Malgers, an executive with Unilever (a transnational corporation known in North America through such brands as Lipton Tea and Lux), uses ecological diction to describe organizational evolution: "Flexibility rather than hierarchy should always be a transnational's motto—today and in the future." He notes, "In all of Unilever's reorganizations, historically, top management has tried to combine a decentralized structure (which has the advantage of providing deep understanding of local markets) with a degree of centralized control. In other words, we strive for unity in diversity."[7]

Trade, Self-Interest, and Globalization

There is confusion over the most appropriate venues for industrial self-interest, as shown by the long and sometimes bitter debates among leading industrialized nation states over trade and economic treaties. An even more disorienting confusion suffuses national and multinational consideration of political relationships, in particular the proper role of the United Nations and "multilateralism" in foreign policy.

All this confusion suggests the real need for a new political economy to adjust our common interests to changing reality. But the imperatives of industrial and capitalist growth do not admit second thoughts: a reflexive embrace of free trade (meaning the unfettered movements of goods and capital) is the *sine qua non* of global integration, i.e., of the heightened competition that is supposed to lead to more goods, more income, and lower prices.

However, as the gap between nations and transnational corporations widens, it becomes more difficult to balance particular local and national interests against common global interests, as shown in conflicts over NAFTA, the Maastricht Treaty

advancing European economic and political union, and the Bolivian round of GATT.

In the United States, the NAFTA debate brought the usually
obscure question of trade policy to political center stage. The argument
concerned not only economic benefit, but also national sovereignty and
the preemption of environmental regulations, social programs, and
worker protections as nontariff barriers to trade. The debate even
included questions about the wisdom of globalization itself, and about
the nature of low-wage competition from countries with far-from-
democratic governments and far-from-free trade unions.

In Europe, community integration was delayed many times.
When it finally came to pass, however, ratification of the Maastricht
Treaty was not celebrated as a triumph. It came a few months after the
collapse of the ERM, which pushed European monetary union and a
central bank into the future. The Economist, an enthusiastic cheerleader
for capitalist globalization, marked approval of the treaty with a cover
showing a pie floating in the sky captioned, "The Maastricht Recipe."[8]

Opposition to NAFTA in the United States and Canada came from
people who thought they were being asked to give up substantial
control over their lives and national culture in return for promises of
unspecified benefits. Similarly, those opposed to Maastricht and the
Bolivian round of GATT were moved by national interests. The French
government, in particular, was under enormous pressure at home to
maintain its subsidies to farmers who would be devastated by low-cost
imports. But those governments whose transnational corporations
would benefit from opening new markets and removal of trade restraints pursued approval of these agreements with a vengeance.*

---

* In the same way, the United States often stops state governments from instituting
environmental, health, and safety regulations that interfere with "interstate commerce"
and the due process clause of the Fourteenth Amendment—written to protect freed
slaves, but also applied to corporations.

Globalization has significance beyond the fact that French farmers or Japanese apple and rice growers may be threatened by lower-cost products. It also means the industrialization of agriculture—dairy cows, for instance, as genetically cloned supercows living on giant, "optimized" farms, their milk production stimulated by genetically engineered hormones. Perhaps in the agro-industrialist's dreams, "dairy" means eliminating cows and building huge factories with genetically engineered udder cells floating in nutrient vats, the milk extracted by filtration.

The Failures of Globalization

As the most recent incarnation of Adam Smith's invisible hand, the global corporations' pursuit of self-aggrandizement supposedly works for the general welfare. The question is whether "welfare" refers to the transnationals or to human and natural ecologies. In our world, the transnational corporations have "rights" to penetrate and dominate new markets; to move capital and profits without restraint; to copyright and patent intellectual property (anything from books and computer programs to the genetic code used to form new products, including drugs, chemicals, and plant and animal varieties). In addition, the globalization of industrial society includes not only the globalization of factories, but the globalization of pollution, of weapons production, of western technocratic management and its communications infrastructure.

In many ways, the new industrialization (aside from nations such as Korea, Taiwan, and Singapore, which enjoyed enormous assistance—for political and strategic reasons—from the West) must be accounted a failure: the gulf between North and South, rich and poor, is widening, not shrinking; the transfer of wealth—in the form of payments on loans lavished upon southern elites by northern bankers, often for weapons and mega-projects—continues to increase. As Jane Jacobs has pointed out in *Cities and the Wealth of Nations: Principles of Economic Life*, placing industrial factories with subsistence-wage jobs in once-rural areas does little to establish the dynamic regions necessary for real and sustainable economic development.[9] What remain are what Jacobs calls "transactions of decline."

The broadening North-South divide further weakens the nation states of the South and increases their dependency upon states of the North. Ours is the era of the refugee: Haitians and Vietnamese fleeing in pitiful boats, political refugees interned in German camps, immigrants from a region (North Africa) once described as part of France, now targets of French fascism.

One illusion of power is that those who are most important can be defined economically—specifically, the governments of the Group of Seven (G-7), the United States, Japan, Germany, Great Britain, France, Italy, and Canada. On another level, those who matter are defined politically, to include nuclear-armed Russia and rapidly industrializing China. These two countries—along with Brazil, with its large economy (and, after the United States, the world's biggest debt)—are sometimes discussed as new G-7 members. G-7 membership was supposed to be based on GNP, but depending on how one counts, Spain exceeds Italy, and China and Brazil have very significant industrialized economies.

The new reality in these countries (and in India) reflects the creation of a substantial low-waged industrial base along with a consuming class of some tens of millions, while average annual incomes and standards of living are declining for the majority of the population. A large percentage of the people in these countries live in squalid poverty, as in the huge slum districts (*favelas*) in Brazil's Sao Paulo—one of the world's largest metropolitan areas with a population projected to be over twenty million by the year 2000—and in South China, where whole landscapes have been transformed to accommodate new factories.

Political questions and their economic implications are marked by a confusing diversity of opinions, both within nations and among the "community" of industrialized nations. The development and regulatory arms of the United Nations, and regional and subregional groups, provide means to expand, integrate, and order the world industrial system. The United Nations is the creature of nation states; its response to globalization is informed by the fact that nearly all national elites support the norms of industrial civilization. But power in the United Nations has never been vested in the General Assembly, where each nation has one vote, but in the Security Council, where major powers hold a permanent seat and veto power. Even this power is not always deemed sufficient. The United Nations has through U.S. eyes been of uncertain value in reliable pursuit of U.S. interests. This lack of confidence is expressed in the right-wing rumblings about the dangers of "multilateralism" and U.S. participation in UN "peace-keeping" missions, even though most have been organized in accord with U.S. policy goals.

Global Choices

Ultimately, those pursuing power must choose between species of global technocratic order—more or less decentralized, more or less dominated by transnationals, more or less government regulated. Ultimately, those pursuing freedom and community must choose between reconciling our lives with industrial society, and trying to limit and transform industrialism. Globalization can be the arena for a decentering and positive transformation of industrialism.

At present, the political leadership of the G-7 countries (mostly self-proclaimed friends of the environment) remain resolutely committed to a policy of industrial and economic growth as measured by GNP. No one voices questions that address the possibility of industrial collapse in conventional political discourse;

instead, we are asked to choose between those who see no real limits to industrial exploitation and the "responsible" environmentalists who offer regulatory mechanisms that codify the rules allowing continued growth of production, consumption, and pollution (or those, such as the Competitive Enterprise Institute, who argue that the "free market" has always been an effective protector of the environment while regulatory schemes merely increase costs and stifle change[10]).*

Barry Commoner has made it clear that regulation is a failure in terms of environmental protection. Neither "hard" nor "soft" industrial paths address issues of social transformation; rather, they offer choices between more or less regulation. Technocrats are willing to impose constraints only to achieve "sustainable" industrial development, not to transform the way of life responsible for the current crisis of civilization.

The new international system needs help to sweep away impediments presented by local communities. It needs standardized protocols for trade and communication, capital flows to accelerate exchange in the global market, and enforcement to assure compliance with the rules of the game (note that nations always, or almost always, pay debts to international bankers and protect foreign investment). Thus, the international system does respect existing power relationships between states, particularly

---

*An example of current free-market reality is a small Czech town, Libkovice, with the misfortune of being located on top of a vast deposit of soft lignite coal, a particularly polluting fossil fuel (although it can be processed to be somewhat less dangerous). In 1992, the townspeople fought a joint Czech government-corporate venture that would have destroyed the town (after relocating the residents) so as to mine the coal more efficiently. In addition to the residents, the graves of between 13,000 and 17,000 Red Army, Polish, Belgian, and French POWs murdered by the Nazis would have to be relocated. The life of the community would be extinguished but, it was argued, for the long-term benefit of the nation and the highest profit for the joint-venture partners. No other soft coal deposits in Czech land can be so easily strip-mined. There was little interest in responding to Libkovice's remaining residents' calls for help.[11]

between rich (that shall be made richer) and poor (that shall come to despise their poverty), so long as these relationships promote economic growth and integration.

Transnational environmental regulation is a new feature of this global integration. For the high-minded, it is an attempt to take appropriate steps to sustain development so both rich and poor can get richer. The 1992 Rio World Environmental Summit provides a good example. The broad principles of the Rio declaration, agreed to by consensus among nations (while the transnational corporations met nearby) recognized environmental responsibilities, but also made it unequivocally clear (in Principle II) that nations had the right to use and exploit resources within their borders, and (in Principle I) identified the primacy of human life above all others in environmental questions—as if human life could be separated from the web of life or was somehow ultimately in conflict with it.

Environmentalists of the rich nations are terrified not only of population growth in the poor nations, but of the possibility that poor nations will, in fact, attempt to do what the rich nations are telling them to do: industrialize and live as the rich do. Elites of the poor nations are told: you must industrialize, monetize, and control population growth so you can repay your titanic debt. But they are also told that they shall not do as we do: North Americans, for example, may cut their forests; South Americans shall not. There is widespread anger in the media about Brazilian deforestation, while clear-cutting in North America, and now in the Siberian forest, accelerates, and Japan drives Asian deforestation as the region's leading consumer of pulp wood and saw logs. In another example, popular concern is expressed over China burning its coal, while Organization for Economic Cooperation and Development (OECD) nations burn incredible amounts of coal and oil. And in its attempt to deal with global warming, the Clinton administration has proposed policies that will give credits to U.S.-based corporations that reduce emissions overseas while continuing business-as-usual at home.

Governments and international organizations provide aid to elites of poor nations and their armies, so long as these elite groups are willing to accommodate the requirements of the industrial order. Every poor nation is a potential site for low-wage factories and for waste disposal; a source for commodities to supply the North (and to be resold in the form of value-added goods to the South). The International Monetary Fund (IMF), the World Bank, and the European Bank for Reconstruction and Development do not merely enforce the monetary and economic discipline of the hard-eyed neoclassical economists; above all, they act on behalf of industrial integration.

Thus, the tension continues: industrialism must go forward yet hold back; encourage uninhibited participation in production and consumption yet deny the South the wherewithal to participate. Multinational and international agencies attempt to apply global technocracy to advance the process of global integration by harmonizing and limiting the power of nation states, and at the same time disciplining (on occasion, by any means necessary) recalcitrant nations in the interests of the more powerful. This was George Bush's New World Order: same as before but more. But the realities of a world of global markets and collapsing nations cannot be constrained by a United States in decline, by a NATO, or by a United Nations as the best available imperial proxy. Chaotic change is the order of the day.

chapter four

CONTESTING ALTERNATIVES: INTRODUCTION

THIS CHAPTER INTRODUCES OUR EXPLORATION of what I see as the three basic alternatives to existing industrialism. Its approach is not in the form of familiar industrial categories. Rather, it is an excursus that extends beyond the confines of predictable argument to touch upon issues and themes that are valuable in seeing our world and its possibilities with new eyes.

Thus we examine questions of theory and ideology, science and the undoing of industrial assumptions, relationship as the generative force of change, and the practice of an ecological dialectic. While abstract, its purpose is to help enliven the concrete analysis that follows with a sense that in searching for a liberatory future we can indeed get there from here.

Antipodes and Possibility

The challenges we face are rooted in both the end of Cold War politics and the deepening ecological crisis of industrial civilization. With the shattering of the binary opposition between capitalism and communism we now see a matrix of antipodes, a panoply of oppositions and relationships: between rich and poor, South and North, industrialized and nonindustrialized, democracy and hierarchy, centrifugal and centripetal forces and formulations (see Figure 4-1 below).

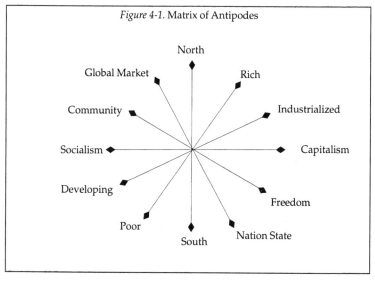

Figure 4-1. Matrix of Antipodes

The dynamics of these lines of social tension represent deep fissures within industrial civilization. Our task is not a matter of replacing one dualism with another, or finding the new demons by using such formulations as "terrorism" or "Islamic fundamentalism" to replace the communist threat in the popular imagination. These deepening fissures threaten to shatter industrial civilization. But they also suggest outlines of possibility.

Three broad themes cohere along the planes of tension, reflecting alternative visions for the transformation of industrial civilization. These are worth examining in detail.

- *Global Management*—strategies for maintaining global industrialism, more or less reformed.
- *Authoritarian Responses*—the embrace of unfreedom as a way to redeem the industrial world.
- *Alternatives to Industrialism*—transformations of the system, ranging from attempts at optimization to ecological societies.

On a basic level, these are responses to industrial excess, choices representing an end to the certitudes of industrial modernity and offering profoundly different futures. This triad is somewhat arbitrary, as the themes overlap to some degree. Global management, for example, may be "greened" not merely by consumer consciousness, but by the environmentalism of an Al Gore, or by attempts at accommodation, such as the one proposed by the German *realo* Green and Social Democratic alliance. Those working to reform World Bank practices may also be part of a transformative movement, and not merely advocates of a global managerial strategy. An authoritarian anti-modernism, such as that of the Nazis or contemporary Islamic theocracies, may also embrace particular versions of a perfected industrial order.

But with due regard for the dangers of oversimplification, this three-part division provides a reasonable way to explore the responses to industrial reality. It provides, for instance, a useful way to examine popular concerns about nationalism and the politics of identity that have surfaced in the post-Cold War world. Instead of focusing on "nationalism" or "identity" as tribal atavisms unleashed by the communist collapse, we can see them as expressions of resistance to global integration and the weakening of the nation state. This resistance is variously expressed: for example, by attempts to attain a mythic social order based on exclusive definitions of a privileged group, such attempts bringing with them the politics of authoritarianism and bigotry. These nationalist and identity tensions are not driven by past antipathies, but by industrial business in the present; they could potentially express an integrative pursuit if they involved ecological social transformation. The choice is not a matter of destiny, but of social practice.*

Understanding the nature and dynamics of these alternatives poses a considerable challenge. We must consider transformative social forces within the context of industrial reality, but we cannot understand them solely within the limits of industrial categories. Our task is to chart a path away from the nexus of industrial power. In so doing, we risk, as Foucault warned, not escaping our miseries, but reinvigorating the themes and strictures of power with a self-defeating reformism. We can, for example, shout about approaching environmental catastrophe and offer what amounts to a more rational, more reasonable, more profitable, more soulful industrialism.

It is indeed hard to predict the form of the butterfly from the segments of the larval worm or the shape of the chrysalis, but the truths of a transformation inhere in the process. Industrialism proclaimed a break with all that came before, an escape from the limits that had structured human life. We seek to escape from the hubris of industrialism.

To begin, we should present some clarifying points. This survey is not a formal methodology or research program, but an

---

* Such themes of identity are also often manifest in political dramas much less apocalyptic than the war in the former Yugoslavia: as part of right-wing "hot button" electoral strategies of division based on race, or in attempts to develop an inclusive multiculturalism (pilloried by the right as an assault upon mainly white middle-class entitlements).

attempt to turn on the light of possibility for eyes blinded by industrial nights.

Caveats and Standpoints: Theory and Reality

Theory is not reality; the world is not reducible to equations, binary codes, or bitstreams of data. The present shimmers; life is expansive, self-conscious of its past, present, and possibilities.

Theory, social or otherwise, is an assertion of truth, subject to the test of falsifiability. Theory as science tends toward the fixed, the mathematical, the inhuman—or more precisely, the not merely human. Science is supported by *data*, not *belief*; in an industrial age of technique, science is privileged truth. Theory, then, is "objective."

Ideology, on the other hand, is supposedly misleading, the province of fanaticism and false consciousness. Ideology leaves us prey to self-delusion, the nonscientific, the unprogressive: theory is to ideology as science is to religion.

Both theory and ideology guide and condition practice. Ideology is more than false consciousness; theory is less than a framework for objective truth. Ideology is the fabric of implicit and explicit claims and beliefs that underlie theory and civilization. Ideology, as the late Alvin Gouldner suggests, can be understood as lying beneath theory; it serves to condition our analysis.[1] Ideology is suffused with belief, and therefore human.

Those in power, whether the petrified ideologists of communism or the less official but no less devoted capitalist intellectuals, argue that the status quo means the demise of false consciousness. Thus, at the height of the Cold War, Daniel Bell wrote about an "end to ideology," meaning an end to communism as alternative to capitalist democracy, and Francis Fukuyama at the Cold War's end offered, more grandly, an "end to history."[2] For Fukuyama, "history produced as a consequence of the unfolding of modern natural science moves in a single coherent direction"[3]—which he also identifies with capitalist, liberal democracy.*

To consider future prospects, we will have to move beyond the belief that this is the best of all possible worlds. To effectively examine contesting visions, we must consider the validity of their claims and the nature of their responses to common conditions. We must step back from the struggles of the moment: the alternatives are rooted in deep social structures that include not merely industrial imperatives, but the human experience that is our social, cultural, and historic legacy.

Change and Science

The industrial world gives change the imprimatur of science—not merely as theory, but as a reliable explanation for social conduct and historical circumstance. Humanity's future is reduced to competing mathematical curves. We have, for example, views of industrialism as an entropic system, using up the earth and its resources, and introducing irreversible disorder; or the idea of dissipative structures that establish a new stability.

The danger of such scientific metaphors, analogies, and appeals to "laws of nature" is clear in such formulations as Social Darwinism (and its recent expression in *The Bell Curve*), which describes a struggle for existence and the virtues of the powerful, or in the murderous eugenics practiced by the Nazis. Science is

---

* Marx and Engels developed a "scientific," as opposed to "utopian," socialism. Theirs was a socialism of inevitability, of history driven by a class struggle—a movement of clarity, not confusion. According to Marx and Engels, revolutionary denouement would deliver communist industrial utopia. Adam Smith in *The Wealth of Nations* also mechanized history: greed was transmuted through the magic of the market's invisible hand into common good. This theory has been refined by generations of capitalist economists and apologists who offer the industrial world as, at bottom, a "humane economy."[4]

used to mask hard social choices beneath complex technical rhetoric. As Jean Chesneaux warns in *Brave Modern World: The Prospects for Survival*:

> Confronted with the complex singularity of our period, the current wisdom also knows how to appeal to the theoretical tools of science proper. However embryonic specialized knowledge in mathematics, physics, astrophysics and genetics may be, any self-respecting "modern" intellectual will readily refer to this systematic thinking of von Bartalanffy, to the dynamics of instability and chaos, to dissipative structures and random fluctuations of Ilya Prigogine, to the mathematical theory of catastrophes developed by René Thom, to the play of bifurcations, to the "fractal objects" of Benoît Mandelbrot, to the black holes of astral space. Familiarization with these new points of reference represents for some a real effort of methodological advancement, even if others are just indulging in fashionable language and letting themselves be awestruck by these strange, seductive, but above all euphoric and reassuring, terms. The sophisticated and somewhat esoteric references arrive just in time; they offer a comforting reading of the contemporary crisis. There is nothing disquieting or unstable in disorder; it is the normal state of things in the immense universe as it is on the scale of the most infinitesimal particles. Once again, our society has only to take inspiration from the world of nature.[5]

We have watched, with murmurs of satisfaction, as science appropriates the terrain formerly occupied by philosophy, now largely banished by academics to exploring texts and language games. In the same fashion, social science collapsed with structuralism, and social scientists are now bogged down with concerns over alternative discourses and the deconstruction of texts.*

---

* And those postmodern theorists who could show how events have repudiated theory have themselves been decentered following the unmasking of deconstructionist Paul de Man as a small-time Nazi propagandist and anti-Semite, and the unmasking of the great ontologist Martin Heidegger as a big-time Nazi sympathizer and collaborator. De Man's pursuits have been described as appropriate for a man with an imperative need to reinvent himself, to stay insulated from his past by faith

So-called pure science has rushed in to fill the void with its claims of objectivity and truth: moral reservations and social concerns are allegedly external to the practice of "pure" (as opposed to "applied") science. Science can offer a worldview that claims to be, in the terms of Richard Rorty, "a mirror of nature." Those who challenge this view are irrationalists, fools, mystics, obscurantists, and—worse—Luddites.With philosophy and social science vanquished, popular, activist, and scholarly imaginations are reduced to choices between good science and bad science, appropriate and inappropriate technology. Global managers, technologists, and scientists offer counsel and ask us to cede our lives to the results of computer models—whether reassuring or terrifying—as a replacement for the practice of democracy and social choice.

Suspension of Industrial Assumptions

Industrial civilization blinds us with the euphoria of the object. If we strip away the mask of comfort and illusion, the magic of steam engines leads to the flash of the hydrogen bomb. Industrial man becomes murdering man; the system of production and consumption is a killing system through its inclination to total domination and ecocide. In the relative calm between episodes of slaughter, those who enjoy the peace of the dominant culture—who are removed, albeit only temporarily, from the contested paths of industrial power through accidents of geography

---

in nearly inexhaustible varieties of interpretations for his life as well as for texts. The case of Heidegger seems to raise more questions. All too many of our philosophers ignore the human specificity of our lives: a life is not just one discourse among many, but the lived expression of dynamic social structures—informed by the accumulated personal and social experience of this and preceding generations that guides our lives and cultures.

or history—can opine, laptops at the ready, about our bright technological future.

Industrial ideology attempts to reduce our prospects to the progressive unfolding of technological inevitabilities. For instance, it claims that with the information superhighway (where interactive television is both *agora* and *polis*), we will transcend our bodies as we leap to commercial cyberspace—eros transmuted to peripatetic electroliths consuming information products at the speed of light. But suppose we assume that our lives have not simply been poured into a technological funnel that renders us blind and deaf to the living world; suppose we see history as more than a swirl downward through this funnel that expels us, homogenized and wasted. Suppose we are, for some moments, no longer good Germans or patriotic Americans who neither see the blood nor hear the screams.

Let us recognize that an industrial consuming class shall always be a small minority of the world's peoples, and its hierarchs an infinitesimally small number. And, further, let us recognize that the imperatives of the consuming class—to expand limitlessly, to struggle for dominance—are the hard, cold death of the child and the bird.

Industrialism undermines the inextricably joined natural and social ecologies. It reduces the natural world, so-called *first nature*, to resources and raw materials, and the world of culture, so-called *second nature*, to a society that defines the industrial as normal and is proud to dominate the living world. The industrial world is the province of method, of matter and reduction, not of life. Industrial bosses want to extirpate limits; their ideologues warn of a fundamental danger to the future of life and propose a solution that a portion of new growth be set aside to assist the poor in striving for the sustainable industrial nirvana of endless growth without consequence (or guilt).

Instead of lending our voices to this bleating industrial chorus, we can ask questions designed to crack open comfortable assumptions (even our own). Suppose that industrial inevitabilities are foremost eschatologies in the self-interest of power—myths about endings and beginnings that immobilize and disempower us. Our future need not be a trajectory of progress, from the flight of an arrow to the gravity's rainbow of a nuclear missile. The world is not a machine, our lives not manufactured products. We can unplug our television sets.

And if our world and our future is not a machine, not a technological inevitability, then we, machine-liberated, must face the primacy of relationship.

Relationship as the Gate to Transformation

"Relationship" is useful not as a concept to uncover value-free truth or to divine the meaning of history, but as a point of entry into the search for direction and agreement.

The concept of relationship supports the politics of renewal; it is the ecological world's expansive response to mechanistic reduction.[6] It is not a politics, but a recognition of unity in diversity from which an ecological politics arises. The importance of relationship is not its power as idea, but the fact that it is essential to an active response to industrial excess. We need to consider the forces contesting to shape our future outside the hidebound definitions of power, politics, and possibility: viewing the world from the standpoint of relationship, we can begin to reveal the prismatic visages of possibility.

Relationship can serve as a bridge between the presumably objective and ineffably subjective, between fated progress and ecological choice. Relationship does not bear the imprimatur of (as Benito Mussolini wrote of fascism) "a formula of truth";[7] rather, it is a matter of engagement and connection with the world. Relationship is the lubricity of circumstance. Relationship is meaningful not only to the life of an ecological society; it is relevant for our considerations of the industrial mainstream and its authoritarian aspects.

Much of the literature of the ecological movement, as broadly defined—from Edward Goldsmith's *The Way: An Ecological World-View*, to Fritjof Capra's *The Turning Point: Science, Society, and the Rising Culture*, to Morris Berman's *The Reenchantment of the World*, to Arne Naess's work on deep ecology, to Henryk Skolimowski's *Eco-Philosophy: Designing New Tactics for Living*[8]—involves detailed discussion of worldviews needed to supplant the scientism and Cartesian dualism at the heart of industrial civilization. For some thinkers, it is easier to understand the contours of thought, the organization of ideas, than the shape of life—as if industrial civilization somehow cohered around the ideas of Rene Descartes, Francis Bacon, and Isaac Newton, and not as a result of stupendous social, political, and economic changes: including happenings as disparate as the Treaty of Westphalia in 1648, establishing the formal basis for what would become the industrial nation state, and the inflationary stimulus from a huge influx of gold and silver following the colonization of the Americas.

This criticism is not to suggest an exclusively materialist conception of history. Rather, it is to suggest that the idealist-materialist dichotomy misses the point, that civilization arises from the most complex interactions. Industrialism no more simply arose when Descartes emerged from his study than it did when Christopher Columbus began the conquest of the Americas. Each of these events, in its fashion, was both creation and creator of its times. Attempts to rank idealist vs. materialist contributions are as unavailing as attempts to separate the influences of heredity and environment: ideal and material, nature and nurture are realized only within the context of dynamic living experience.

Using relationship as a portal to understanding allows us to recognize a multiplicity of shifting forces and influences—for example, to see that ideas express not simply personal thoughts, but social formulations and lifeways. The artifacts of human life are not found simply in material culture, but in our lives and ideas. Recognizing a multiplicity of influences does not mean that we have to codify them or anoint some hierarchy of forces by privileging, for example, economic relationships, as do marxists and capitalists.

Moreover, a focus on relationship as central to understanding change subsumes a recognition that change is basic and fundamental. Relationship is the generative force of change: events are not simply caused; life is the result of connection, influence, and intimacy on many levels. Relationship is at the root of dialectical change: when excess leads to a countervailing response, people's lives, not history, are at work. The conduct of the industrial world leads to responses, among them the "ecological response"; but the ecological response is clearly not the sole, necessary, or privileged answer to industrial reality. The processes of change itself vary and evolve; these are human processes, and not the expression of some abstract and timeless logic of history.

Industrialism, on the other hand, views change as the "logic" of progress and struggle. As practiced by marxists, such a dialectic is negative, produced by conflict, and inevitable. The industrial dialectic is exclusive, the province of the either/or, yes/no logic of computers and commissars; it elides "struggle" with "conquest"—conquest of nature, of peoples, of the planet; it makes endless choices between either A or B, and orders the results hierarchically. But the logic of history and of change in human lives may be more analogous to the "logic" of the weather—a logic rooted in the dynamic relationship between life and planet, and subject to both celestial forces and innumerable local perturbations, from footsteps to the flapping of a butterfly's wings.

An ecological dialectic rejects not struggle, but the endless slaughter of industrial negation—this is its dialectical origin. An ecological dialectic is inclusive, chooses both A and B; it generates matrices of relationships, not hierarchies of subservience. This is the logic of conversation, of ecosystems, of interpretations—not a timeless expression of progress and perfection, but the contingent expression of life. Such a dialectic does not anoint any predetermined future. It may, however, help make an ecological future possible—in the same way that hard, "objective," mechanistic science inclines us to pursue industrial ends, but cannot, by itself, assure industrialism's future. Science need not be industrial science; likewise, an appreciation of relationship need not lead to an ecological civilization. The future is in our hands and our hearts.

chapter five

CONTESTING ALTERNATIVES: GLOBAL MANAGEMENT

THIS CHAPTER CONSIDERS GLOBAL MANAGEMENT as one of the three basic alternatives for the future of industrial civilization. It attempts to anatomize the logic and common sense of industrial managers.

Global managerialism offers a further intensification of industrialism and its markets. Global managers embrace market-driven growth and technological innovation as the solution to our problems, and not as the path to deeper troubles.

Global Management

Global management is the base case for industrialism's future. As a corrective force, global management attempts to apply industrial means to modify the consequences of industrial ends. For the global manager, the leveling action of markets combined with the wonder of technology will help heal the wounds of industrialism. This belief means the manager must first free the forces of the market and technology, then manage (but not control) industrial change.

The global managers act from within government and business, and from advocacy and advisory organizations that represent managerial capitalism, bureaucratic hierarchies, and the professoriate. In broad terms, their approach implements the neoliberal agenda for growth and limitation: it is reform from above, not a challenge to the prerogatives of power. Managers enlist the powerful by appealing to their self-interest, and seek the support of activists to press for the steps needed to make the industrial order "sustainable." Global management focuses on technological innovation, regulatory design, and social changes required to accommodate the world to "rational" industrial and market imperatives.

The insightful global manager, like Peter Drucker in his *Post-Capitalist Society*, sees in the weakening of nations and the rise of subnational organizations a new venue for reforming the corporate industrial state. This faith in progress and markets often has a Panglossian tone—"This is the best of all possible worlds"—meaning there are no acceptable alternatives. Global managers construe tensions within the system in terms of the values of those in power. They redefine the essential relationship of the poisoned to the poisoners, of communities fighting industrial abuse: resistance is a misguided impediment to development or, at best, an impulse for reform, not real change.

Neoliberalism

Global management must be understood within the context of its guiding ideology, neoliberalism. In application, this ideology is a species of traditional liberalism informed by a new awareness of limits. Liberal doctrine sees price signals sent by competitive markets as a way to encourage growth and efficient utilization of resources, and thus sees a need to expand market forces. Global management has an unquestioned commitment to industrial growth expressed through a militant internationalism, support of expanded trade, the development of international and regional organizations, and a global militarism to defend the status quo.

Neoliberalism accepts the need for prudent regulation of industrial forces, but only as a corollary to the interests of growth and power. Thus, after triumphing over labor, environmentalist, and populist opponents of NAFTA, Bill Clinton could say the treaty represented both beneficial growth and the opportunity for true environmental reform—that is, NAFTA would increase the aggregate industrial social product (by whom, and at what cost and for whose benefit is not discussed) and encourage compliance with existing environmental regulations. In these matters, global management supports not a generalized world system, but the major industrial powers and their multifarious corporate and financial entities. Despite occasional heartfelt pleas for reform, management is a political or economic actor in the interests of a dynamic status quo. While many exponents of global management may use revolutionary rhetoric, their practice has to do with such measures as developing and expanding markets in rights to pollute.

For neoliberals, value is equal to price. They determine the value of species to be saved from extinction by what must be paid for their protection. They determine the cost of pollution by the price paid for emission entitlements, sold by those who pollute less to those who pollute more.

Neoliberalism has a particular political resonance in the United States and other capitalist and neocapitalist nations, particularly in Russia and the former Soviet Republics and European satellites, the states of the so-called near abroad. Neoliberalism does not recognize limits to market forces, but only to the efficacy of government action. For neoliberalism, government action is necessary largely in the event of market failure, to assist, as William

Ruckelshaus suggests, in "bending the market" to help meet environmental and social needs.[1]

Neoliberalism in Application

Scientific American for September 1989 contains a classic exposition of the science and politics underlying managerial neoliberalism. In an article entitled "Managing Planet Earth," William Clark of the Kennedy School of Government and editor of *Environment Magazine* writes of the need "to get on with the task of responsibly managing planet earth,"[2] that is, he explains, to manipulate the world for continuing industrial use. He introduces discussion of atmosphere, climate, water, biodiversity, human population, agriculture, energy, manufacturing, and sustainable economic development, in turn, to help develop a comprehensive view of management strategies.

Following Clark's introduction, in agriculture, Pierre Crosson and Norman Rosenberg of Resources for the Future in Washington, D.C. argue that world food production could grow to feed a world population of ten billion in 100 years (2089) with environmental damage less than is "apparent" at present. They believe that global use of high technology agricultural research stations will lead to genetically engineered nitrogen-fixing corn (thereby alleviating the need for fertilizers), drip irrigation systems to conserve water and limit salinization, and integrated pest management techniques to reduce pesticide use. The market, they argue, will allow proper price signals to be sent to encourage farmers to adopt necessary new techniques throughout the world. Of social impediments to agricultural plenty, Crosson and Rosenberg write:

> Markets do not function effectively, however, unless clear property rights can be established in resources to be exchanged. This is easier to do for land than for water or for genetic resources, partly because parcels of land can be readily identified and stay in place. As a result land markets operate in many areas of the world. When land is sold in these

regions, landowners reap the benefit of good land management...

Markets in water and in genetic diversity are much more difficult to establish...As it moves the same water can be used repeatedly by different individuals or institutions...Since the essence of property rights is exclusive use, markets for water are poorly developed. Most of the world's water...is distributed by publicly administered systems. Because these systems are subsidized...this is a signaling failure...

Water subsidies are deeply rooted in social and political traditions of long standing. Their removal would encounter fierce resistance...The challenge to policy makers is to design policies that carry the needed signal without provoking unacceptably high levels of conflict.[3]

Crosson and Rosenberg go on to discuss the application of market forces to genetic diversity, suggesting that people around the world who care, for example, about tropical rain forests might buy development rights from the owners of the rain forests to protect them, and that debt-for-nature swaps are an appealing idea.*

In fact, market prices for water are not simply established as a rational way to allocate resources. Water pricing may be an artifact of the development of an industrializing, export-oriented economy. For farmers, the industrial market has meant denial of the right to use water for food production, particularly on common lands and small holdings. Marketed water goes to the highest bidder—to those producing commercial cash crops, particularly

---

* Note that this formulation reduces biodiversity to signaling problems, in the hope of identifying social needs as individual needs expressed through the market. But this idea presupposes, among other things, that traditional communal peasant village life can be transformed to the point where industrialized western ideas of individual interests have meaning and have been reduced to a desire for maximum cash income. To industrialized eyes, "social" does not refer to the village or region with sustainable lifeways, but to the national state, in which prices are set by the global market. Lifeways that have been sustained over long periods, where balance is the product of nonmarket social forces, are deemed incapable of responding effectively to industrial dislocation, and so must be led by managerial wisdom into lives of cash and competition.

crops for export or those that require further value-added processing. Water becomes the property of those who can pay market
prices or make the capital investment needed for wells and irrigation systems. A water market is a response not to natural scarcity,
but to scarcity resulting from industrialized farming. As a sad
corollary, water-deprived farmers become wage laborers on cash-
crop farms. This is as true today in parts of India or in the southwestern United States as it was in Spanish Andalucia 100 years ago.

The market price of water reflects long-term relationships
between government and large landowners/industrial farm-
ers/food processors. It does not consider the ecological and social
damage wrought by the transformation to an industrial agriculture. For example, in the Jodhpur district of India, according to
Michael Goldman, most available water is controlled by large
landowners (with government collusion) and used to irrigate chili
peppers, a cash crop, while the common land of local farmers lacks
water for essential food and fodder.

> The consequences of the appropriation of the groundwater
> have been dramatic: Peasant families have lost their access to
> groundwater and have had to watch their herds die, land
> deteriorate, and their families and communities split up. They
> work as casual low-paid laborers on the chili farms, in the
> quarries, or in the informal sectors of the cities. The privatiza-
> tion of the rural commons is intensifying exploitative social
> relations and degrading ecological relations elsewhere, just as
> such trends are impacting this community. No terrain or
> production relation can be properly understood in isolation.
> The desert's mines, capitalist farms, "famine-relief" projects,
> and urban centers analyzed separately do not sufficiently
> portray the interactive dynamics at work, as is true when
> analyzed as a holistic set of contradictory processes.[4]

Conspicuously absent from Crosson and Rosenberg's work
is any discussion of the effects of cash cropping for the global
market on nations pressured by the World Bank and IMF to raise
hard currency (at egregiously unfair terms of trade) to pay their
debt for past and current development projects, and for weapons.

And while they make much of wonders to come from genetic engineering, the authors ignore the risk of relying on a few privately owned hybrids to replace genetically diverse local varieties—hybrids that could be eliminated by as yet unknown diseases, by droughts, or by heavy rains, and that may need high levels of fertilizers, pesticides, and herbicides (supplied by manufacturers such as Union Carbide at Bhopal). For example, much current effort in genetic engineering is directed not simply to creating a deep red-looking tomato for winter supermarket shelves, or to making plants resistant to pests, frost or drought, but to rendering plants herbicide resistant, able to withstand far greater doses of chemical weed killers than existing varieties.

Under NAFTA, the "price signals" embraced by global managers are likely to force perhaps one million of Mexico's corn farmers off their land and into toxic urban mega-slums, or north to the United States, as they are unable to compete with industrialized U.S. producers. Crosson and Rosenberg do conclude that agricultural problems are more social than technical, but this conclusion reflects not so much awareness of global inequities and alternative development paths as support for measures that sweep aside social impediments to growth.*

Regulation and Prohibition

Because global managers see the market as the most useful stimulus for growth, they focus on mechanisms that encourage market activity and deal with market failure. They limit social choice to market decisions: global managers find no merit in democratic social choice as a way to shape the production system. This focus explains the recent efforts to establish markets in

---

* A similar argument is a favorite of the nuclear industry: even as all their waste dumps leak, nuclear advocates swear that the problem is simply to find the political will to do what is technologically justified.

pollution rights or pollution taxes, purportedly based on the level of abuse the global environment can "sustain." In practice, this policy means defining certain rates of environmental degradation as acceptable. The unasked question is, acceptable to whom, besides those who manage and those who profit?

These measures are supposedly interim steps, a bridge (of indeterminate length) to the time when market forces will lead to development of new processes less costly than buying rights to pollute. Global managers consider such measures superior to existing means of regulating pollution (such as end-of-the-pipe or top-of-the-stack devices), which have proved expensive for polluters and capable of little more than reducing the rate of pollution increase.

Occasionally, global managers accept prohibitions in response to industrial realities where real change must occur quickly. An example is the Montreal Protocol, an international agreement by nations to gradually eliminate production of freons and other chemicals in an effort to slow and perhaps eventually stop the destruction of the earth's protective ozone layer. The protocol is predicated on the assumption that chemical companies will be able to develop refrigerant chemicals with less or no propensity for ozone destruction. Such prohibitory actions come after the fact—after grievous environmental insult—and focus on particularly damaging industrial processes.

Where complex regulations are in place, managers need to craft ways to balance growth and limitations. A good example is the so-called ecosystem approach to nationalize regulation advanced by the Clinton administration. This approach is intended both to reduce the cost to developers and ease permit approval, and to allow particular regulations, such as the Endangered Species Act, to be ignored in a given ecosystem. Such an approach will clearly facilitate managed development at the expense of wildlands and wildlife. It means negotiating a "compromise" with developers that permits species survival, at least for a time, and protecting (as opposed to preserving) a fraction (or some attributes) of undeveloped lands. Such arrangements may limit short- or medium-term exploitation and place ecosystems within a comprehensive managerial framework whose long-term impact can range from beneficial to catastrophic. This plan has drawn opposition not only from defenders of wildlands, but from those wary of greater government involvement and from protectors of private property (including corporate and industrial landowners), who see any regulation as a "taking" without compensation and due process.[5] In essence, ecosystem protection absent real community control recalls U.S. government treaties with Indian nations: the imperatives for growth offer little real choice.

The neoliberal managerial agenda is typified in such tortuous affairs as "Option Nine" to regulate logging of old growth forests in the Pacific Northwest. Options one through eight, which struck various balances between conservation and logging, were presented in 1993 by a panel chaired by a respected U.S. Forest Service scientist. The timber transnationals and their friends in Congress found these options unacceptable, so the Clinton administration crafted and imposed Option Nine. This option offers some conditional protection of old growth forest, but, according to Larry Tuttle of the Oregon Natural Resources Council, does not "permanently protect a single tree from logging."[6] The market is bent slightly, but the forest remains at risk.

All of these strategies are in sharp contrast to those that flow from the community. A strategy based on community ownership and stewardship of the land—through community or cooperative ownership—would work to keep land and forest as a truly sustainable part of a living community.*

---

* Compare this ideal with schemes to buy "development rights." These schemes are designed to stop the transfer of property to developers who cut trees to build vacation houses and subdivisions, thereby gaining the highest (short-term) monetary return. For example, when developer Charles Rancourt bought 500,000 acres of forest land in Vermont and New Hampshire from Diamond International, the

The Clinton administration's record, even before the 1994 advent of a right-wing Congress, was largely in accord with a neoliberal and pollution sensitive regulatory approach. The administration supposedly banished those, such as Bush administration former White House chief of staff John Sununu, who deny environmental realities. In fact, the changes are more in kind than degree, and sometimes the changes are matters of nuance. In 1992, Senator Albert Gore wrote in his book, *Earth in the Balance*, of the imperative need for an environmental global Marshall Plan and the reduction of greenhouse gas emissions. Reality arrived in October 1993 when Vice President Gore and President Clinton presented *The Climate Change Action Plan*. This document offers a pallid combination of technical and regulatory measures to marginally reduce U.S. greenhouse gas emissions to 1990 levels by the year 2000. In other words, success will be measured by reducing an anticipated 8 percent increase in emissions to levels already projected to be unsustainable. Yet Clinton and Gore state in italics, "*This plan harnesses economic forces to meet the challenges posed by the threat of global warming.*"

The Climate Change Action Plan reflects the administration's political judgment of the weakness of the environmental imperative. It is also classic managerial neoliberalism, relying largely on market forces, with modest aspirations for palliative improvements on the margins of current activity. The pre-1990 greenhouse

---

New Hampshire state government bought development rights of key parcels (at substantial expense). To stop second-home and recreational development, the New England states formed a study committee to consider the future of the forest with representatives of Vermont, New Hampshire, Maine, and New York. To protect the forest, the committee recommended in a 1993 report the use of tax incentives (i.e., expenditures) to encourage transnationals and others to maintain long-term ownership of large parcels, state financing to buy development rights in the event of sale, and a "national outdoors stamp" to finance conservation investment. Government is moving very slowly to implement the recommendations. A less popular alternative to transnational ownership is state or federal land purchase, which is viewed as a loss of tax revenue. Community stewardship is not considered a viable option.[7]

gas levels become a sort of unwritten entitlement. The plan makes no mention of reducing vehicle emissions by mandating an increase in gas mileage—a position supported by Clinton as presidential candidate and by Gore in *Earth in the Balance*. The plan's transportation measures include fuel economy labels for tires, encouraging telecommuting, ending federal tax subsidies for employer-constructed parking, and a plan to encourage development of state transportation efficiency programs. Also missing is any effort to achieve widespread use of photovoltaics or wind generation, except for a "renewable technology consortium" involving the U.S. Department of Energy and private utilities, to encourage commercialization.

Some of the plan's projections seem fanciful. For instance, one proposal asks for $55 million in federal seed money for the fiscal years 1995-2000 to encourage states to set up revolving funds for public building energy-management programs. This seed money, it is alleged, will stimulate $2.5 billion in nonfederal investment by states and localities, and yield a 30 percent reduction in energy use in 10 percent of public buildings, resulting in a substantial reduction of carbon-equivalent emissions.

In other words, the proposal suggests that one federal dollar will bring $45 in spending on energy conservation in public buildings. After more than a dozen years as an energy consultant for schools, hospitals, and local governments, I'm quite skeptical of these claims. They ignore substantial impediments, including insufficient tax funds to form loan pools, lack of expertise needed to identify projects, and the difficulty of measuring energy savings. Conservation loan pools may be an excellent idea, but they are unlikely to bring the projected results on the basis of a little seed money.

The Logic of Global Management and Managers

The industrial logic of the global managers rests on a triad of beliefs: first, confidence in the technical nature of industrialism; second, faith in the ability of the market (or the bureaucracy) to generate technical solutions to technical problems; third, therefore, the belief that social problems can be solved if there is sufficient political will to overcome resistance to new technical solutions. The global manager resolutely denies that industrial production is the source of the problem, not its solution.

Many advocates of global managerial strategies who may be considered (or consider themselves) enlightened reformers—such as Lester R. Brown of the Worldwatch Institute, Ruckelshaus of the Global Tomorrow Coalition, and Vice President Gore—speak of the necessity for dramatic environmental change. They present data on the impending global catastrophe in progress and even, though to a lesser degree, touch upon its social concomitants. In strikingly similar terms, they call for a nearly immediate global environmental revolution.

Ruckelshaus writes:

> Can we move nations and people in the direction of sustainability? Such a move would be a modification of society comparable in scale to only two other changes: the agricultural revolution of the late Neolithic and the industrial revolution of the past two centuries. Those revolutions were gradual, spontaneous and largely unconscious. This one will have to be a fully conscious operation, guided by the best foresight that science can provide...[8]

Lester R. Brown writes in the 1992 *State of the World: A Worldwatch Institute Report on Progress Toward a Sustainable Society*:

> There is no precedent for the change in prospect. Building an environmentally sustainable future depends on restructuring the global economy, major shifts in human reproductive behavior, and dramatic changes in values and lifestyles. Doing all this quickly adds up to a revolution, one defined by the need to restore and preserve the earth's environmental systems. If this Environmental Revolution succeeds, it will rank

with the Agricultural and Industrial Revolutions as one of the great economic and social transformations in human history.[9]

The "revolutions" described by Ruckelshaus and Brown are, above all, managerial revolutions, led by those who have managed and profited from the social and environmental catastrophe in progress. As managers, they see "environmental systems" as things that can be taken apart, examined, and optimized, instead of as an "environment"—a sensuous, living whole. Brown discusses societies mobilizing to bring about the changes needed, then asks, "What if national governments were to take unilateral actions to help restore the planet's health? What if Japan were to launch a program to reverse the deforestation of the planet?" He goes on, "If we are individually wealthy, counting ourselves among the 202 billionaires and the three million or so millionaires in the world, should we continue doing business as usual?"[10]

Despite grand rhetoric, Brown and Ruckelshaus make no suggestions on how to help catalyze fundamental social change, which must come from below, from a real transformation in the way we live. They appeal to the enlightened self-interests of the industrial class, and attempt to mobilize public support for the reforms required to redeem the future of industrial society. Their prescriptions for change are like the health plans presented in 1993 that attempted to provide universal coverage and cost controls without challenging the basic entitlements of the major players.*

---

* The nature of corporate and managerial environmentalism is clear in the trade magazine *Environment Today*. Here is the "real" world managers face: the bewildering government regulatory regimes profoundly shaped by the polluters and pollution treaters; the ongoing policy debates; the occasional public intervention; and, above all, a cavalcade of machines, procedures, devices, and services designed to store, transfer, destroy, detoxify, minimize, and reclaim toxic materials, effluents, and other substantial effects of industrial activity. The idea of this environmentalism is change on the margin: remedy the worst excesses, and, above all, expand opportunities for vendors, consultants, bureaucrats. This is the environment as a venue for doing good by doing very well, not as the contested terrain of people's lives. The grassroots struggle, invisible in the magazine's pages but epitomized in the growing global environmental justice movement, is not a matter of seminars and sales.

Global managers, seeing industrialism heading toward the precipice, respond by demanding even more growth. They are like a fire brigade in the midst of a fire storm that neither cuts breaks nor uses water, but tries to encourage the spread of the flames, in the belief that once the world is ablaze the fire can somehow be both sustained and controlled.

Sustainability and continuing industrial growth are not in conflict for global managers. As Gro Harlem Bruntland, former chair of the World Commission on Environment and Development (and Norway's prime minister), notes, "The commission found no absolute limits to growth. Limits are indeed imposed by the impact of present technologies and social organization of the biosphere, but we have the ingenuity to change."[11]

Reformers-as-managers are inclined to accept definitions offered by economists who are accustomed to reducing the world to questions of input, output, and value. For example, British Green economist Michael Jacobs writes:

> Sustainability means that the environment should be protected in such a condition and to such a degree that environmental capacities (the ability of the environment to perform its various functions) are maintained over time: at least at levels sufficient to avoid future catastrophe, and at most at levels which give future generations the opportunity to enjoy an equal measure of environmental consumption.[12]

While this argument is based upon intergenerational equity, it is suffused with the assumption that current industrial practice could be or should be sustained. From an ecological standpoint, sustainability should refer to the well-being and resilience of the interlinked natural and social ecologies, and has little to do with parsing the limits of environmental consumption. Managers and economists are always considering incremental effects—the effect of spilling or burning one more barrel of oil—instead of questioning the wisdom of a system based on petrochemicals.

For the global managers, talking seriously about limitation and redistribution is unnecessary. Rather, their dialogue is about redirecting and managing: if population is to double, then world output must quadruple, with lessened environmental insult. In this scenario, once dynamic industrial expansion begins in the nonindustrialized world, a relatively small annual increase (e.g., 3 percent) will lead first to a doubling (in twenty-four years) and then a quadrupling (in forty-eight years) in output and wealth; enough to raise the poor to a respectable level of consumption.*[13]

The major problems, to global managers, are "signaling" difficulties, which interfere with the market's ability to transmit true costs, and social impediments to rationalization. The alternative—ecological lifeways that question the wisdom *and* the possibility of an industrial growth solution—is anathema to global managers: it would require transforming the patterns of the rich so that they consumed less and produced less (but also worked less, and so presumably lived better), redefining the relationship between rich and poor from one of exploitation to a partnership to speed alternatives to industrial development.

Industrial Distinctions and Global Management

Even within the context of their market never-neverland, global managers fail to recognize the difficulty posed by the differential exploitation inherent in the industrial system. Marx understood exploitation as the controlling dynamic of capitalism based upon class, but its industrial expression is broader, including distinctions based upon race, sex, religion, ethnicity, age, etc. Under industrialism, some are always relatively better off and others relatively worse off: the air, water, food, and land may be poisoned for all, but some enjoy filtered air, bottled water, pure food, and

---

*Even before that, enlightened global managers see the need to raise the not-so-poor to something approaching the level of the rich—for example, the European Community seeks to raise levels of consumption and production in Spain, Portugal, and Greece as part of economic and political integration.

private preserves. Industrialism tends to magnify and expand the distinctions of privilege both by creating new capitalist markets for what was once free and relatively pure, and by intensifying marks of status. To be poor in our time means not simply to lack money and the ability to buy manufactured goods. In industrial terms, to be poor means to be bereft of almost all means for personal and social sustenance, to be cast into an increasingly hopeless world of hunger and homelessness.

Thus, for example, subsistence farmers in the mountains of Central America are increasingly forced to work as day laborers on coffee plantations for cash wages, picking the coffee cherries during the three-month harvest. Whole families often work six days a week and are paid about a dollar a day. For some in Nicaragua, it is work on a cooperative organized after the Sandinista revolution, when their own land tenure was protected by the state. But for most, it is an increasingly tenuous existence ruled by the international coffee market, where fortunes are made by speculators, distributors, marketers, and the large landholders who follow managerial recommendations and apply modern techniques to coffee growing to boost productivity.

To understand the industrial world in this way is not nostalgia for an idealized preindustrial life giving way as a consequence of progress. The goads to industrialization that the rich impose upon the poor—structural adjustment policies, debt payments, unfair conditions of trade—are adopted and internalized by the elites of poor nations; and these policies do, in fact, encourage the poor to attempt to duplicate the journey of the rich, a journey based upon massive exploitation of people and the living world. Thus, the problem is not that the industrializing poor reject the rich nations' injunctions, but that, for most of the poor, industrialization has simply failed. And utter ruthlessness in attempts to meet industrial goals, whether or not informed by managerial wisdom about "sustainable" growth, often fails.

In China, for example, managerial success is fueled by cheap labor, government support, astounding social dislocation and environmental pillage. The dictatorship, in its wisdom, set free the commercial energies of a dynamic Chinese civilization in some business matters; and this freedom has created booming regional economies, as in the coastal provinces of Shangdong, Fujian, and Guandong. Opening itself to the industrialized world (initially through the overseas Chinese business community in places such as Hong Kong and Singapore), China has employed its comparative advantages through increasingly sophisticated factory production based upon state support, a huge labor force without wage or health and safety protection, and lack of environmental regulation.

But this boom occurs in the midst of staggering poverty and depends upon a "floating population" of dispossessed peasants, an estimated one hundred million people searching for any work. In an increasingly cash-dependent economy, income gaps are widening. About one billion are impoverished, about fifty million are members of a modest middle class, and another one hundred and sixty million are judged no longer poor.[14] These figures would seem to threaten the stability of the Chinese state: growing disparities in wealth, the increasing weakness of the dictatorial center, and an enormous, unprofitable state-subsidized industrial sector are not ingredients for long-term health any more than they were in the Soviet Union. (It is true that in China, unlike the former Soviet Union, an industrial sector has to an extent broken free of the dictatorial core. This is not, however, enough to ensure long-term national political stability.)

Thus, despite the supposed "rationality" of industrial market and planning mechanisms, the inherent tendency of industrialism is to create new and deeper distinctions between privileged and deprived. (Environmental discrimination—siting the most toxic facilities in the midst of the least powerful communities—is a classic expression of this tendency.) "The poor will always be with us," is the song of the powerful—and an anthem that sustains and propagates industrial abuse to the ultimate detriment of everyone. We can hardly expect change to come from those who benefit from "our way of life"—regardless of the fact that we are all being slowly cooked in the same large industrial pot. Change comes not from the torpid movements of the few and the comfortable, but from the many struck most clearly by necessity.

Technocratic Eschatologies

Global managers exercise real power over the policies of industrial civilization. But conflicting imperatives between growth and limitation, and the contradictory character of neoliberal versions of sustainable development, make it difficult for these managers to exhibit a united front. Thus, there are sometimes strong differences of opinion about the likelihood of alternative futures, and consequently about what policies are both proper and possible. This is not, however, an open debate; rather, the future is mystified—the product of magical, but wise, market forces colliding with mysterious, but irrational, political forces.

Growing tensions make global managerialism increasingly untenable, and push people and events toward alternatives, manifest in attempts at a perfected industrialism, and the poles of authoritarian and ecological responses. As the center shakes, global managers' interest in alternative technocratic eschatologies, science's version of endings and beginnings, is heightened.

Global managers' worldview is often reduced to a predilection for competing curves. The technocrats offer three basic visions of the future:

- The exponential
- The logistic
- The catastrophic

Each of these alternatives can, in broadest terms, be represented by a simple equation and presented graphically as a curve that reduces social reality to Cartesian coordinates, the mechanism of fate. For the exponential and logistic views, change and rates of change are more or less comfortably related to existing conditions. Change may accelerate or decelerate, its consequences may or may not be predictable, but all this fluctuation is generally linear and within the boundaries of the familiar. At any given point on the curve, the near future will not be dramatically different from the present. The catastrophic view introduces the nonlinear, the discontinuous, the uncertainty of dramatic change. It offers a world of sudden danger and transformation—the domain of the moralist, the scientist, the revolutionary, the social eschatologist. Technocratic eschatologies are, at bottom, social expressions, although the assumptions and agendas are cloaked in mathematical and scientific language.

It is true that particular social and biological patterns approximate a familiar curve over a certain time—e.g., the boom, bust, recovery cycle of capitalist economies. But this tendency does not necessarily describe the future, nor necessarily apply to phenomena outside the frame considered. The power of technocratic eschatologies is to confuse and silence the populace with the pronouncements of the diviners and priests of science and industrialism.

That certain processes and dynamic events tend to be cyclical should enhance, not end, the conversation. To demonstrate, for instance, that our universe began with a big bang and that the density of matter will, in billions of years, result in a grand cosmic implosion as the universe rushes back to a null point, does not mean that everything else in the meantime is superfluous and unworthy of consideration.

The Exponential View

Classic industrialism embraces (and the global manager aspires to embrace) the exponential vision of the future (see Figure 5-1). Production and consumption is ever increasing; all industrial activity is productive (even sterilizing Alaskan beaches to "clean up" oil spills). GNP forever doubles and redoubles.[15]

The exponential view attracted warnings of apocalypse long before Earth First! and Worldwatch. In 1798, Thomas Robert Malthus (at the age of thirty-two) warned the world of the doleful fit between population, which will grow exponentially, and food supply, which can at best expand only arithmetically. "Famine seems to be the last, the most dreadful resource of nature. The power of population is superior to the power in the Earth to produce subsistence."[16]

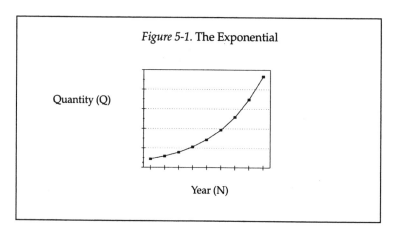

Figure 5-1. The Exponential

Quantity (Q)

Year (N)

But Malthus and his successors go beyond this grim view. They share a faith in stasis and Thomas Hobbes' view of life as nasty, brutish, and short. Malthusians of various stripes not only find the exponential view unrealistic and fated to be undermined by poverty, hunger, and ignorance; they see that humanity's attraction to exponential expansion undermines any hope for betterment. For Malthus, "the passion between the sexes" poisons prospects for "the perfectibility of man." This view is a most traditional, patriarchal inversion of love to slavery, transmuting sex from joy to burden.

These dour predictions are rooted in grave beliefs about an immutable "human nature" that is remarkably consistent with the relationships of industrialism between classes and among nations and people. Alternatively, for other Malthusians, lack of balance is a result not only of biology, but of numerous, and often maladaptive forces inherent in human society and intelligent self-consciousness. Catastrophic famine is but one possibility. Casting Malthusian skepticism about the sustainability of limitless increase aside, the most resolute industrialists act as if they believe that production and consumption can increase exponentially forever, that greener pastures will always be found, that water, air, and land will be forever free to use and despoil.

The Logistic View

Theorists of sustainable industrialism, such as Herman Daly,[17] embrace the logistic curve as a realistic alternative to exponential increase and collapse (see Figure 5-2).[18] The curve follows an "s" shape: a period of slow growth is followed by rapid expansion, leading in turn to slow growth, then to no growth or at least relative stability. This curve is a familiar description of the capitalist business cycle where the slow or no-growth period is supposedly followed by a renewed upward spurt. It is also a familiar pattern for population growth and stabilization in biology. In one form or another, the logistic curve is embraced by various groups of reformers and ecological revolutionaries (i.e, those who want dramatic transformation of industrial reality).

The logistic view implies, but may go beyond, maintenance of the status quo or redistribution within fixed boundaries. It can reflect a structure governing a constrained industrialism, such as bidding, as Daly suggests, for rights to deplete nonrenewable

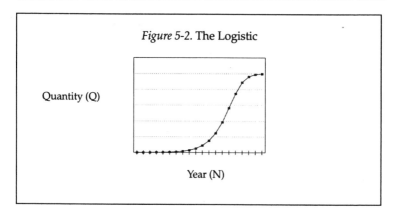

Figure 5-2. The Logistic

Quantity (Q)

Year (N)

resources. While its advocates allow for much dynamism, the logistic view is rooted in the embrace of limits that are anathema to industrialism: this is the politician's nightmare of a "fixed pie" and endless zero-sum struggles for bigger slices.

But the logistic curve need not describe current consumption and production as an aggregate entitlement to be maintained—"sustained"—and distributed or redistributed by markets (or planning or war). The logistic view can also include the result of a social transformation to ecological society. It could refer not to the biosphere's alleged carrying capacity for pollution or for use of resources, but to stabilizing industrial activity at a much lower level of insult to the biosphere, and to uncoupling much of human activity from standard industrial and economic formulations: writing poetry and raising children can be accounted as creativity and love, not as production and reproduction.

The Catastrophic View

Prophets and scientists offer the catastrophic curve of life (see Figure 5-3) as a cautionary possibility, and it sometimes seems as if radical ecologists who advocate a return to the Paleolithic almost welcome this possibility. It is also admired by anti-modern reactionaries, including some religious fundamentalists, and by intel-

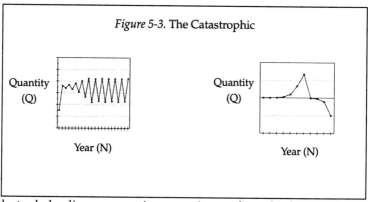

Figure 5-3. The Catastrophic

lectuals leading peasant insurgencies, such as *Sendero Luminoso.*
Catastrophe is the negation of the normal, of the islands of stability
in the midst of a universe in motion. Its message is not welcomed
by power—and is sweet music to those who believe they have
nothing to lose.

Technical arguments for the catastrophic view include requisite computer models. Thus, in *Beyond the Limits: Confronting Global
Collapse, Envisioning a Sustainable Future,* Donella and Dennis
Meadows and Jørgen Randers suggest that if current trends continue, the interactive effects of increasing resource use and pollution, combined with growing population, will lead inevitably past
the point of sustainability—and the biosphere's carrying capacity—sometime in the mid-21st century.[19] The threat is not simply
one of decline, but of grave instability and collapse. Thus, time
governs the catastrophic view in a way denied in the exponential
and logistic worldviews. It is very hard to predict what specific
straw will break the camel's back—it only becomes increasingly
likely that another added to the burden will do so.[20]

Sophisticated computer models, such as that employed in
Beyond the Limits, allow investigators to take the world apart,
determine significant variables (e.g., population and food supply), add in factors that influence those variables (e.g., the
amount of arable land, supply of fertilizer, temperature changes,
carbon dioxide [CO_2] concentrations, etc.), then put the world

back together and draw conclusions based upon interactions between variables and contributory factors. Such models are, of course, limited—by imperfect knowledge of existing conditions; by misunderstanding of contributory factors or of interactions between variables; by exclusion of what cannot be quantified (e.g., changing human behavior or technology); by the tendency to view coincident events as causal and linear; by limitations of mathematical models; by the biases, conscious and unconscious, of the analysts; and *ad infinitum*.

If happy predictions of exponential industrial growth are over-simple, world computer models quickly become recondite and impenetrable, changed over time but never fully understood by any person. Computer modeling on a world scale becomes a sort of divination, the programmer a modern Pythia staring into the earth's navel at Delphi. As someone who has devised simple computer models for energy use in buildings such as college gymnasiums, I can testify that it is quite sobering to see the disparity between model and measured data, or to realize that when data and model do correspond it may be the result of errors canceling each other out to yield a correct total.

There are difficulties with computer doomsdays beyond modeling problems. The first may be described as Sununuism (for John Sununu): an insistence on postponing action in the face of threatened damage until it is too late to prevent disaster.

A second, and more subtle, difficulty is this: What if prophecy fails? What if catastrophe does not occur, or if warnings are heeded only to the extent of avoiding immediate collapse? Global warming and ozone depletion, for example, may not result in sudden changes, but only contribute to a continuing insidious degradation of the biosphere.

A third problem is that models of catastrophe tend to silence people. True, the model maps physical effects, but these effects are the result of social behavior, not of unmediated natural phenomena. We can be disarmed by the mathematical aggregate and forget that the behavior of the crowd is extraordinarily malleable: even empires, as we have seen, can be brought down by the courage of individuals suddenly manifest in the collective truth and power.

Prophecy is, at best, a daunting task—as the joke goes, many economists can be credited with predicting six recessions out of the last three. In 1967, William and Paul Paddock wrote a book, *Famine - 1975*, in which they predicted :

> 1975 will be a crucial year in the world, crucial because the world food shortage will then dominate the headlines and the results will be in full view. The present downward trends cannot be reversed, nor can they be dusted under the carpet. Those who say there are too many variables in the future to forestall food deficits ignore the present trends.[21]

In 1992 (in the midst of mass starvation resulting from civil war in Somalia), Robert W. Cates, director of Brown University's World Hunger Project (echoing Crosson and Rosenberg's 1989 optimism) stated:

> Famine has ended in India and China. The long term trend is down. We are in an extraordinary, critical moment right now. We can see the end of famine in the world. It's almost breathtaking to think we can do that by the end of the decade.

And looking toward the 21st century, Cates said:

> The proportion of the hungry is being cut while the number of hungry [about 500 million persons] stays the same or rises. Population growth and agricultural intensification are the big questions. We have to triple or quadruple food production if the ranks of the hungry are to be reduced in the face of the predicted doubling of world population by early next century.

But in 1994, Worldwatch's State of the World reported that fish harvests have leveled off; per capita grain production has fallen 11 percent since 1984; fertilizer use has declined 12 percent (indicating, according to Worldwatch, that production limits have been reached); fresh water is increasingly polluted and scarce; and erosion, over-grazing, deforestation, and mismanagement have ruined five billion acres of land since 1945. "As a result of our population size, consumption patterns, and technology choices, we have surpassed the planet's carrying capacity."[22]

The forest is burning. But it is very hard to determine precisely how fast the fire will spread, whether it will lead to total devastation, or whether a saving rain will preserve an important remnant. To wait and watch the fire from a distance until our predictions prove accurate means more than just closing the opportunity for change and courting catastrophe. It assumes separation. But we are not separate from the earth. We are in its midst. We are a part of the living world. The fire will make us respond, computer programs or not. Our lives are sufficient evidence of the need for change; there is no need to join the argument about just where or when the biosphere will become sufficiently poisoned and degraded to require action.

I am not disparaging the efforts of those scientists and computer modelers—prediction can be a spur to effective action. But solutions to the problems of industrialism will not be solved by embracing any particular mathematical model and technical solution.

An Example of the Catastrophic View: A Global Warming Scenario

In 1992, Dr. Jeremy Leggett, a British scientist and scientific director of Greenpeace International's Atmosphere and Energy Campaign, outlined what may be called a "nightmare global warming scenario." This scenario was based on a projection of known, but as yet unquantified, biological feedback mechanisms identified by the Intergovernmental Panel on Climate Change (300 atmospheric scientists from forty countries).[23]

This scenario is a plausible extrapolation from what is known: it reflects both the magnitude of the possible risks courted by industrial humanity, and the inadequacy of the global managerial perspective when circumstances go beyond what is viewed as industrially acceptable. However, even if this scenario is completely accurate, industrial managers can always point to enough uncertainty at each step to justify inaction.

Global warming is the result of the release into the atmosphere of "greenhouse gases," i.e., gases that are relatively transparent to the passage of energetic short-wave solar radiation (sunlight) and, at the same time, reflect back much of the longer wave infrared (or heat) radiation generated when sunlight strikes the earth. The most significant greenhouse gas is CO_2, which has been released into the atmosphere in huge quantities as a by-product of burning fossil fuels in automobiles, power plants, and industrial processes such as steel production, and by wood burned for fuel and forests burned for land-clearing. In 1950, 1.62 billion metric tons per year of carbon (gigatons carbon or GTC) were released from burning fossil fuels; by 1991, this figure had increased to 5.854 billion tons per year.

To get some sense of the significance of this number, we need to know that the preindustrial atmosphere contained an estimated 580 billion tons of carbon. Thus, we are now adding about 1 percent of the preindustrial carbon total to the atmosphere yearly. Current atmospheric carbon levels are 750 GTC, a 29 percent increase from preindustrial levels. In only thirty-two years since 1959, when continuous recordkeeping of atmospheric carbon dioxide began, concentrations have increased 12 percent from 316 parts per million (.0316 percent) to 355 parts per million (.0355 percent). Other greenhouse gases include methane (CH_4), a product of natural decay and fermentation released in large quantities from concentrated livestock production, and the chlorofluorocarbons (CFCs) that are also responsible for the destruction of the ozone layer.

The precise global dynamics and possible effects, both long- and short-term, of huge increases in greenhouse gases are unclear. There is a natural cycle that keeps CO_2 concentrations relatively balanced. Huge amounts of CO_2 are dissolved in the oceans, 39,000 GTC with about 90 GTC exchanged each year between atmosphere and ocean. (CO_2 in water forms carbonic acid—this is why steam heating condensate pipes often corrode unless the boiler water is deaerated.) Huge amounts of carbon are also locked up in submarine methane hydrates, ice-like solids made up of water crystals and trapped methane gas, on the Arctic continental shelf.

Carbon is also found in the bodies of all living things, from giant redwoods to microscopic creatures (an estimated 750 GTC in land plants and 1,500 GTC in soils; annually 100 GTC is exchanged between the atmosphere and land plants.) The normal carbon-based system includes the use of CO_2 by plants, which release oxygen as a by-product that is then used for animal respiration (which, in turn, yields CO_2 as its by-product). The carbon taken up in the bodies of living creatures is also released in the form of methane as they die and decay.

Atmospheric scientists argue that climate stability can likely be sustained if levels of human CO_2 production are somewhat below the emission levels seen in the 1950s. At present rates, by the middle of the 21st century, most climate scientists predict substantial increases in global temperature.

How significant these increases will be, and the nature of their impact, is the question. Jeremy Leggett warns that such global warming *may* disturb major sinks for carbon in Arctic tundra and, through a complex series of interactions, result in runaway warming that would continue even if human CO_2 and all other greenhouse gas emissions dropped to zero.

Leggett's "putative" logical chain of events includes:

- As the oceans warm, they are less able to absorb CO_2.

- Warming oceans are more thermally stable. This stability reduces the circulation of nutrients and decreases the biomass of the photoplankton, thus further damaging the ability to absorb CO_2.

- Ultraviolet radiation from the damaged ozone layer, particularly severe in polar regions, further damages the photoplankton. The net ecosystem balance between respiration (CO_2 emitted) and photosynthesis (CO_2 used) now tilts toward respiration, and more CO_2 is released into the atmosphere.

- As the temperature rises, Arctic tundra melts and releases huge amounts of methane. Under certain conditions, wet, flooded soils can release 100 times more methane than dry soils.

- At this point, drought in many areas from warming and associated climatic changes further retards photosynthesis.

- Changes in the chemistry of the atmosphere deplete the cleansing hydroxyl reservoir that oxidizes methane and other greenhouse gases.

- Ozone in the troposphere, a greenhouse gas at lower levels of the atmosphere, is increased as a result of carbon monoxide and nitrous oxide from growing automobile exhaust.

- The Arctic ice cover begins to thin and retreat. This thinning reduces the albedo (the net reflectivity of the planet), thus leading to further warming.

- Finally, huge amounts of methane trapped in the Arctic continental shelf in the form of methane hydrates are released from under the permafrost and in shallow Arctic waters.

Leggett concludes, "In emergency session the UN brings in sweeping measures for world-wide greenhouse gas emission reductions. But it is too late. A runaway greenhouse effect has been generated."

This chain of events is a dark possibility. It is not a prediction. It does make clear that industrial civilization has put into question not just the prospects for human society, but planetary processes hitherto the domain of natural rhythms and geological time. Industrialism is betting that its resolute commitment to continuous growth can somehow be managed to avoid catastrophic consequences.

The world has 4,000 GTC in proven fossil fuel reserves; we cannot decide their future use, the production of further CFCs, and the mass burning and clear-cutting of forests on the basis of maximizing industrial production and consumption, profits and power. Industrial civilization entertains a hideous risk if it continues each year to pour 5.8 billion tons or more of carbon into the atmosphere. Whether industrialism's technocratic eschatologies are reassuringly exponential, cautiously logistic, or righteously catastrophic, social behavior, as well as the reality behind imperfect mathematical models, will determine the nature of alternative futures.

chapter six

CONTESTING ALTERNATIVES: AUTHORITARIANISM

THIS CHAPTER EXAMINES AUTHORITARIANISM as a contesting alternative for the future course of industrial civilization. Authoritarianism is a strong and desperate response to the not-so-tender ministrations of the forces driving and intensifying the globalization of industrialism.

It is a difficult chapter in that it considers in detail the polar opposite of an ecological democracy. The reader may choose first to read some or all of the subsequent chapters—Seven, Eight, and Nine—that address building an ecological democracy before becoming immersed here in consideration of the dynamics, politics, and philosophy of democracy's authoritarian opposition. This chapter's conclusion, however, is optimistic, examining the disabilities of authoritarianism and the opening for the pursuit of liberation.

Authoritarianism

Authoritarianism is again ascendant, promising redemption from the agonies and insults of industrial civilization through order and blood. It is a fervent movement that offers an ecstatic transcendence suffused with a sort of religious valence.

Redemptive authoritarianism is also a way to organize civilization—it has an ideology, principles, practices—and, at bottom, it is a product of industrialism: both a reaction to abuse and an expression of the desire for change. It cannot be dismissed as an "uncivilized" aberration or anachronism.

Whether it is called fascism, nationalism, militarism, or theocracy, redemptive authoritarianism is capturing the energies of young people, and the yearnings for power of angry and tormented men, such as Russia's Vladimir Zhirinovsky and his followers; and it is attracting opportunists, such as Italy's Silvio Berlusconi. Authoritarianism's allure reflects not simply the fall of European communism, but the deepening crisis of industrial civilization.

We are most familiar with this authoritarianism in its fascist guise. But the phenomena is much broader than that, and its motivations and historic resources extend far beyond anti-communism. Redemptive authoritarianism is a particularly totalizing pursuit. Unlike global management, it aspires to much more than influence; unlike ecological liberation, it does not want to free humanity. To redeem is to make amends and deliver from sin, to restore, to make worthwhile. The sins that authoritarianism seeks to redeem are those of industrial modernity; the redemption it offers involves the creation of new men and women, not simply new political orders.[1]

Authoritarianism and Nationalism

The end of Soviet totalitarianism did not bring liberal capitalist nirvana, but has instead seemed to unleash a wave of vigorous authoritarian and neofascist movements. Clearly, those cheering the desperate promises of an authoritarianism of the Right did not learn the bitter lessons of totalitarianism.

Many now say, in the new controlling myth, that history and nationalism merely paused for a time—ethnic animosities were frozen by the Cold War and its global bipolarity, and directly suppressed in the panoply of national groups under Soviet domination—but that with the Cold War melted, nationalist antipathies were released raging upon the world. Assessing nationalist particularism, historian Tony Judt writes:

> Taken separately, each of these developments has a distinctive and local origin and explanation. But taken together they point to a shift in the emphases of public life and language in contemporary Europe....Everywhere there has been a growing absorption in what Freud called the "narcissism of minor differences." None of this began recently, born again as it were in 1989. Nationalism in Isaiah Berlin's words is not "resurgent"—it never died.[2]

The image is of history as a great basin filled with the fluid of nationalist passion and irrationality, broken open by the communist collapse. Accordingly, the hopes for democratization or neosocialist reconstruction have fallen before the resurgence of the most intractable human habits. The implication is that communism has been vanquished and terrorism rejected as inadequate as a geopolitical organizing principle, so nationalism and Islamic fundamentalism have emerged as the central threats to capitalist liberal democracy: nationalism replacing communism as the enemy within, and fundamentalism supplanting communism as the foreign threat.

If this is a myth, it is based on some impressive realities. In Europe, only weeks before the fiftieth anniversary of the liberation of Rome, billionaire Berlusconi swept Italian elections with an improbable and short-lived right-wing coalition, including members of the fascist National Alliance Party, the political heirs of Mussolini. Genocidal war in the name of ethnic cleansing grinds on in the former Yugoslavia. In Russia, the neofascist Liberal Democratic Party of Zhirinovsky is a major contender for power. An ethnically based Slovakian state has appeared. France has passed laws threatening to jail those who pervert the French language with prohibited Anglicisms and is increasingly hostile to dark-skinned, particularly North African, minorities. A redemptive authoritarianism in the name of Islamic fundamentalism is a significant political force throughout much of the Muslim world. And in the United States, neo-Nazi David Duke was almost elected governor of Louisiana as a Republican candidate; and Pat Buchanan, nationalist and sometime racist and anti-Semitic propagandist, ran well, to the surprise of the experts, in the 1992 Republican presidential primaries.*

Nationalism in Context

Despite these realities, all this activity represents much more than "the return of nationalism." We must reject the idea that nationalism is an ahistorical or perennial force: the political, economic, social and historical context of our world does not allow a replay of the 19th century. In the 19th century, nationalism was an organizing principle, a centripetal force supporting the nation state as the proximate universal for industrial civilization. But in our era of global markets and weakened nation states, nationalism is a disintegrating, centrifugal force.** Dozens of new "nations" based on ethnicity and language and demanding

---

*On the intellectual fashion front, Regis Debray, once given to praising Third World deliverance, is offering a biography of Charles de Gaulle and his redemptive national vision.[3] And on this side of the Atlantic, academics, historians, and denizens of think tanks discourage volumes on nationalism in the post-Cold War world.

** The growth of the ultra-nationalist militia movement in the United States is another expression of the reaction to the forces of globalization—in this case, given to conspiracy theories about a UN takeover, gun control, and mysterious black helicopters carrying foreign troops preparing for the takeover.

independence are a reaction to, and defense against, the forces building global markets and diminishing the prerogatives of the citizens of existing nation states.

In other words, the nation is now more an expression of defensive particularism than the aggressive assertion of a new order. In essence, the nation is separating from the state: the nation defines itself by blood and language in an attempt to retrieve and protect community and freedom from the power of the industrial world system. But this effort has a very limited understanding of freedom and a very particular definition of community.

This movement is a third wave in the creation of nation states. The first saw the rise of industrial nations in the 19th century following the American and French revolutions; the second came after World War II, a time of decolonization, neocolonialism, and development whose energies are largely spent—although the development dream lumbers on. The third wave, in a time of globalization and instability, emphasizes national assertion rather than the creation of nation states from old colonial principalities. The new nationalism—in Serbia, Georgia, Armenia, Azerbaijan—has been a path to impoverishment, conflict, and social disintegration, not state building.

Hungary or Poland, released from Soviet domination (and support), can struggle toward acceptance in the European community as a source of low-waged-but-skilled labor, trying to escape the essentially Third World status of, for example, Mexico in relation to the United States. But Serbia, Armenia, Albania, or the new Central Asian states face grim prospects, even without ethnic conflict in part fomented by cynical leaders as a way to retain power. Thus, for example, Serbian outrage at a history of abuse is not only a club used by the government of Slobodan Milosevic: it would come, even without war and international blockade, from the unhappy prospects facing the Serbs, whether as dominant partners with the Montenegrans within a rump Yugoslavia, or as citizens within a greater Serbia carved by force from Bosnia and Croatia.*

It is not surprising that peoples released from the choking "internationalism" of the Soviet Union are ready to embrace blood and language to define a nation in response to an indifferent global market. The market did not provide succor; industrialized capitalist states did not, and could not (even if they had tried much more diligently), provide a soft economic landing and smooth political transition for an area stretching from the Pacific to the Adriatic. In Poland, Hungary, and Lithuania, market "freedom" has actually brought the former Communist Party, in a new social democratic incarnation, back to power as defender of working people and advocate of a more humane market economy.

The nationalism of this third wave does not have to pursue the paths of blood and soil, but the present reality provides, at best, a limited chance to fulfill conventional dreams of building a nation state. The Soviet collapse was not only a rejection of totalitarian brutality, but an expression of the Soviet Union's failure to adapt to the transformations marking the close of the epoch of industrial modernity. Now some of the new states must struggle against both the fetters remaining from Soviet rule and the very same unpromising realities of the late 20th-century international political economy that helped bring down the Soviet Union.

Redemptive authoritarianism thus reflects an inability to confront, or even fully realize, the new realities of global industrialism. Instead, this postmodern nationalism often chooses to make war against an available other. This authoritarianism is further encouraged when people and nations are choked between the

---

* A doleful legacy of Cold War militarism is that these nations-become-states are often heavily armed—sometimes even with nuclear weapons, as in Ukraine. Combined with the exploitation of ethnic antagonisms, the existence of such armed states certainly makes it likely that the dream of self-determination will yield to the desperation of authoritarianism and revenge.

depredations of a capitalism that denies community and limits freedom to those successful in the market, and authoritarian socialist orders that deny freedom and permit community only in the context of totalitarian order. At the extreme, this nationalism becomes genocidal, destroying the very human particularity it is supposed to represent. Instead of a vital community, genocidal nationalism embraces a purified, mystical land where human evil, personified as a mythic Other, is banished.

Nationalism can assert vernacular values and local customs in opposition to the rationalized order of empire and oppression. But nationalism can be corrupted if it is based not on shared locality and experience, but on an abstract conception of blood, a mystical community bound by reactionary rage against a hypothesized other.

Genocidal nationalism, then, does not represent the irresistible return of long-repressed ethnic hatreds. Rather, it flows from the conflicts and agonies of modernity intensified by authoritarian regimes. Such reactions are not limited to states that capture and channel the impulses of rage, like Serbia or Rwanda. In the United States, they are expressed in highway shootings, "drive-by" killings, and the hate unleashed against the poor welfare mother.

The Idea and Dynamics
of Redemptive Authoritarianism

The authoritarian alternative seeks redemption through order. This is a particular kind of order, a response to the excesses of industrial civilization; it is intoxicated with the search for perfection, for the unattainable. Order replaces freedom and is seen as a rite of purification—though its fulfillment can bring utter corruption (ethnic cleansing is anything but clean). While all of life is ordered in dynamic unity, the order of redemptive authoritarianism is one of static separation: despite all attempts at unity—the uniforms, the flags—order and perfection essentially repel one another.

Although supposedly a resolute opponent of industrial abuses, redemptive authoritarianism embraces the values of industrialism—the steel triangle of hierarchy, progress, and technique. It also takes advantage of the social energies of ethnic animosity, religion, racism, anti-Semitism, anti-capitalism, and anti-communism, while capturing the allegiance of those driven by the popular sentiments of the moment.

The ideal of redemptive authoritarianism is not merely to transcend the cruelties and banalities of industrial reality, but to supplant conventional conservative appeals in the name of traditional virtues, nationalism, militarism, and patriotism. (In the United States, with its individualist traditions, militant anti-communism has served as proxy for a state-based fascist movement.) Thus, fascism was designed to save European capitalist nations from both communism and capitalist modernity: its immediate goal was to save the capitalist nation from Bolshevism, but from the beginning it shared the Bolsheviks' contempt for the bourgeois state. Fascist authoritarianism was at once the industrialists' defense against working people and the working person's betrayed defense against the abuses of the industrialists.

Redemptive authoritarianism uses violent revolutionary methods, as in the toppling of the Shah of Iran by the Islamic movement of the Ayatollah Khomeini, or of Italian democracy by Mussolini and his black shirts; but it is reactionary and counter-revolutionary in intent. Through the medium of the state, redemptive authoritarianism aspires to restore all to harmonious perfection (though its means are often far from harmonious). It is anti-modern, despising those who would accelerate the rationalization and intensification of industrial progress. It defends supposedly traditional verities by any means necessary. Like ordinary conservatism, authoritarianism wants to defend the past, but it also wants to expunge the sins of industrialism. Class division, poverty, and personal and collective humiliations are to be ended, the nation and its special people purified and renewed. Redemptive authoritarianism is more than discipline and hierarchy; it is order in terror of disorder and difference—the embrace of unfreedom.*

Authoritarianism and Totalitarianism

Simple authoritarianism's ambitions are more modest. It is a way to discipline and destroy opponents of the regime, and to establish conditions for maximizing production and consumption—in other words, to suit the needs of those in power, at least in the short run. It provides a structure useful for rapid, state-led industrialization. It also potentiates the impulses of the ultra-nationalist, the militarist, the anti-communist. (Thus, in post-communist Russia, many yearn for a strong man to fill the role of an Augusto Pinochet in Chile, the colonels in Greece, or the generals in Argentina.) Simple authoritarianism in general applies power from above and enriches particular social groups—the ruling families, the army, the corporate allies of the regime.

Totalitarianism, in contrast, is characterized not simply by hierarchy and dictatorial leadership, but by the state's absorption over time of nearly all aspects of civil society and, in turn, by the absorption of the state by the ruling party personified by its leader. In these respects, the conduct and aspiration of the Nazi Party in Germany and Communist Party in the Soviet Union may be said to have been broadly similar.

---

*Redemptive authoritarianism goes far beyond a cynical attempt of those in power to reach an accommodation with revolutionary order to preserve their prerogatives. The Pahlevi regime of Iran, for example, resolutely authoritarian and resolutely brutal, was attacked from the Right in the name of an anti-modern theocratic order. The democrats and socialists who joined in the revolt against the Shah soon found that the revolutionary regime substituted a new kind of tyranny for the old.

Redemptive authoritarianism tends toward totalitarianism but is not necessarily identical with it; it tends toward fascism but is broader and more diverse, as in strains of Islamic fundamentalism. Authoritarian or totalitarian states seek to incorporate other states as vassals, not as partners. This aspiration was the Nazi ideal, and the Soviets, despite their avowed "internationalism," had little difficulty incorporating satellite states after World War II. Those communists who challenged Moscow, as in Yugoslavia and China, became targets for Soviet ire.

The Authoritarian Assertion

The contest for industrialism's future is not between the status quo propped up by global management and chaos, but between the assertions of authoritarianism and the promise of ecological transformation confronting the attempt to maintain business more or less as usual.

Industrialism was built upon dismantling the moral confidence that supported the existing hierarchical order of the world. The scale of nature—the great chain of being in an earth-centered universe of fixed hierarchies, stretching not only from vegetation to man, but to the circles of hell below and the angels in heaven above—was broken by the industrial, political, and philosophical revolutions of modernity.

Technique established industrial order and, mixed with capital, yielded industrial hierarchy—not the hierarchy of divine providence, but of technique and progress in an expanding universe. This technique was not art, but mechanization, scientifically approved rationality, labor turned to metal. Thus, industrial technique committed the classic sin of separating knowledge from wisdom. Industrialism's torrent of objects, its poisoned fruits, have not yielded human happiness, balance, or harmony. Redemptive authoritarianism is a quest for a return to Eden through a new order, but in a way that intensifies the very same sins.

Of course, a global managerial technocracy requires order, too: managers seek participation and acquiescence; they profit from influencing and, to a degree, controlling the course of events. But their order is instrumental—to perpetuate both managerial control and the industrial system—and within these broad limits, the global manager will permit, even facilitate, a rather complex matrix of dynamic industrial hierarchies within the state and in the corporation. Thus, protection of freedom of association and contract are cornerstones of capitalist industrial democracy. Global managers may turn to strict regulation, even to war, to maintain the power relations supporting the industrial system. At times, they will employ crusader zeal (for example, anti-communism) that threatens nuclear annihilation—but only after less costly means have failed.

Today's redemptive authoritarianism, while it masquerades as anti-modernism, uses industrial technique and managerial wisdom to maximize production-consumption and accumulate wealth. It does not simply ask for obedience, but grants "freedom" to act in concert with industrialism's goals. This works to further mystify the nature of industrialism, by transforming the venue for freedom from the market to a state defined in fascist, theocratic, or militarist terms. The new order thus rains contempt upon the corrupt exercise of freedom represented by choices in the marketplace and the selection of parties on the basis of their ability to improve "the standard of living." Authoritarian values are meant to supplant these false freedoms of consumption.

The techniques of industrialism lend themselves to this message. For example, the media can unite and manipulate those torn apart by the industrial state. Thus, Joseph Goebbels discovered sixty years ago that it was possible to sell Adolf Hitler to an impassioned crowd in the same way that you could sell a Ford. In a world with, as Joshua Meyerowitz of the University of New Hampshire suggests, no sense of place, one can find home in a new authoritarian transcendence.[4]

There are many examples of this collaboration between media and authoritarian values. To watch an evening of U.S. commercial television is to be bathed in a fascist aesthetic of violence, power, and sexuality, a lustful sacrament that inculcates not only desire, but obeisance to powerful instruments. In Italy, Berlusconi, who owns all three commercial television networks, rose to power after a two-month media blitz based on images of national pride and vague promises for national restoration. Similarly, in the United States, Ross Perot became a viable presidential candidate because his wealth gave him great access to free and paid media. But despite his billions, Perot, lacking absolute media control, could not succeed. With his quirkiness, and his penchant for charts and lectures, Perot was a bit too much of a florid American character to claim he personified universal American virtues.*

The Redemptive Quest

At its core, redemptive authoritarianism aspires to recapture the past glories of an idealized preindustrial Golden Age. This aspiration may be romanticism, but the process of its realization is far from romantic: the quest operates through the nation state ruled by a cultish elite and its supreme leader. Ultimately, such a quest

---

* Part of the persistent appeal of redemptive authoritarianism is no doubt rooted in the human psyche, but it would be a mistake to consider this as a purely psychological or social-psychological phenomena. Such dynamics are beyond the concern of this work, but it is worth noting Karen Horney's view that perfection is one of the two basic organizing principles for the modern neurotic personality (the other being the appeal of love).[5] The tensions inherent in industrial civilization provide by themselves a broad base for some of the appeal of redemptive authoritarianism. But the personal is also political, that is, social: the mass appeal of neurotic perfection can be manipulated and mobilized by those afflicted with the more extreme and painfully bound personal energies, as described by Wilhelm Reich.[6] As a totalizing practice, redemptive authoritarianism, like industrialism itself, is a complex social creation that touches all or nearly all aspects of social practice and beliefs. Redemptive authoritarianism in this sense reflects, but cannot simply be reduced to, the aggressive reassertion of patriarchal values, the exaltation of patriarchal power *over*, at the expense of ascendant feminist values which, in part, means the rise of a facilitating and empowering practice of power *to*.

for perfection means we must redeem ourselves from ourselves. This impossible task accounts for authoritarianism's unquenchable rage. The system captures and uses potent human energies—including the symbolic and ritual dedication of religion, and the magical wish fulfillment of infantile dreams and pagan ceremonies enlisted to facilitate the brutal and murderous excesses of the redemptive authoritarian state.

In his great allegorical novel, *The Plague*, Albert Camus shows that the redemptive authoritarian impulse is all too much a feature of the human condition, not something that can be expunged. He concludes, as the plague ends:

> And, indeed, as he listened to the cries of joy rising from the town, Rieux remembered that such joy is always imperiled. He knew what those jubilant crowds did not know but could have learned from books: that the plague bacillus never dies or disappears for good; that it can lie dormant for years and years in furniture and linen-chests; that it bides its time in bedrooms, cellars, trunks, and bookshelves; and that perhaps the day would come when, for the bane and the enlightening of men, it would rouse up its rats again and send them forth to die in a happy city.[7]

In redemptive authoritarianism, the perfect One is defined by its opposition to the corrupt Other, the supposedly irredeemable source of evil. The mythic state is not only cleansed of corrupt ideas and behavior: the human Other must be identified and destroyed. This is central. Punishment, defilement, and murder are the fulfillment of the authoritarian dream; murderous lunacy against the Other becomes the common passion of the state, unimpeded by historical experience or empathy for suffering.* Like the

---

* Thus, Russian nationalist Zhirinovsky can proclaim his admiration for Hitler, despite the Nazi slaughter of tens of millions of Russians. Likewise, some Israeli settlers praise as a redeemer one of their number, a physician, who shot dozens praying at a mosque because he wished to prevent Israeli-Palestinian peace. And Palestinian suicide bombers attacking buses are, in turn, regarded by some in their community as martyrs.

desires of capitalism, this passion is an expression of limitless ambitions; its goal, however, is not profit, but perfection.

The redemptive authoritarian moment is suffused with the impulses for revenge—not only to expunge past humiliation, but to eliminate present insults at the hands of real or imagined villains, i.e., to identify and expunge evil at a personified human source. It is all the better if this evil Other is unarmed. So the Nazis, for example, found it expedient to blame the humiliation of Germany in World War I and its aftermath not on their own imperialists and officers, nor on their enemies, the French and British, but on Jews and communists (tools of the Jews) at home.

In the United States, Khalid Abdul Muhammed, national assistant to Minister Louis Farrakhan of the Nation of Islam, facing a history and present of relentless, institutionalized white racism in an overwhelmingly Christian nation, can also find the Jews responsible—not only for the present plight of African Americans, but for slavery (claiming, for instance, that Jews owned 70 percent of the slaves in the old South).[8] Thus, behind the pain of African Americans, Louis Farrakhan and Khalid Abdul Muhammed find not just Jews, but *the Jew*—an Other of historic resonance for the white, European, Christian civilization that built the United States. This belief is not merely a response to the pain of racism; it is the adoption, conscious or not, of the master's bigotry—and serves a purpose similar to this bigotry for authoritarians in search of a convenient and relatively powerless Other.

Black nationalists drawn to a redemptive authoritarian movement do not simply seek African-American dignity. Their goal is power, both personal and organizational—first within the community, and then in white America. Self-assertion is a logical response to the often bitter African-American experience, and many African Americans are receptive to the positive aspects of the nationalist message. Their common experience helps explain why many African Americans have difficulty responding to white demands to chastise nationalists for bigotry, particularly when white racism goes unanswered and unpunished. Anti-Semitism, however, is part of the problem of oppression and not a venue for anyone's liberation.

The Authoritarian Quest in the Context of Modernity

Mass murder did not vanish with the advent of industrial civilization, or with the defeat of Hitler; instead, it has been industrialized and continues to be perfected along with the development of weapons. However, genocidal passion cannot be attributed to technology or limited to authoritarian regimes: genocide is a social act. As Aimé Césaire suggests in his *Discourse on Colonialism*, Hitler "applied to Europe colonialist procedures which until then had been reserved exclusively for the Arabs of Algeria, the Koolis of India, and the Blacks of Africa."[9]

While the ability to define, persecute, and exterminate an Other is central to the redemptive quest, it is also of much broader use to the ongoing conduct of industrial civilization.* This practice is neither confined to the periphery of civilization (where we are assured "life is cheap") nor to authoritarian regimes: advanced democracies also bomb, poison, and starve with impunity for reasons of state (and to provide "object lessons," as in Iraq). The creation of the Other in terms of race, sex, religion, and ethnicity is a part of progress, facilitating the devastation, dispossession, and cynical manipulation of a populace by a ruling group. As we have also seen in Chapter Two, industrial progress is indeed a matter of

---

* The dynamic tendency of the living world is toward evolutionary elaboration and recombination, but industrial progress is not merely a manifestation of evolutionary possibilities. It is a social creation. It has a variety of expressions, both social and technological. But its excesses are in essence those of humanity, and not technology run wild. This view contrasts to that of Heidegger, whose notions of a pervasive and autonomous technology serve to obscure, for instance, the nature of the Holocaust as a complex social act. Heidegger seems to pluck technique from the context of the social formulation of industrialism, and to miss the social valence that results from technique's relationship with progress and hierarchy (and its expression in the Nazi regime that, for a time, he willingly served).

creating new things and new men and women—but only if they fit
the chosen molds. As we have seen in Chapter Two, industrial
progress is, in part, a war against particularity, against differences
that fall outside current definitions of the acceptable. The world is
not only made safe for technology; wilderness and the Other, both
without and within, are domesticated or destroyed.

As Jean-Paul Sartre noted in *Anti-Semite and Jew,* bigotry, the
acute consciousness of Otherness, at least provided the French
anti-Semite with membership in a mythical community based on
blood and native virtue, a community within which all daily
failings and degradation were momentarily forgotten. Sartre
wrote:

> Anti-Semitism is not merely the joy of hating; it brings
> positive pleasures too. By treating the Jew as an inferior and
> pernicious being, I affirm at the same time that I belong to the
> elite. This elite, in contrast to those of modern times which are
> based on merit or labor, closely resembles an aristocracy of
> birth. There is nothing I have to do to merit my superiority,
> and neither can I lose it. It is given to me once and for all. It is
> a *thing*.

> To this end he finds the existence of the Jew absolutely neces-
> sary. Otherwise to whom would he be superior? If by some
> miracle all the Jews were exterminated as he wishes, he would
> find himself nothing but a concierge or shopkeeper in a
> strongly hierarchical society in which the quality of "true
> Frenchman" would be of low valuation, because everyone
> would possess it. Thus the Anti-Semite is in the unhappy
> position of having a vital need for the very enemy he wishes
> to destroy.[10]

Thus, murderous bigotry, central to redemptive authoritarianism, is the basis of a socialism of fools, an extension of and cause
for the worst excesses of industrial civilization. This is the community evoked in different ways by such figures as David Duke, Pat
Buchanan, and Louis Farrakhan in the United States, the Afrikaner
Resistance Movement (ARM) in South Africa, Slobodan Milosevic
in Serbia, and Jean-Marie Le Pen in France.

The Authoritarian Nation State

The authoritarian alternative for industrialism's future is not limited to fascist conceptions. While ostensibly attempting to redeem the common man or woman (usually man) from industrialism's depredations, authoritarianism relies upon one of industrialism's basic creations, the hierarchical nation state.

Quoting Terence, Italian fascist philosopher Giovanni Gentile (1875-1944) writes:

> *Nihil humani a me alienum potu.* [I count nothing human alien to me.] And since we can also say that the State is man, it follows that nothing human can be alien to the essential nature of the State. For the State includes, unifies, and fulfills every human activity, every form or element of human nature so that every concept of the State that omits some element of human nature is inadequate.[11]

In this view, human unity in diversity is to be realized not from the Platonic transcendence of earthly illusion described by Plotinus as the one manifest in the many, or by Benedictus de Spinoza's idea of the essential unity of "G-d or nature," but within the state. In his *Ethics*, Spinoza, writing on the cusp of modernity, found god as the "indwelling and not the transitory cause in all things." That is, "Whatever is, is in G-d." (I prop. 18). For redemptive authoritarianism, whatever is, is in the state.

Again, according to this view, the industrial world that was grotesque, uncontrolled, unjust, and confusing is to be made right through the venue of the all-powerful state. Yet despite its power, this redemptive authoritarian state cannot be merely paternalistic and relatively benign. Its power is to be spiritually redemptive, *not* redistributive of existing wealth.

Since the new state embraces core industrial values and power relationships, it can find fulfillment only by focusing on symbolic victims who must be sacrificed to achieve the purification of authoritarian order. Thus, Muslims are slaughtered in Bosnia in the name of a greater Serbia; thus, the Nazis committed genocide against Jews and others deemed defective and subhuman; thus, the Khmer Rouge annihilated the middle class and the literate. Such impulses are not peripheral to redemptive authoritarianism and its state, but central. Thus Hitler wrote:

> As National Socialists we see our program in our flag. In the *red* we see the social idea of the movement, in the *white* the nationalist idea, in the *swastika* the fight for the victory of Aryan man and at the same time the victory of the idea of creative work, which in itself always was and always will be anti-Semitic.[12]

This is the lunacy at the heart of redemptive authoritarian ideals. Such sentiments may well be a pathetic projection of psychopathology, but in view of their author's rise to power and domination of the state embodying these ideals, they must be considered part of the attraction of the Nazis. Thus, the ravings of a contemporary Russian fascist such as Zhirinovsky should be understood as an integral part of his appeal as leader of the Liberal Democratic Party and a man with a reasonable prospect of being elected president of Russia.

The Jews of the Warsaw ghetto in April 1943 and the Muslims of Gorazde in Bosnia huddled in the rubble of their devastated city in April 1994 both faced death not because of what they had done, but because of who they were. The Nazi war against the Jews aimed and the Bosnian Serb war against the Muslims still aims unambiguously at the total removal and obliteration of an ethnic group and its culture. In both situations, urgent appeals were made to the world as the noose tightened.[13]

The Theocratic Alternative

One manifestation of redemptive authoritarianism as an anti-modern movement is a theocratic state such as the Iran of the Ayatollahs, a state openly hostile to both capitalism and socialism, and to the great powers that once contested for influence over Iran as a strategic principality.

Islamic fundamentalism as a political movement is not necessarily violent, authoritarian, or even classically theocratic. Its
leading supporters—as in the case of fundamentalist Algeria before the military denied its electoral victories and opportunities for
democratic governance—can, in fact, be advocates of open elections and parliamentary rule, advancing a political and moral
order in response to the failures of capitalist and socialist industrial
modernity. However, the nature of this movement and the forces
driving it, and its potential for constructive change, have received
little serious attention in the West.

Mary Anne Weaver in a report from Cairo provides a graphic
example of the complex forces at work:

> Imbaba, only a bridge away from the affluent island of
> Zamalek, is one of Cairo's most dismal and sprawling slums,
> holding some eight hundred thousand people. In its stark,
> sometimes tottering houses, built of stucco or brick or of
> corrugated iron and mud, line a labyrinth of open sewers and
> unpaved alleyways. The alleys are so narrow that they are
> little more than dark, hidden passageways.

> ...The Islamists, led by the [Muslim] Brotherhood had built
> their own social and welfare system here. Gama'a-controlled
> popular mosques had set up discount health clinics and
> schools, day-care centers, and furniture factories to employ
> the unemployed, and they provided meat at wholesale prices
> to the poor. Despite an aggressive ten million dollar
> [government] social program launched by the last fall, the
> Islamists' institutions remained generally far more efficient
> and far superior to run down government facilities. Along
> with the collapse of every secular ideology embraced by
> Egyptian politicians during this century, it was government
> repression and ineptitude, far more than the militants guns
> and bombs that were fueling the Islamic flame.

> ...Throughout their areas of control, they imposed Islamic
> law by fiat. In Imbaba, the Islamists had, for all intents and
> purposes, created a state within a state. Then in December of
> 1992, the government moved in, in an abortive attempt to
> crush the Islamic groups. It was a virtual invasion, of some
> fifteen thousand troops. Raids have occurred intermittently
> ever since.[14]

Redemptive theocracy, as in Iran, fuses moral order with state order to make war upon modernity. While fascism identifies the dominant political party as the incarnation of the people's will and spirit, and the state as the path to spiritual renaissance, redemptive theocracies use an active religion, purged of modernity and liberalism, to govern the political as well as religious order. Nazism, with its theatrical neopaganism, had a certain theocratic dimension. It was to an extent anti-Christian and anti-modernist, with much parading about of symbols of an idealized pagan past. Nazism identified Christianity with its Jewish antecedents and rejected much doctrine that conflicted with a belief in violence as the expression not of sin, but of deliverance.

Of course, such a rejection of modernity is selective. It does not involve rejecting useful military and industrial accoutrements; and it is strongest in the case of such cultural movements and artifacts as the emancipation of women, western music, and commercial culture—drugs, sex, rock 'n' roll, and Coca-Cola. For example, in Algeria in 1994, Islamic radicals, who had been driven underground by the government, shot and killed two women, ages nineteen and twenty, waiting at a bus stop, because the women did not cover their heads in public in conformance with the killers' idea of Islamic modesty.[15] Thus, for some authoritarian fundamentalists murder is a step on the path to moral and political rebirth.

Such a belief is at once apparently sincere and cynically self-serving. Personal and institutional corruption inevitably attends not only arbitrary acts of murder, but also the simultaneous wielding of great state and institutionalized religious power. A redemptive theocracy, despite its contempt for modernity, is pushed by reasons of state to pursue industrial ends through industrial means. Thus, it too embraces the ideology of hierarchy, technique, and progress, though it may give a moral gloss to the workings of the machine. Authoritarian theocracy is a dead end as a real alternative to industrial modernity.

Triumph of the People or Triumph of the Will?

Certainly, all social movements can draw upon a cultural legacy of transcendence—philosophical, mystical, and otherwise. Social movements can also politicize personal transformation: empowerment, the political face of transcendence, is basic to their success. Social movements are thus more than intellectual exercises or logical arguments for change.

Empowerment is not taught. It is the experience of acts and their consequences; the result of taking personal and collective risks, facing the fear of jail, death, injury, loss of job, housing, and friendship—and finding courage. Empowerment is also the lever that upends empires, that transforms lonely individuals into a potent collective force. Empowerment, not force of arms, led to the election of Nelson Mandela in a multiracial South African democracy.

By choosing resistance over acquiescence and facing fear, an activist gains the ability to put consequences in perspective. At some times, in some places, holding a sign at a legal demonstration may be an act of bravery—though years later, the same sign-holder might find the risk of arrest for a political act more energizing than fearful.

For an individual actor, empowerment is conditioned by the support of people who can be trusted. The experience is at least superficially similar in any grassroots social change movement, so there is the possibility of abusing this experience. When Mussolini tells of his black-shirted followers writing "I don't give a damn" on their bandaged wounds, we can understand the feelings of commitment, bravery, and empowerment—even though these feelings are focused on fascist ends.

What distinguishes libertarian from authoritarian groups, the Clamshell Alliance from the Moonies, is not only a principled commitment to nonviolence and a respect for the essential humanity of others, but the practice of internal democracy—a practice that involves wide-ranging discussions about the organization as well as group actions and policies. In authoritarian groups, empowerment is part of the hermetic mystification that separates the anointed from the Other; it is used not to question, but to march in lockstep to fulfill the leader's dreams. Thus, authoritarianism not only demands blind obedience, but also denies the questioning, feeling parts of its followers.

The empowerment of individuals potentiates the creation of passionate crowds. These are "open" crowds in the term of Elias Canetti, that is, crowds that will grow to absorb the energies of all they can touch directly or metaphorically. Authoritarian and dictatorial revolutionaries feed and encourage the ecstatic fires of their crowds to destroy or supplant all that *is*—in order to replace it with the order that will be.

Transformative social movements are not only terrifying to the managers of the status quo, but deeply sobering to anyone who reflects upon the risks and responsibilities of change. Such reflection and self-limitation—driven by conversation, ethics, democratic practice—can condition the destructive impulses of mass movements by undermining dogma and by adjusting practice to evolving realities. This is the underlying strategy of liberatory movements.

Change is driven by an untenable reality. It can catalyze forces of freedom and of repression: change unleashed and corrupted by revolutionary apocalyptics, as in Cambodia's Khmer Rouge or Peru's *Sendero Luminoso,* is a fearful thing; and fear of the unmediated crowd is at the root both of the sort of conservatism that looks upon change with a jaundiced eye, and of the democratic prudence guiding the practice of liberatory movements for social change.[16]

All democratic and libertarian organizations inevitably face the problem of making decisions. Authoritarianism, on the other hand, resolves that problem by bowing to the will of the leader on all questions. According to authoritarianism, empowerment exists only insofar as it meets the hierarch's demands; freedom in action is limited to the struggle against the adversary who must be destroyed. Thus, redemptive authoritarianism is a vampire preying upon human aspiration and emotion, and draining them of living and liberatory content in the interest of a triumph of the will of the anointed leader.

Conclusion: Disabilities of Authoritarianism

Does willingness to dispense with the complicating niceties of grassroots democracy make redemptive authoritarianism a contender for the future of industrial civilization? Are its weaknesses greater than the empowerment it offers? Can it overcome the resistance of those unwilling to cede their freedom to its notion of community?

Despite their appeal to rage and bloodlust, redemptive authoritarian regimes have had rather pinched careers, resembling in a way their conception of human freedom. Once in power, the life cycle of such regimes typically resembles that of Francisco Franco's Spain, evolving from vigorous and murderous fascism, to corrupt and cozy corporatism, to a simple managerial repression primarily interested in holding power, to exhaustion and dissolution—ending with a whimper instead of a bang. King Juan Carlos, chosen to be Franco's successor, has instead helped lead Spain toward parliamentary democracy and a social democratic government.

Redemptive authoritarianism is ultimately ill-suited for the imperatives of industrialism. The industrial impulse encourages at least the framework of freedom to excite and channel desire toward industrial ends. The globalizing aspects of industrialism, the weakening of nations, the instant transfer of capital, and the organization of communication all work against the privileged refuge of authoritarianism.

This is not to imply that liberal capitalism will lead to paradise, but to suggest the underlying weakness of the authoritarian model. Redemptive authoritarianism attempts to use industrial means and structures to somehow avoid the snares and consequences of the industrial ends that brought it to power; but it is hobbled because, by its nature, it can rely upon neither freedom nor community.

In sum, redemptive authoritarianism is the assertion of power against change; its medium is mythic nationhood fused with the modern state. This corrosion of the impulse for order embraces an idealized and mythic freedom and community with no power for constructive change; the very order it embraces closes the door of opportunity for awakening from the industrial nightmare. Redemptive authoritarianism leads not to redemption, but to delusion and desolation. In contrast, as we shall see, an ecological society represents a liberatory and participatory transcendence that involves not the futile pursuit of perfection and order, but the nurturance of freedom and community writ large.

chapter seven

ECOLOGICAL DEMOCRACY AND CIVIL SOCIETY

THIS CHAPTER DETAILS HOW TO BUILD an ecological democracy from the reality of industrialism. It addresses ecological democracy as an expression of the complex dynamics of civil society. It examines the concrete experiences of three cooperative social systems as examples of emerging ecological democracies: the Mondragon cooperatives, Seikatsu Consumer Cooperative Club, and Co-op Atlantic.

Democracy is not engendered by reform from above, but by insistent action from below. An ecological democracy arises from popular ferment, aspiration for a better life, intolerance of the abuse of power, and collective and personal determination to build a just and enduring community. It is the product of civil society, that realm of community and individual self-assertion that lies outside domains of ruling power. In our time, civil society has given us Solidarity in Poland and the Velvet Revolution in Czechoslovakia, the African National Congress and the astonishing establishment of a multiracial South African democracy, the democratization of Argentina and Chile. A revivified civil society has fostered social miracles, toppled regimes of seemingly implacable power.

The flowering of civil society was potentiated by liberal capitalist democracy, but the social forces it represents transcend capitalism. The mission of civil society is not satisfied by founding nominally liberal capitalist democracies to supplant totalitarian and authoritarian regimes. In the global crisis of industrial civilization, civil society stands between people and the giant bureaucracies of states and corporations; it represents the possibilities for community response to the excesses of business and government. Civil society and its creations are not contesting for power, but working for community and freedom.

Civil society generates community associations and grassroots movements. But these movements (as Adam Michnik noted of Solidarity) seek only a limited revolution to reform relations between power structures and communities.[1] Ecological justice movements, worker and community struggles for safety and dignity, Green parties, radical and reformist environmentalists, people working in a myriad of associations and movements for peace, freedom, justice—all of these groups express this desire. In the United States, civil society is the bearer of popular anger against continuation of business-as-usual—an unfocused demand for change that can be captured by ambitious plutocrats, such as Ross Perot, and hard-eyed conservatives, such as Newt Gingrich.

Ecological Democracy

Ecological democracy as an expression of an ascendant civil society is based on limiting and then transforming industrial abuse. It is decentralist, flexible, and devolutionary in an era that engenders such characteristics. In this sense, the breakup of empires and nations that has accompanied global industrial political economy also represents the opportunity for democratic transformation. By weakening the nation state on a number of planes, globalization invites diverse community self-assertion.

Prospects for the rise of ecological democracy are represented by a confluence of forces: the dynamic importance of city regions as engines of economic organization and community possibility; the democratic idea; communication and information technologies that *can* encourage the expansion of community. In the United States, democratic forces are manifest in the direct democracy that still exists in New England town meetings, the expansion of plebiscitary state referenda (albeit abused by right-wing manipulators), and the consensus process of many grass-roots organizations.[2]

The transformation of industrialism to ecological democracy rests upon three broad themes arising from actions of civil society: association, cooperation, and confederation.

Association

Ecological democracy is predicated upon the growth and empowerment of democratic, community-based associations. Association is the blood and sinew of civil society: it potentially encompasses all social and economic activities, ordinary and extraordinary, including not only human-service activities—schools, health care, housing, sports, arts, banking, fire and police protection—but nonviolent, direct action to protect the community from polluters, as well as farming and fishing, and other services and businesses of all sorts. Associations can be political organizations, community groups, social clubs, non-profit corporations, local government organizations, or businesses small and appropriately large. They are the basic venue for moving power away from state and corporate bureaucracies. For an ecological democracy, association is also the gate to transforming the industrial state and revivifying community, the first step toward building an ecological commons.

The concept of association has a long and varied pedigree: from anarchists to free-market libertarians, to guild socialists, to democratic pluralists, to populists, to corporatists, to council communists, to nationalists of many stripes, to varieties of fascism. Association as political myth is the basis of the social contract, the defining notion for a well-ordered society. In other words, association as an idea does little more than recognize some degree of organization independent of the state.

In practice, association can range from the radically democratic to blatantly authoritarian. For anarchists, it is a means to replace the state; for corporatists and guild socialists, a means of balancing the interests of groups and classes within a continuing process of negotiation, as in German codetermination and the new ideas of associative democracy of Paul Hirst and John Mathews. For market libertarians, association allows the expansion of market activity that the state does not approve; for Green social ecologists, it is the means for expanding local power, pursuing relative self-sufficiency, and abolishing the market in favor of local planning, as in Murray Bookchin's libertarian municipalism.[3]

For an ecological democracy, association, through cooperative and confederative efforts, diminishes the power of the central state and capitalist market. Association is not a magic wand; but associations, because they are nested within civil society, are at least conditionally shielded from state and corporate bureaucracies. Their goal is not to seize or abolish state power, or to substitute planning for market mechanisms, but to transform both state and market. This goal is not a utopian trope, but an amplification and redirection of forces unleashed in the process of globalization that have pushed both state and market into smaller, confederated units.

In form, ecological democracy driven by association can range broadly, from arrangements resembling the Swiss confederation to multiple and parallel organizations of community and state power centered on continuing dialogue and the pursuit of dynamic equilibrium.

Hirst's and Mathews's Associative Democracy

The most significant explorations of association as a transformative, albeit reformist, venue for the modern capitalist industrial state are those of Australian John Mathews in *Age of Democracy: The Politics of Post-Fordism* (1989) and Paul Hirst in *Associative Democracy: New Forms of Economic and Social Governance* (1994).[4] Both outline compelling designs for shifting the focus of government from the center to community associations that will gradually supplant both government and private corporations. Their view is rooted in the existing practices and politics of social democracy and labor, but is separated from the decentralization sought by Green parties and ecological justice movements more interested in transformation than reform.*

Both Hirst and Mathews see the state as, in a sense, hollowed out, with most of its functions eventually transferred to democratic community groups that people are free to join or leave. In return for tax support, these groups must meet certain broad goals, exercise financial responsibility, and maintain a one member-one vote democratic governance. According to Hirst:

> Associationalism challenges both the centralization of the state and its claims to "sovereignty." It proposes that authority be as far as possible divided into distinct   domains,

---

*Hirst and Mathews address association in the context of existing industrial political dynamics and suggest reasonable points of departure for grassroots organizing. This focus can help move the policy debate toward the building of ecological democracies from below. Grassroots transformative movements need to do more than follow Rene Dubos's dicta of working locally and thinking globally: while working in our communities, we must also proceed on an agenda addressed to larger spheres. Local success enables meaningful action through broadening circles of cooperation and confederation; we must think in terms of bridging the gap between local models and international questions.

whether territorial or functional, and that authority should be as localized and as small scale as possible.[5]

For social services, associative democracy offers what Hirst calls "thick welfare, thin collectivism." Through a gradual decentralization process, driven by citizen initiative, comprehensive social benefits would be provided to members by a wide range of democratic community organizations and agencies. To receive tax support, organizations would have to meet certain standards; for example, schools would have to meet student performance and curriculum standards. (Such associations need not be supported by taxation, but may, in fact, arise from independent social and economic action as with the cooperative systems examined in this chapter; or they may resemble community organizations, such as trusts in Britain, that have helped revitalize communities without tax dollars.) Also crucial to Mathews's and Hirst's visions is the institution of a guaranteed minimum income for all adults to eliminate basic poverty and replace many welfare functions. (Mathews, but not Hirst, considers the more liberatory prospects of a social wage system as described by André Gorz.)

In broad compass, then, associative democracy is an attempt to redirect the capitalist industrial state toward a democratic cooperative commonwealth with power largely, but not entirely, shifted to civil society. Associative democracy aims to move from domination by large firms and government bureaucracies to a much more convivial, local, cooperative, and responsive social and economic order.*

Associative democracy is not another name for privatization and libertarianism: it rests upon social action by groups of individuals and a socially mediated market-and-welfare system. In a

---

* Although associative democracy has British roots in the Guild Socialism of G.D.H. Cole and the writings of Harold Laski and John Figgis, Hirst sees it as an evolutionary doctrine that need not be explicitly socialist and can appeal to many who mistrust government and believe in local initiative.

way, this model is radically conservative, as it calls for dramatic weakening in the power of government; but it departs from the conservative agenda in that it empowers democratic community groups, not private or corporate authority. Associative democracy is based on transferring power from government and market to community; the New Right agenda, on the other hand, is predicated upon weakening government but empowering market forces, and identifies all that is private, including transnational corporations, with civil society and a realm of freedom.

Mathews and Hirst see associative democracy as a cogent action plan for social democratic/labor parties. In the United States, with only parties of the Right and farther Right, such ideas certainly merit consideration from desperate politicians searching for an alternative to the politics of cruelty now ascendant. A program to transfer power to democratic community associations, as an alternative to abolishing or privatizing government services, should appeal to citizens fed up with business-as-usual and stale dogma.

Moreover, associative democracy has a potentially strong economic program. Its appeal rests upon the manifest superiority of cooperation as the basis for economic activity—both at the level of the firm, as reflected in a plethora of pseudo-cooperative management initiatives, and at the level of the nation, as seen in the prowess of the relatively more cooperative and corporatist systems of Japan and Germany. If such partial and pseudo-cooperation works well, why should people not be interested in trying the real thing?[6]

As I have argued earlier in this book, the dynamics of the industrial world system will increasingly sharpen disparities between rich and poor, while increasingly making the future unsustainable—economically, socially, and ecologically—for poor *and* rich. Merely developing a more equitable way to manage a destructive system will not solve the problems of either group. Thus, democracy cannot settle for being "associative" within a destruc-

tive industrial state: the radical pursuit of both democracy and
ecology is necessary for the attainment of either.

In short, our efforts must transcend reform. Understanding
association as the basic pillar for ecological democracy is vital, but
we must give freer reign to our imagination. Mathews and Hirst
provide practical points of departure, but they do not look carefully enough at the instability of the industrial system or the
possibilities for liberatory transformation. Cooperation and democratic devolution must *transform* the social order into a system that
rests upon sustaining the inextricably linked natural and social
ecologies, an order based upon peace and justice, freedom and
community, unity and diversity.

Association and Ecological Democracy

An ecological democracy views association as the beginning
of transformation. For an ecological democracy, an associative
democracy is important as a program for the devolution of power
to be advanced from below, from the arena of civil society. The
motive force for change lies within the associations of civil society—diverse and squalling, blunt and disorderly, somber and gay,
but rooted in local conditions, not the calm platitudes and lies of
economists and politicians.

The diverse needs of communities and their associations are
reflected in the program of equally diverse Green, ecology, environmental, and ecological justice movements—all with differing
philosophies, worldviews, plans and demands, but all calling for
social, political, economic, environmental, ethical, and spiritual
change.[7] Clearly, the response of association to the crisis of industrialism can be perverted by authoritarian nationalists, misguided
populists, and fascists; but it can also cohere into a movement for
liberatory transformation.

Of course, not all members of Green movements embrace
associative democracy. Green thinkers and organizers have devel-

oped a range of critiques of industrial civilization and its capitalist and socialist manifestations. These critiques address state and market, social life and political life, technology and science, ethics and spirit. The more radical critiques have great scorn for those who seek power on a national or state level, like the German *realos*, and who find themselves dealing with social democratic politicians. Rudolf Bahro, who moved from being a heterodox East German socialist to a West German Green radical and theorist, wrote in 1984 (the year before he resigned from the Green Party over its reformist direction):

> What is fundamentalism? Externally it puts ecology before economics, and fundamental long term interests before immediate short term ones. (Priority does not mean exclusivity, but keeping to a rank order.) Similarly to survive it has to be a policy with a spiritual impetus and a moral standard.

> Anyone among us who wants to carve up an up-to-date plan for overall repair, which means quite automatically a solution in grand style from above, presupposing a well-oiled state, has not understood at all that a world is disintegrating, that this disintegration is the best thing about it and we must say "Yes" to it and assist it as far as possible.[8]

It is important to embrace Bahro's idea of the need for fundamental change, but his negative vision of disintegration can be both a strategic and tactical error. There is a crucial distinction between commitment to transformative change and a rigid fundamentalism: we need to do more than suggest that the industrial system must disintegrate before we can rebuild in the ashes. It is perfectly reasonable to recognize the folly of a Green political movement devoting its efforts to playing modest parliamentary roles that marginally improve the conduct of business-as-usual—efforts that actually help the industrial system fulfill its own imperative need for limits to the extent necessary to continue operations. But fear of co-optation should not keep a vibrant grassroots movement from advancing, on a national level, a constructive and gradual program of radical reform. Associative democracy can thus be an interim step on the path to a truly ecological democracy: it is both valid on its face, and valid for creating the opportunities for deeper cooperative and confederal action. We need a constructive program that allows meaningful interim steps.*

Association in civil society involves more than a banal rearrangement of what *is*. Association unbound can be understood as relationship and an ecological way, reflecting an ethics as well as a politics; association is a prologue to epochal change. To appreciate what is at stake here, we should recall the words of Murray Bookchin, founder of social ecology:

> Mutualism, freedom, and subjectivity are not strictly human values or concerns. They appear, however germinal, in larger cosmic or organic processes that requires no Aristotelian G-d to motivate them, no Hegelian Spirit to vitalize them....To vitiate community, to arrest the spontaneity that lies at the core of a self-organizing reality toward ever-greater complexity and rationality, to abridge freedom—these actions would cut across the grain of nature, deny our heritage in its evolutionary processes and dissolve our legitimacy and function in the world of life. No less than this ethically rooted legitimation would be at stake—all its grim ecological consequences aside—if we fail to achieve an ecological society and articulate an ecological ethics.[9]

---

*Political reform can proceed through different, though complementary, grassroots views. The experience of the grassroots anti-nuclear movement suggests that there can be a broad compatibility of interests between those waging a nonviolent, direct action campaign and those working as legal interveners. For example, the Clamshell Alliance launched its nonviolent campaign against the construction of the Seabrook nuclear power plant in New Hampshire after the state ignored Seabrook town meeting votes against the plant and the Nuclear Regulatory Commission issued a construction permit. At the same time, the Seacoast Anti-Pollution League (SAPL), working in the regulatory arena, raised objections to this specific plant. SAPL's measured practice and Clamshell's radicalism proved to be an effective combination. Despite some years of friction, it eventually became clear that SAPL was actually fighting for more than a safer nuke in another location, and that Clamshell was, in practice, fighting for something less than the prompt abolition of all nukes and the comprehensive development of community- controlled renewable energy resources. The efforts of Clamshell and SAPL were both relevant and, in fact, tactically and strategically complementary (a fact not always appreciated by partisans of both groups all the time).

A Contract with the Community: Associations and Community Democracy

Applied community empowerment and democracy in the current U.S. context rests upon three broad pillars: social development, economic development, and gradual adoption of the social wage. The community empowerment model means the pursuit of justice, and not simply the exercise of compassion. Although social and economic development are presented here as separate points for clarity, they are, in fact, interrelated and interdependent. They need be pursued together.

The three basic elements of a community empowerment strategy:

- First, to establish, with tax support, democratic community associations and organizations. These would gradually come to perform social functions, from schooling to providing health care, housing, and other forms of social welfare. Power would be devolved from bureaucracies of government and large corporations to communities through existing and effective community institutions.

For instance, instead of the government privatizating school systems, community groups, together with teachers and their unions, would create a range of community-controlled schools, often connected to other community institutions. Community health clinics would operate not on the basis of bureaucratic rules and Medicaid treatment, but as community-owned institutions providing comprehensive individual and public health care—working, for example, with other community institutions, such as co-ops and small businesses, on drug treatment, addiction prevention, and deleading apartments. Instead of using food stamps for supermarket food purchases, we could develop community-supported agriculture and city-rural partnerships that assist community development, provide superior nutrition, and give a measure of local food security.

- Second, to encourage the parallel and interrelated growth of community-based and -controlled democratic economic institutions: co-ops, nonprofit corporations, municipal corporations, micro-enterprises, and small businesses of all kinds (including banking, production, retail, and service businesses and institutions).

Cooperative community economic development would be supported in several ways: financially, by providing capital and working capital, and recycling and reinvesting community income and savings for the benefit of the community; technically, by making assistance available at all stages from business start-up to break-even to the revitalization of mature firms; educationally, by providing training, both formal and informal, through schools, at work sites, and in homes through television and distance-learning programs.

These community institutions would at the same time be pursuing a social development agenda that would complement and potentiate work on economic development. When examining community needs, we must understand the dynamics of money-flows through communities. Typically, in poor communities, consumer spending and social welfare transfer payments do not go to community-based, -owned, or -controlled businesses or institutions, *and* are not reinvested in the community. With integrated social and economic planning, the community can realize gains both from recirculating funds among community businesses and institutions, *and* from having funds reinvested as community-based capital.

Existing examples of community economic development cover a broad range, including the work of Chicago's South Shore Bank on housing, the Industrial Cooperative Association on community job creation and preservation, the Institute for Local Self-Reliance on solid waste recycling and processing and on economic development. The aim for community empowerment is to knit these examples together into a coherent whole of complementary cooperative and cooperating institutions.

Federal funding for local community development does not necessarily mean a soft budget constraint, where additional funds will usually bail out failure; rather, it means providing the resources community groups need if they are to have a realistic chance of succeeding in implementing plans for which they are held accountable. We need to avoid the kind of debacle that federal deposit insurance meant for unregulated savings and loans, while at the same time assuring that community plans are not strangled or set up to fail by regulatory micromanagement, political interference, or inadequate financial, technical, or educational resources.

- Third, to investigate the social wage—the idea that each person is entitled to a share of the social product—as an underlying transitional principle. The social wage (discussed further in Chapter Nine) means a basic income for a predetermined amount of socially useful labor, as broadly and democratically defined, from all those able to work (such labor can include, for example, community volunteer work).

To take full advantage of the productive capacity of new technology, and to avoid the further division of our society between a wealthy few and an impoverished many, we need to transform our understanding of what is meant by full employment and of the nature of the connection between work and wages. Reduction of the work week, job sharing, and the social wage must be part of our long-term vision.

The social wage could eventually replace much of traditional welfare payments, providing the economic basis for a decent life for all in exchange for responsible effort. While not essential at the first stage of community economic and social development, the social wage, or some related practice, is necessary in the long run to respond to changing economic and social realities.

In this regard, it is crucial to appreciate structural as opposed to cyclical economic changes. For example, in New Hampshire, 38.4 percent of new jobs (6,613) created in the recovery of 1991-93 were in industries in which average pay was under $15,000 per year, below the poverty line for a family of four. Jobs in this low-income category increased 7.7 percent from 1991-93, while the number of jobs paying above $35,000 per year *declined* by 3.1 percent.[10] These state findings reflect national trends: during the "recovery," from just January 1993 to March 1994 layoffs of over 5,000 workers announced by major corporations (from General Motors [69,650] to Lockheed [5,600]) amounted to 475,790 lost jobs.[11]

Implementation: An Organizing Agenda

To turn theory and program into practice, I suggest the following. It is relevant to the current political universe defined by the Gingrich-led Congress, with its focus on block grants to states, and the devolution of federal power and responsibilities to localities and to businesses.

· Attempt to make federal funding and the award of block grants dependent upon creating and implementing community, social, and economic development plans made by democratic community organizations and assemblies.

· Research and develop with community groups a variety of model plans—including a wide range of actions and their synergistic integration between economic and social development—for different kinds of communities, based on real communities and real institutions. This would serve as an organizing, education, and policy tool.[12]

· Develop model standards for community organizations that would receive tax support to help assure they are open, democratic, and accountable.

- Convene working groups, build coalitions, and hold conferences to advance the community democracy and empowerment agenda, both for organizing and policymaking purposes.

- Focus the issue on justice and the ability of individuals and families to build safe, sane, and sustainable lives. The issue ultimately is the ability of people to constructively and creatively take control of their lives in their communities.

Cooperation

Cooperation, the second broad theme in the transformation to ecological democracy, is more than a means of describing an organization's internal workings. Ecological democracy is predicated upon a great expansion of cooperation. Cooperation is the social and economic force behind the growth of community associations, the catalyst in the creative actions of associations and their members. It is both *social creativity*—the growth of new lifeways, of neighborhoods and communities—and *economic creativity*—the ways and means of making a living through the growth of community–based cooperative business enterprises. In an ecological democracy, cooperation is not merely a way of accommodating ourselves and our communities to goals established by state bureaucracies, but a social force integral to community well-being.

Such cooperation is a matter of necessity. It is a key response to the crises of modernity. In this sense, the industrial state becomes the catalyst for the creation of its antipode, the dynamic cooperative commonwealth.[13]

Cooperative social systems have already developed as expressions of the expansion of voluntary, self-governing associations. Three examples discussed in this chapter—Mondragon cooperatives in the Basque region of Spain, Co-op Atlantic in Canada's Atlantic provinces, and the Seikatsu Consumer Cooperative Club in Japan—are expressions of grassroots responses to the excesses of the industrialized world and examples of emergent ecological paths for those seeking alternatives to conventional development. They are evocative examples, and worth investigating, but do not represent the limit of possibility for building an ecological democracy. These systems suggest how civil society has begun to limit and redefine the economic and political nature of industrial civilization. They represent the emergence not simply of a third way of industrialism between capitalism and socialism, but of a third force between the individual and the corporation/nation state.

These systems are characterized by direct democracy (one person-one vote), and by bringing cooperative forms into all aspects of life and cooperative concerns to discussion of issues at every level, from local to global. They offer a possible means for democratic and sustainable development for the poor, and a method to limit, regulate, and change industrial civilization.

In a general sense, cooperative social systems lie within the broad discourse of those calling not simply for a more just or perfected industrialism, but for transformative and ecological social practice. This is the critique expressed by elements of the Green and radical ecology movements, in works such as *The Development Dictionary: A Guide to Knowledge as Power* edited by Wolfgang Sachs, and by thinkers and organizers such as Vandana Shiva, Ashis Nandy, Ivan Illich, and Gustavo Esteva.[14]

Several existing community-based cooperative systems transcend a narrow enterprise consciousness. The three discussed here represent important successful examples of the pursuit of freedom and community in various cultural contexts, examples that converge on the practical ideal of democratically transforming the conduct of industrial civilization.

The Mondragon Cooperatives

The Mondragon cooperative system was born in the late 1940s as a community-funded apprentice school for mill workers in the industrial town of Mondragon in the Basque region of the Guipuzcoa province in northeastern Spain. Today, the Mondragon system has over 26,000 workers and more than 150 cooperative businesses, ranging from heavy industry to cooperative department stores with $3.1 billion in 1993 sales, a bank with billions of dollars in assets, a research center, a social insurance and health system, and housing and educational institutions from preschool to postgraduate technical education.

The elaboration of the Mondragon system represents more than economic achievement. It is an expression of democratic cooperative entrepreneurship that has facilitated not only business, but the building of a system. Through a complex matrix of affinities and relationships, Mondragon has closed the circle of power between the efforts of working people and the health of their communities, opening the door to community-based development that extends far beyond the economic sphere.[15] Especially since the co-op bank, *Caja Laboral Popular*, was established in the late 1950s to serve the needs of the rapidly growing and capital-starved industrial co-ops, Mondragon has crafted an ongoing series of cooperative and democratic responses to the problems of capitalist industrialism.

Each co-op is the basic unit of democratic decisionmaking. A co-op can decide to enter into a number of relationships with other Mondragon co-ops, for example, joining a group organized by business type or location. Co-ops can also sign a contract of association with the co-op bank and with co-ops offering entrepreneurial assistance, co-op social insurance, research, and education. Mondragon has embraced cooperative principles, including one member-one vote; open enrollment; recognition of education as a crucial task; and solidarity between co-op members, between co-op and community, and within the global cooperative movement. Each member pays a one-time membership entrance fee (which in large measure can be paid from *anticipos*, essentially equivalent to wages). Co-op membership cannot be sold.

Broad policy questions for the cooperatives are decided by the Co-op Congress. Its decisions must generally be voted upon by each co-op. For example, the Congress may decide to change the maximum pay differential from lowest to highest paid cooperator, but implementation depends on a further vote by each co-op.

In *We Build The Road As We Travel* (1991), I considered Mondragon not only as an outstanding example of a democratic, labor-managed social system in a market economy, but as a model of a successful response to the forces transforming industrial civilization; a success that is not only economic, but based on the conscious pursuit of both freedom and community. Since then, the Mondragon system has been wrestling with the effects of Spain's integration into the European Community (EC), which has removed protective tariff and nontariff barriers, and with the European recession, which has had a marked effect on the Basque economy (of which Mondragon represents about 5 percent). Heavy industry and metal working have been particularly affected by the globalization and dispersion of high-technology production.[16]

These pressures have led to a number of decisions that are controversial. They include strengthening the integration of co-op groups to make them more competitive with transnational competitors;[17] expanding the highly successful retail co-op system beyond the Basque region in joint ventures with other co-ops and with nonprofits that may not allow workers to become members immediately; increasing the maximum wage differential within co-ops to attract skilled technicians and managers; acquiring a foundry from its capitalist owners to expand and consolidate co-op production facilities, with only a slow transition to co-op status. With these changes going on, the year 1994 was one of considerable economic progress by the co-op system.

Some observers, such as Baleren Bakaikoa,[18] view these changes as undermining Mondragon's cooperative nature. Within the co-ops, some members, such as José Maria Mendizabal, argue that the changes reflect creative cooperative adaptation to new economic and political realities, and are within the Mondragon cooperative principles: "To create employment, especially industrial, enhance cooperation and educate people in solidarity."[19]

At many points in the past, critics have charged that the co-ops are succumbing to one or another of the supposed immutable laws of individual behavior or the capitalist market. But so far, the Mondragon co-ops have demonstrated an ability, through open and vigorous discussion, experimentation, and adjustment—the pursuit of *equilibrio*,[20] or dynamic balance—to find solutions in accord with their cooperative principles.

In broad terms, Mondragon's difficulties reflect, on one level, a failure of the cooperators and the cooperative movement to successfully encourage the development of other industrial cooperative systems that could act supportively in times of economic and political crisis. Mondragon provides support structures that keep individual co-ops from being swept away in a capitalist sea, but Mondragon as a whole is without the safety of a fully developed network of co-op systems. In other words, as globalization accelerates, Mondragon's difficulties reflect the need to expand and strengthen cooperation, not some inherent disability.

Mondragon's retail cooperative is moving to expand and protect itself in concert with other retail co-op systems, but such opportunities are rare in industrial and financial areas. Still, Mondragon is responding to current economic and political dynamics by seeking new alliances, and developing new ways for cooperation to expand in response to the challenges of globalization.

Seikatsu Consumer Cooperative Club

Founded in 1965 as a buying club in Tokyo for families to buy pure milk at affordable prices, the Seikatsu ("lifestyle" or "life-way") Consumer Cooperative Club evolved quickly into a group concerned with building alternative production, consumption, social welfare, and activist networks. By 1992, Seikatsu, with 225,000 participating families, had total sales of $700 million, and included 161 related worker collectives with 4,200 worker owners.[21]

Seikatsu represents a marked departure from traditional models of both cooperative and business development. It was organized primarily by women and relies on a decentralized small-group structure based on the *han*, an association of eight to ten neighbors that facilitates local control and bottom-up decision-making. Over the years, it has evolved from a buyers' club to an organization that forms producer co-ops, and it has an active peace and ecological political program.

The stated goal of the club's members is to create a new civil society. They write, "We want to speak out against the evils of industrial society, and also to create a sustainable communal society in its place. We hope to breathe fresh air into a lifestyle of individual autonomy in cooperation with others."[22]

Members pay dues of about $100 annually; average member investment is now about $500. These funds are used to capitalize co-op activities and provide some financial assistance to related worker collectives.

As Seikatsu moved from being a network of buying clubs, with all work done by members, to offering goods and services to the general public, it began to organize workers' collectives, starting with a snack bar and retail store in Yokohama. These collectives, begun on the initiative of members, are managed on a one person-one vote basis. Technical assistance is provided by an independent Workers Collective Association. As capital is not available from conventional Japanese banking sources, most funding for expanding worker collectives is generated by collective members, with some assistance from Seikatsu. Lack of a reliable funding mechanism limits Seikatsu's ability to fulfill its ambitious agenda.

In Japanese terms, Seikatsu clearly represents a response to industrial society, inspired and led by women. Ninety percent of its active members and 80 percent of its board members are women; its worker collectives are predominantly composed of women (although men are encouraged to join). Most paid administrators have been male, but female participation at this level is increasing.

Many collective members work part-time. Wages average $5 an hour. The largest collectives are no longer in food service, but in home care for the ill and disabled, many of them elderly. The Tokyo *Himawari* collective has 140 members, and the Yokohama *Himawari* collective has 122. Home care services are provided by contract to Seikatsu social welfare organizations, financed by Seikatsu group-insurance plans that cost members about $4.50 per month.[23]

Seikatsu must also be understood in the context of the Japanese cooperative movement. Although little known in the United States, where Japan is seen largely as the progenitor of a new style of state-mediated capitalism, the consumer cooperative sector is another example of the dynamism of Japanese society. Its values and purposes are far different from those pursued by the country's corporate giants. For example, in 1990 the Japanese Consumers Cooperatives Union (JCCU), founded in 1951, had 674 member organizations with 14.4 million members, or one in five Japanese, with sales equal to 2.5 percent of total Japanese domestic retail trade. In all, 44 percent of co-op sales were generated by *han*-based buying clubs, and 56 percent from retail stores. The first purchasing co-op on the Rochdale model was founded in Kobe in 1878; today the Kobe Consumers Cooperative, with over one million members, is the world's largest cooperative. The JCCU also sponsors or cosponsors annual conferences on the abolition of war and nuclear weapons.[24]

Co-op Atlantic

Co-op Atlantic is a cooperative social system serving the Atlantic provinces of Canada: Labrador and Newfoundland, New Brunswick, Nova Scotia, and Prince Edward Island. Founded in 1927, Co-op Atlantic is one expression of a dynamic cooperative movement in Atlantic Canada that is best known for the Antigonish Movement started in 1928 in Nova Scotia by Moses Coady.[25] Co-op Atlantic serves the needs of its owners—161 retail, producer, agricultural, housing, and fishing cooperatives, and a co-op newspaper. Like Mondragon, Co-op Atlantic is a second-degree cooperative providing assistance and coordination to member co-ops. It wholesales groceries, hardware, petroleum, dry goods, and livestock supplies; it provides assistance with management, training, and planning to members; and it operates Atlantic People Housing Ltd., a subsidiary that manages and constructs co-op housing. In 1993 Co-op Atlantic wholesale sales to member co-ops were in excess of $440 million.

Co-op membership includes over 168,000 families of primary producers and consumers representing more than 500,000 people. Member co-ops have over 5,000 workers and over $300 million in assets. Co-op Atlantic food stores now account for 19 percent of all food sales in Atlantic Canada. Efforts are underway to expand into other business and production areas.[26]

Each co-op is basically self-managing and democratic in operation, as in the Mondragon system. However, Co-op Atlantic consumer co-ops are owned by members in the classic Rochdale fashion, not by workers as in Mondragon. Of the eighty-eight retail co-ops, twenty-nine use an innovative and dynamic "direct charge" system in stores open only to co-op members. This system requires substantial capital investment (a

$30 initial investment, and a weekly contribution of $1 or $2 until the total reaches $600 to $800) and entitles members to significant discounts on food and grocery purchases, and discounts on other items ranging from gasoline to appliances. Members also contribute $2.50 to $3 weekly to cover operating costs, including overhead, administration, facilities, and supplies. These costs are charged equally to all members regardless of the amount purchased, thus the term *direct charge*. The result is a well-capitalized co-op whose members have made a clear financial as well as social commitment. Most direct charge co-ops are very successful and have a long waiting list for members.[27]

Co-op Atlantic has difficulties, as does any cooperative system. One area of tension involves relations with workers, who are in the traditional role of employees in the member-owned retail co-ops. This dynamic is acknowledged by Sidney Pobihushchy, former Co-op Atlantic board chair and professor of political science at the University of New Brunswick.[28] In addition, the Atlantic provinces are considered, in the Canadian context, relatively underdeveloped and poor. The region has been a source for raw materials and commodities—particularly lumber, agricultural products, and fish—and a market for manufactured goods. Much of the economy is dominated by large, often family-controlled corporations. These economic relationships have led to a dependency on federal welfare payments, substantial migration, and pressure on resources and the environment.

The Co-op Atlantic system was, in part, a response to such unfair terms of trade and corporate domination, an attempt to achieve greater equity and gain community control. Recently, however, the economic/political situation has been further complicated by the United States-Canada free trade agreement and NAFTA (vigorously opposed by Co-op Atlantic), and by the collapse of the Atlantic ground fishery (e.g., cod, haddock) due to overfishing. Moreover, Quebec secession, which many consider a real prospect, could splinter the Canadian state, and end or greatly reduce welfare and development from Ottawa.

In the face of all this, Co-op Atlantic in 1990 and 1991 passed *A Proposal for Renewal* calling for integrated community-based co-operative development in all phases of the economy. This plan is explicitly based on community-controlled capital, a broad concept of community control, environmental responsibility, and intense education. To implement this ambitious plan, Co-op Atlantic has begun organizing Co-op Development Boards on a community basis that include not only Co-op Atlantic members, but other co-ops. The first step has been the establishment of co-op funeral homes to provide death with dignity.

A basic principle of this plan is for existing local co-ops to invest part of their surplus in community producer co-ops, and for members of producer co-ops to become more fully integrated as members of consumer co-ops. This principle reflects both the Mondragon idea of planned cooperative entrepreneurship and the Seikatsu manner of developing producer co-ops to meet the needs of retail co-ops. Co-op Atlantic is also interested in exploring relationships with U.S. co-ops. For example, at the 1994 annual meeting of Northeast Co-ops (a New England-based natural and organic network) in Amherst, Massachusetts, Sidney Pobihushchy spoke of bringing U.S. organic products to Atlantic Canada, where mainstream agriculture is heavily involved with petrochemicals.

Confederation

An ecological democracy is organized on the basis of confederation, the third broad theme in society's transformation. Confederation is not simply a matter of formal relationships between governments. It embraces a limited degree of sovereignty and association, a reflection of the balance between the interests of the one and the interests of the many that is central to ecological democracy. Confederation is the broad mix of social connections that form the dynamic matrix of an ecological society, involving groups on all levels and of all sorts. For example, confederations concerned with children will include relations between schools, parent groups, hospitals, daycare centers, and cooperative economic groups.

Confederation means multiple alliances. The efflorescence of confederal power weakens the power of government and corporate bureaucracies, and strengthens the power of communities to protect an ecological commons from exploitation and abuse.

Thus, the elaboration of democratic and community-based associations, cooperation, and confederation are the practices of an ecological democracy. Such a democracy limits and transforms industrialism, and evolves into an open network of community-based and protected ecological commons. Association, cooperation, and confederation together represent the ongoing elaboration of civilization's web and a beneficent increase in social complexity.

Ecological Circle

A basic departure from the underlying industrial ideology informs the social practice of ecological democracy. Where industrialism sees the world as a machine grinding life into the pulp suitable for governments and corporate bureaucracies, the ecological way, in its diversity, may be said to be guided by basic principles of unity that I term the "ecological circle." This circle includes:

- The practice of a moral ecology, that is, the lived awareness that actions have profound consequences that we both can and must consider and act upon.

- Unity of experience and relationship that reflects both our intellectual and sensuous connection to one another and to a living, evolving world.

- The inextricable connection between the one and the many that draws together in living experience the parts and the whole, the universal in the particular, friends and community (see Figure 7-1).

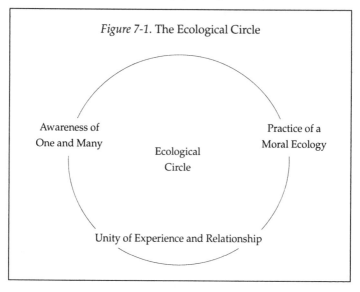

Figure 7-1. The Ecological Circle

Awareness of
One and Many

Practice of a
Moral Ecology

Ecological
Circle

Unity of Experience and Relationship

Moving toward an ecological world does not involve merely the clash of ideas. The world will change not by philosophical legerdemain, but by comprehensive social transformation in which descriptions of changing ideology are a reflection of profound changes in the way we live. Ecological values can inform our actions and choices both consciously and unconsciously, but value finds meaning through action—the practice of association, cooperation, and confederation. The problem with the global factory, hierarchy, and technocracy is not just that they are morally, politically, and socially bankrupt, but that they are failing. Ecological democracy does not merely mean turning industrialism toward justice, peace, equality, and harmony; it entails the profound social transformation required to make our goals both possible and attainable.

Freedom and Community

An ecological democracy is not concerned with a hollow universalism that attempts to repress difference, but with the particular expression of diverse communities. These need not be communities of sovereign (or would-be sovereign) territory: community can be defined through myriad forms of association and identity. True community means voluntary association that cannot exist without freedom. True freedom means the ability to pursue human values, not just individual assertion or accumulation; such freedom exists and flourishes within the embrace of supportive, democratic community.

Industrialism must keep freedom and community at arms' length, as if they were the opposed poles of magnetic bars, for the joining of the two would threaten the unhappy tension that industrialism depends upon. Industrial "freedom" is bound by consumption and production, by the market or the state; it is obedience, not real freedom. It is *industrial* freedom, essential for the creativity, the entrepreneurial energies needed to push the industrial machine to new heights—the freedom to work and shop, to make and use, to produce and possess.

Industrialism depends upon community as well—the community of the industrial organization where human energies are harmonized for production; the community of the nation state that establishes laws and customs for industrial organization; the community of multinational and transnational organizations to impose and enforce industrial norms on an ever broader scale. Thus, industrialism hobbles freedom and community to facilitate and protect its goals, to sustain its growth, so that we—the global "we"—can continue to do business. This is relationship reduced to monetized exchange, a world where love, sun, fresh air, and clean water have a price. In the capitalist industrial world, we are free to buy, but not free to be.

Ecological democracy is built on many individual and community initiatives. This is community in the sense of free and unmediated association of those who live, love, work, and play together, community related to the local, the face-to-face and human scale. But community-based activity is not necessarily limited to local scale: in a world of instantaneous telecommunications, locality can sometimes mean electronic propinquity, as with the interactive computer bulletin board that connects people around the world.

The integrity and democratic rights seen at the local level are the basic building blocks for structures of cooperation and communication that can be global in scope. But a community-based system means that each level makes only those decisions it is required to by its role, no more. Community experiments—such as the Mondragon system, developments in India's Kerala state, home health care co-ops in the South Bronx—are each part of the solution to the problems of industrialism. None is *the* solution, but together these and related themes yet to be created can form the basis for an ecological democracy. This system can be seen as an ecological model, with each type of community effort filling one niche in the social matrix that forms an ecological society.*

For a New Political Economy

The importance of cooperative social systems is not merely their economic success, but their significance as creative and amelioratory responses to industrial reality. Association, cooperation, and confederation in action are not means to better accomplish industrial ends; they are the counterweight to the consequences of

---

* "Matrix" here means the net formed by the disparate connections of different parts of an integrated whole. It is used instead of "order"—which denotes arrangement and is perfectly consistent with the patterns of a living world, but has been infected with the meaning of rigid hierarchy, not only socially, but biologically and historically.

industrial activity. As we have seen, industrial economics always presents choices as either/or decisions: either deal with scarcity, or impose stifling limits upon industrial conduct. Ecological democracy, in contrast, represents a both/and way of thinking: both address problems of scarcity and embrace essential limits on industrial activity.

Ecological democracy means the conscious melding of the political and social with the economic. In this context, democracy is not merely a way to manage the economy; ecology is not merely a way to guide conduct. Ecological democracy achieves its ends not by using accounting conventions to hide the true costs of industrial production and consumption, but by adhering to democratic and ecological values that are essential for the pursuit of freedom and community.

The confederal structures of ecological democracy will reflect recurring patterns of local necessity. This is the motive force behind Mondragon, Co-op Atlantic, and Seikatsu, and thousands upon thousands of others. As these groups cohere into exquisitely varied structures, they will share a basis in civil society, local community, and democratic action.

The transformation of industrialism means the rise of a new political economy, one rooted in respect for the interdependence of social, political, and economic realms, and their connection to the encompassing social and natural ecologies. In reaching toward this new political economy from within industrial society, we cannot simply grasp the levers of power, nor can we ameliorate industrialism's excesses through regulations and exhortations to good conduct. Rather, a new political economy must be based upon the building of a democratic community that engages and transforms the economic and social realm. In an ecological democracy, market and planning mechanisms are clearly rooted in political choices and social values. These choices and values can be mystified, as they often are in industrialism, but they cannot be banished. This was clear enough to the founders of modern economics, who understood they were not describing abstract laws. The fascination with production and consumption is a way to hide the social choices and values that privilege exchange over value, and money and power over life.

An ecological economy is essentially based upon value instead of exchange. Exchanges do take place, but in the context of the community organized around an ecological commons; the market focuses upon social as well as economic value. This is a break from the industrial view: in the capitalist world, life is monetized and ethics are separated from practice. In an ecological democracy, the question is not simply, what is the price? but, what is the effect? In such a system, we are not what we do or what we buy; the focus is on consequences in real terms, on social benefit, on ecological effects. This focus includes, but is not limited to, concern with pollution and resource depletion, and effects upon other species and future generations. Such judgments cannot simply be internalized in the price system; they depend on social choices and explicit planning. The focus of an ecological economic system is upon effectiveness and value, not on production and consumption.

Scarcity and the Market

To accept the industrial worldview is to embrace both endless need and ceaseless growth, as well as the ideal of a global market as the proven means to satisfy endless need. This is the world international banker Walter Wriston of Citibank rhapsodizes about: a democracy whose ballots are the daily transactions of global currency speculators voting through their video terminals. Yet it is clear that endless growth is, sooner or later, unsustainable. So the question becomes, will there be a soft or hard landing when the system encounters limiting realities?

It is clear that the unhindered operation of the global market driven by the price mechanism is not sufficient to meet the needs of all peoples in all places at all times—witness, for example, how governments have protected and assisted markets in now-prosperous industrial states; witness the current reality of impoverishment and failure at the hands of the market. Not only is appropriate and aggressive social mediation necessary, but, if done well, it brings superior results in both the short and long term.

Scarcity and growth are not necessarily logically related. A scarcity of unpolluted air, water, and soil, for example, calls for less, not more, industrial activity. For industrialism, scarcity means the opportunity to sell a new product, not an existential reality; so we can buy clean bottled water, organic food, and soon clean air. In fact, there are many other possible responses: scarcity of cash can be helped by barter; scarcity of energy by conservation and efficiency; scarcity of time by rest and reflection. All these responses may markedly improve people's lives, but may also decrease their "wealth" and their contribution to the GNP. If the root problem is material scarcity, then it can be solved by redistribution from rich to poor, instead of further industrial activity.

Limits

Industrialism makes war on scarcity by maximizing production and consumption—but this maximization leads to a new scarcity, created by depletion and pollution, and a need to establish limits. The question of limits, both social and material, does not just pose a fundamental challenge to the rights of accumulation and property that are the pillars of capitalism. Limits pose a basic challenge to the underlying imperatives of industrialism itself—whether capitalist or socialist.

Limits are not merely regulatory measures imposed by the state (liberal, socialist, or otherwise), by oligopolies, or by unions, associations, and communities. Limits challenge the industrial system by disrupting and interfering with the maximization of production and consumption: they require not merely restraints on markets, but on industrial activity.*

Civil society and/or government can impose, by law or custom, constraints upon industrial activity that distinguish between common interest and self-interest, between short-term and long-term benefit. This constraint may be prudent even in terms of neoclassical economics: for example, maximizing short-term gain by cutting all trees, butchering dairy cattle, fishing species to extinction, and burning all the oil will lead in the slightly longer term to starvation and impoverishment. But limits also are the creation of industrial activity itself: the contamination of air, water, and soil makes manifest the inherent limitations of a living world. Thus, it is increasingly understood that limits are a necessity if industrial conduct is to continue.

The challenge to the global crises of industrial civilization posed by the rise of an ecological way cannot be resolved by lessening the destructive nature of business-as-usual, nor by imposing new regulatory schemes on capitalist markets. An ecological worldview represents a new moral economy.

The economic and political question we face is not whether or not to limit industrial civilization, but what the nature of those limits will be: how they are chosen, how imposed.** In considering the concept of limits, then, we must deal with all its component discourses and themes, not just the economic realm. These issues include:

---

* Adam Smith did not argue that market activity was necessarily good—he was, after all, a moral philosopher—but that market activity, in general, was the best means to achieve the valid ends of eliminating scarcity and poverty.

** The industrial leader must perform an impossible trick: standing with one foot on the racing horse of growth, whipping the horse on, and the other foot on the horse of limits, pulling the reins to slow it down. This ends with a wild tumble or a lopsided shuffle.

- Market interference in a global market economy. The myth is that markets are both responsive to demand and, therefore, to social need. Adam Smith raised this topic in his classic discussion of the inland (domestic) corn market and starvation in *The Wealth of Nations* under his "Digression Concerning the Corn Trade and Corn Laws." Smith concludes,

The interest of the inland dealer, and that of the great body of the people how opposite soever they may at first sight appear, are, even in years of greatest scarcity, exactly the same.

- Yet the capitalist reality is one of persistent famine, typically resulting not from absolute scarcity but from a combination of lack of funds to buy food, distribution problems, and social dislocation resulting from war and civil strife—problems for which the capitalist market has few solutions.[29]

- Market interference in the context of great wealth and poverty as a social question and a matter of political economy.

- Market limitation and market abolition as part of a socialist challenge to capitalism.

- The confusion between limits on capitalist market conduct and limitation on industrial conduct whether capitalist or socialist (that is, limiting the conduct of capitalists, as the Soviet system made clear, does not necessarily mean limiting social or environmental depredations).

- The imperatives of the nation state to limit the destructive consequences of industrial activity in its own interest. State action to limit markets in response to the clamor from below (and above) is hardly a new phenomenon.*

---

* In 1800, in response to severe food shortages and public unrest, England's Chief Justice Lord Kenyon found that hoarding for profit should be declared illegal, as "a thing most essential to the existence of the country."[31]

· The limits resulting as unintended consequences of industrial activity and population growth and those resulting from the imposition of market-driven, socially developed, and state-imposed constraints on industrial conduct.

The evolution of association, cooperation, and confederation, the growth and elaboration of cooperative systems, the pursuit of freedom and community, and its manifestation in the development of democratic limits to industrial conduct are basic venues of ecological democracy. The change is both gradual *and* qualitative. It is change that will be reflected in the appearance, development, and coherence of ecological commons to challenge the power of industrial pursuits and prerogatives.

chapter eight

THE ECOLOGICAL COMMONS

BUILDING AN ECOLOGICAL DEMOCRACY from within our world means first limiting, then transforming the conduct of industrialism—withdrawing from industrial imperatives that reduce all aspects of life and land to inputs, and re-creating the realm of social, economic, and political action.

Ecological democracy will cohere and evolve within an ecological commons. In this context, a commons is a socially enclosed, that is, protected, space or realm of activity where individual rights and responsibilities are balanced with those of the community of individuals that use the commons. The community may be a neighborhood, town, region, nation, continent, or planet.

As an idea, the commons means more than simply physical space, like a grazing commons or fishing commons, the Greek *agora* or public square, or a market commons. Nor is the commons a free resource to be plundered or drawn upon at will, where a limitless number of sheep may graze or limitless amounts of waste may be dumped. Citizens or community members are entitled to use a commons, but they are also responsible for the nature of that use and must perform part of the upkeep needed as a consequence.

An ecological commons is sustainable because the community has democratically chosen limits to its use. In the context of human civilization, the commons is our shared biosphere, and its ecological sustainability must depend upon social choices informed by ethics and norms, not by the blind operation of economic or ecological "laws."

For an ecological democracy, both the social and physical space of community must be protected from industrial exploitation. Regulation is not enough; as Barry Commoner has forcefully demonstrated, it largely moderates abuse on the margins (and, even so, is bitterly opposed as government interference). A much broader challenge is required: lives and lands must be protected, re-enclosed, by boundaries of community practices and norms. Placing social and physical limits upon industrial civilization means reclaiming, restoring, and sustaining revitalized ecological commons.

In an agricultural world, freedom, sustenance, and dignity were intimately related to the ability to use land fairly. There was a balance between rights and responsibilities in many preindustrial communities, but this balance was not the result of idealistic beneficence. Rather, neighbors living and working together could see and be seen, and each had an individual and community interest in the long-term health and fair use of the commons. The rise of industrialism meant enclosure—removing land and its bounty from community access.

Industrial Enclosures

The rise of capitalist industrialism meant not only turning the commons into private property, but subjecting its present and future use to market forces and the "rational" desire to maximize production. The landless were reduced to laborers upon the land or in the new workshops. They no longer worked to grow food or make things they needed; they now worked for cash to buy, rather than to create or trade for, necessities. These themes continue today as global industrial development proceeds with a vengeance, bringing privatization, cash economy, and wage labor to the world. They continue within the center of the industrialized world as well: even clean air is now enclosed, to be bought and sold by polluters making deals in a market; and knowledge becomes an item of an industrial commerce that encompasses genetic material and includes attempts to sell that of "interesting" individuals, such as members of isolated indigenous groups whose genome may have marketable qualities.*

The rise of industrialism is also contemporaneous with the rise of the nation states. These states—whose expansive interests largely coincided with those of the merchants, industrialists, and land barons—used their power against common rights and regionalism. Their official ideology followed the path established in *Leviathan* by Hobbes, who argued that great state power was needed to overcome what he viewed as the inherently centrifugal and destructive forces of humanity. Thus, partisans of the nation state would argue that the state was required to save humanity from itself.

The commons—the idea of local integrity, local autonomy, and local customs exercised for purposes at odds with the ends of industrialism—is then anathema to modernity and the nation state. An ecological commons means the reassertion of the rights of commoners.

---

* A very substantial literature discusses the English processes of enclosure and privatization of land, the destruction of the rights of skilled artisans and their guilds, the imposition of state power over local custom, and attempts at resistance.[1] But these themes were repeated with variations elsewhere in the commercial and industrial revolutions.

The Commons is not a Tragedy

There has been considerable confusion in recent years about the relationship between freedom, responsibility, and the commons. In a well-known essay, "The Tragedy of the Commons," biologist Garrett Hardin concluded that the freedom of the commons must be tempered by coercion to avoid the catastrophic results of pollution and overpopulation. "The rational man finds his share of the cost of the waste he discharges into the commons is less than the cost of purifying his wastes before releasing them."[2] Clearly, Hardin's "rational" action refers to the short-term thinking of economic man in the industrialized world. Hardin is writing not about the long-term existence of a socially regulated and sustainable commons, but about open access areas in the midst of industrial private property. These are particularly subject to abuse: Hardin's pessimism arises from his understanding that these areas are open to assault by the logic of industrial society because Adam Smith's "invisible hand" is unable to bring society to sustainable equilibrium.

In a later amplification of his essay, Hardin concludes, "Beyond the limits of his confining skin, no man can own anything. 'Property' refers not to things owned but to the rights granted by society; they must periodically be re-examined in the light of social justice."[3]

The idea of a nested and overlapping series of social and economic commons, ranging from the local to the global, is central to the concept of an ecological democracy and a community-based economy. These are commons governed and regulated by social and individual choice, informed by a new ecological ethics, and expressed through self-management, regulation, and law. Thus, an ecological commons is preeminently a democratic social system, but it can also be a market system and a planning system informed by the pursuit of the ecological interests of individual and community. It does not depend upon the magical balancing effects of the blind pursuit of self-interest.

Property and the Commons

The "commons" is a standard for social use, not an explicit theory of ownership. In an ecological world, property ownership carries with it not only rights of use, but the responsibilities of trusteeship; in such a world, neither individual, nor public, nor cooperative ownership in the abstract is inherently more desirable. The commons is built and maintained by social norms, not legal forms. Thus, an ecological democracy encourages the general growth of both personal and community property rights, instead of a concentration of private ownership in the hands of the rich or public ownership in the hands of the state (see Figure 8-1).

Figure 8-1. Predominant Forms of Property Ownership

Industrial Society
Private *or* Public

Ecological Democracy
Personal *and* Social

The concept of "personal property," as opposed to "private property," is illustrative. Industrial private property is rooted in Roman law, an expression of conquest and exclusion. Industrial capitalism has tended to concentrate both ownership and power in the hands of the rich, while industrial socialism has concentrated ownership and power in the hands of the party and an industrial elite, termed variously the "new class" or *nomenklatura*. In both systems, a small percentage of the population effectively controls vast assets and material resources.*

---

* Like many of my neighbors, I have a small retirement account and own shares in

Private property in our system means more than the right to live secure in your home, drive your own car, and profit from the fruits of your labors; it also means the right not only to own land, but, unless specifically forbidden by law, to devastate, despoil, and poison that land and the living things on it, as well as the common air we breathe and water we drink. Private property means the right to profit from the labor of others through ownership—not only from wage labor, but by buying the "goodwill" of a business that can be sold and, in effect, taking a mortgage on the labor of individuals who may not yet have been born.*

Thus, private ownership confers not just the right for personal and family dignity and security in a community of other free people, but also the option in an industrial market economy for spectacular abuse. This opportunity is justified as being a stimulus for general wealth creation, an entrepreneurial prod, but its weakness is that it externalizes the true cost and consequences of action.

By designating property as *personal* instead of private, an ecological democracy recognizes an essential connection between the use of property and community well-being. An ecological democracy can make social choices to encourage personal ownership and participation in a broad range of activities; personal property should not be limited to a conception of chattel, of portable or ephemeral items, but redefined to recognize the broad

---

a "socially responsible" mutual fund that has holdings in a few dozen large corporations; this is poor evidence of my participation as an owner of these corporations. Similarly, the bank that holds the mortgage on my house and profits from my monthly payments diminishes the significance of my "private" ownership. I do not intend to disparage pension funds or home ownership, but it is important to note that, for the vast majority, these private rights are bracketed by the holders of real power.

---

* In capitalism, "goodwill" is monetized by selling the reputation of a company that is based on the efforts of workers in the past. It is workers laboring for the new owner who must work to pay for this premium. In Mondragon-type co-ops, in contrast, workers gain or lose based only on their own work through a share of their company's profits or losses. When they leave the company, they do not encumber the labor of future workers.

range of rights and responsibilities that ownership and community participation entail. An emphasis on association, cooperation, and confederation, in fact, will tend to expand participation in personal ownership in the broad range of associations. Personal ownership of housing, land, and small businesses certainly will thrive; over time, personal ownership (and personal security) will expand dramatically with the growth of voluntary associations.

The traditional industrial dichotomy between public and private property is rooted in exclusive concepts of ownership and power. In an ecological democracy, on the other hand, the concept of property is redefined to reflect a more limited and more balanced set of individual and community rights and responsibilities. In an ecological democracy, all property will be seen as having attributes of both personal and social or community property, protected by both individual and community. Social or community property need not imply state or bureaucratic government ownership. So-cial property can be, for example, the total of the individual own-ership of a community-based cooperative system, as at Mondragon. Social property can also be municipal or neighbor-hood property, such as schools, a recycling center, or a solar thermal cogeneration plant. But the existence of social or community prop-erty need not mean the elimination of personal or family owner-ship, or loss of the ability to receive income from one's labor. It does limit the ability to use, dispose of, and despoil property and the commons—but this is social stewardship, a part of ownership: a balance of freedom to use and responsibilities to maintain the commons for both community and individuals.

For example, a Mondragon cooperator pays a fixed member-ship fee (about one year's earnings) to join the co-op and receives, in addition to what amounts to wages, a share of the cooperative's annual profit or surplus, or is charged with a share of the co-op's losses. But the cooperator may not sell that share and profit from the company's "goodwill"; a cooperator who leaves or retires receives his or her share of accumulated profits, plus interest, and a pension.[4] The person who replaces the departing member pays the membership fee and begins anew to accumulate surpluses or losses. In short, the co-op is a sort of self-perpetuating, quasi-social property. It can be sold only with agreement of a high majority of all cooperators. It plays a social role both in terms of defined responsibilities to the community, and as a consequence of individual ownership and use. As socially rooted personal property, it lacks the implied unlimited and isolated rights of the industrial private. Such a system of community personal property is built, not cobbled together from a combination of sentiment and government fiat.

Dynamics of the Ecological Commons

The ecological commons is more than a new social contract or an ephemeral projection of a common goodwill. The challenge of the ecological commons is to move in our view of the world—a world experienced in our practices, values, social structures—from the industrial concept of resource to the ecological one of a living community.

Understanding the commons helps demystify the conceits that explain the market and social relations of industrial capitalism as effects of economic "laws" instead of social choices. In her insightful book, *Governing the Commons: The Evolution of Institution*, Elinor Ostrom discusses common pool resources, but the success of the commons she discusses has everything to do with community.[5] On the basis of many case studies, she describes certain principles for governing. Such community-based social choices maintain and protect the commons through ongoing discussion and equilibration that work not only to facilitate the use of the commons, but to resolve the inevitable conflicts and disputes. I believe these principles can be of more general social applicability beyond resource commons, from which they have been derived. These principles, based on the experience of successful and failed commons, provide a good sense of vernacular community democracy in action:

- *Boundaries.* Both those who participate in the commons and the boundaries of the commons itself must be clearly defined.

- *Local conditions.* There must be congruence between appropriation and provision rules—how and when the commons is used—and local conditions.[6]

- *Collective choice.* Those affected by the rules can participate in making and changing them.

- *Monitoring.* Those who use the commons, or are accountable to those who do, shall monitor the commons.

- *Sanctions.* Sanctions for violating the rules of the commons are to be appropriate to the seriousness of the offense and administered by those using the commons, or by monitors or officials accountable to them.

- *Conflict.* There must be a quick and low-cost means of resolving conflicts between those using the commons and/or the officials monitoring and regulating the commons.

- *Rights to organize.* People using the commons have a right to devise their own institutions unencumbered by outside authorities.

- *Nested enterprises (for commons that are part of larger systems).* All rules and customs governing the commons are organized in multiple layers of nested enterprises or systems that allow appropriate decisions to be made at the level most directly involved.

What is at work in Ostrom's commons is the creation and maintenance of a community social space in which the resources in question are not just a pool to be exhausted or preserved, but the common ground of life for the participants. Naturally, such social systems stand outside the conventional industrial hierarchical organization. The successful common pool resource systems Ostrom discusses are exceptional not simply because they rely neither upon state nor private governance, but because they represent social choices that allow groups to protect their lives from the values and behavior of industrialism. It is ironic that it now requires Ostrom's analytical rigor to prove it is "realistic" for communities to manage their lives in ways that resemble the dominant form of human social organization before the rise of the nation state, private property, and industrialism.

The Commons in Action

A good example of a commons in action is the inshore fishery at Alanya, Turkey studied by Fikret Berkes. In the early 1970s, overfishing and competition led to decreased catches, increased costs, hostility, and sometimes violence. Of the approximately 100 fishermen, half were members of a co-op, many using two- or three-person boats with nets. Over more than a decade of trial-and-error efforts launched by members of the co-op, a system was developed to allocate fishing rights and govern the fishing commons:

- Each September, a list of all licensed fishers in Alanya is prepared.

- Local fishing sites are named and listed. They are spaced so that the nets of boats will not interfere with each other. These fishing sites will be in effect from September through May.

- In September, local fishermen draw lots and are assigned to fishing sites.

- Every day from September to June each fisherman moves east to the next fishing site. From January to May, the fishermen move west. Fishermen thus both fish different sites and have an equal chance at catching fish that migrate east to west between September and January and west to east between January and May. The rotation system allows boats to watch their neighbors and makes cheating difficult.

- The signed agreement of annual fishing sites is registered at town hall. National legislation has given co-ops the jurisdiction over such local arrangements. Disputes are resolved by the fishers themselves.[7]

The Commons and Diversity

As the Alanya example suggests, the ecological commons is, at bottom, an exercise not in resource management, but in social reconstruction. This exercise means moving toward an extraordinary diversity of community lifeways. The ecological commons is not limited geographically: the social space of the inner city will be quite different from that of the rural mountains, but that does not mean there is no organic connection or mutual interdependence between city and country. Community and commons evolve as part of the living world: their relationship and network are dynamic, not hierarchical.

The nation state is not likely to vanish quickly; but as its prerogatives are reduced by the imperatives of industrialism, the nation may be weakened in a beneficial way if it gradually withdraws its grasp of absolute power over community lifeways. As the trappings of nationhood (e.g., large standing armies, a unitary justice system, centralized fiscal controls) recede, the strength of community institutions and groups and of international cooperation will expand.

Creative proposals will abound. For example, Frank Bryan and John McClaughry in their book *The Vermont Papers: Recreating Democracy on a Human Scale*[8] suggest "shires" in Vermont, based on greatly expanding the power of county-size regions, to make government at once more intimate, since it is closer to the people; more effective, since it eliminates much of the bureaucratic structure; and more frugal, since people see more clearly and directly what they spend and how they pay for it.

In very different circumstances, the disintegration of the former Soviet Union has led not only to the development of new nation states from the constituent republics, but to the appearance of many autonomous or semi-autonomous districts and regions based on common ethnicity, culture, history, and geography. These exist at varying degrees of tension with the central government, and present the possibility of new confederal relationships, as well as the threat of bloody conflict (as in Chechnya).

In Green political circles, the idea of bio-regions is popular: natural regions based on watersheds, topography, history, and affinity rather than traditional political subdivisions. These are evocative ideas but should not give way to an ecological determinism dedicated to purely "natural" divisions, or to a new form of political uniformity. The bio-region can represent the idea of a social space, one in which the integration between humanity and nature is consciously considered and embraced as essential to the mutual well-being of both.

Ecological transformation carries the notion (E.F. Schumacher's "subsidiarity") that each level of functioning is empowered to make decisions appropriate to its scale of operation.[9] The ecological commons is not based upon the imposition of technocratic administration; it is more community based than class based, although clearly it will lessen class distinctions. It reflects a transformation out of the reach of those intent on maintaining the hierarchical structures of industrial power. The elaboration of the commons perforce involves a variety of actors in very different communities responding to their particular experience. These will be the new agents of change.[10] It is not limited to expanding the idea of a revolutionary industrial worker to include service workers and the Xerox line to supplant the assembly line.

The increase in social complexity that accompanies the ecological commons—the growth of civil society, democratic self-management, confederal forms, and a welter of agreements and relationships—marks the reversal of industrial globalization and its market as an ordering and homogenizing force. Such a tendency is, of course, already reflected in the centrifugal forces expressed by the rise of identity politics, and by the devolution of nations and empires. Beneficial change can no longer be simply identified with the seizure of power (by bullet or ballot) and redistributive justice. We must deal with questions that apply to both our societies and our movements: What do we do? How do we do it? Why do we do it? We must provide credible answers in theory and in fact, or the ecological democracy described here is likely to remain just another utopian chimera of human aspiration—a creation of hope without action.

The Commons as Network

The building of an ecological commons may be described through contrasting models and metaphors.

Industrialism		*Ecological Commons*
Bank	versus	Library
Ladder	versus	Network

The library and network as operating principles are logical expressions of the logic and dynamics underlying an ecological commons. They represent a basic departure from the either/or logic of industrialism where the corporation/nation is a universal and the atomized individual the particular.

The ecological universal is freedom; the particular, community. The guiding principle is inclusive both/and logic in which particular and general exist in dynamic tension. Ecological both/and logic is a relationship between entities in a time of

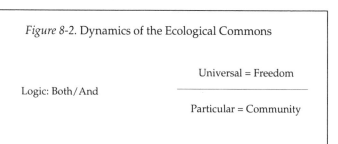

Figure 8-2. Dynamics of the Ecological Commons

Logic: Both/And

Universal = Freedom
_____
Particular = Community

shifting alliances and combinations; its political application is confederation.

Industrialism seeks to control and profit from the sale of information in databases, allowing access only to those with political privilege and/or who are able to pay fees. The controlling metaphor for the ecological commons, in contrast, is the library—an open institution where information can be used. Library use entails responsibilities and rules of behavior, but unlike the data bank libraries seek to maximize use and facilitate interconnection.*

The network provides the strength of market relations, but does not work to maintain privilege or to mask the cost of so-called externalities. Rather, the network of the commons is conditioned by customs and responsibilities made explicit through transparent

---

* The attempt to assert proprietary rights over information and discussion—for example, the FBI's blundering short-lived campaign to impose Cold War protocols on programmers and data as a threat to proprietary informational rights—resembles the elegant operation of centrally planned economies. The failures of such tactics were reflected in the fate of the once vaunted "fifth generation" computer project, Japan's attempt to leapfrog computer technology by isolating workers from the global conversation of programmers, designers, and computer users. The fifth generation project bogged down in many dead ends and was finally abandoned; but the plan reflects the organizational principle of industrialism—a hierarchical ladder that is not only a rigid system, but spectacularly disempowering. Such failures are the reason modern corporations attempt to embrace their version of "cooperation" and give divisions the ability to function relatively independently to approximate principles of networking freedom.

and democratic planning. Networks need moderators/facilitators; hierarchies need enforcers/managers.

Alternative Political Economies

Network planning affects behavior, investments, and customs codified through agreements. Technological developments—a computer in every home, interactive television, the ability to obtain and manipulate huge amounts of information—need not be employed in the interest of industrialism. Indeed, the power of information technologies has led some socialists to suggest the use of computer networks and interactive television for making decisions about what shall be made and what shall be consumed—thus eliminating the need for markets (Michael Albert and Robin Hahnel in *Looking Forward: Participatory Economics for the Twenty First Century* call this "participatory planning").[11] The problem with such a system is not so much the question, could it be done? as the question of, why would we want to do it?

The debate in academic and popular left circles following the repudiation of really existing socialism has focused less on radical transformation than upon choices among species of market socialism in an industrial context. The discussions are suffused with the discussion of feasible design,[12] and the discovery of the market as mechanism by Marxian economists and radical social democrats.[13]

One alternative to market socialism is a sort of participatory planning, first outlined by British marxist Pat Devine,[14] focused on planning of major capital investment to replace capital markets. This idea was followed in 1991 by Michael Albert and Robin Hahnel's plan for a computer-mediated planning and regulatory system for all aspects of production, consumption, and the organization of work. What is striking about Albert and Hahnel's proposal is that in the name of absolute fairness and improved efficiency they have created a system that offers a startlingly unitary hierarchical order, one that brooks no alternatives and requires all to participate (although they argue that the system will eventually be democratically chosen and put into motion).[15] In other words, while attempting to rid the world of the scourge of capitalism and markets, Albert and Hahnel embrace a concentration of social energy in a system that, although decentralized, is one grand hierarchy. Perhaps this system would allow decisions that would undo the industrial routine — but the logic informing their system, like the ideas of Pat Devine, is rather productivist.

In these schemes, the firm is the focus of personal and community identity—inefficient (or polluting, or unnecessary) firms are generally not closed, but negotiate for their continued existence and a share of the social product. The workplace is democratized, but the struggle for existence seems to be focused on the firm and the interest of the state, region, and nation.

Both market socialists and anti-market planners too often focus on ways of perfecting, not transforming, an industrial social order. New decisionmaking processes, established to govern "sustainable" industrialism, will, they argue, resolve social, economic, and environmental problems. The ecological commons, in contrast, is focused on the appropriate and overlapping world of communities. This is true internationalism, based on allegiance not to some abstract ecology, but to the living particularity existing in communities.

Ecological Commons in Global Context

As ecological catastrophe approaches, it is the height of irrationality to add the straw that breaks the camel's back. It clearly makes no long-term economic sense to treat businesses, communities, and resources as cows to be milked as long as possible and then slaughtered. Yet it is important to realize that such behavior is just as clearly in the economic interest of those for whom industrialism has become a matter of personal conquest and maximal short-term gain. This is the logic behind plans to accelerate pollution and exploitation to gain transitory advantage before the expected collapse. This is the path followed by U.S. capitalism in the 1980s, the path of junk bonds, leveraged buyouts, and financial manipulation. The logic of industrial global integration favors currency speculation and forest obliteration over sustainable production. It signals the collapse of a longer term industrial rationality and an embrace of frenetic postmodern eschatology.

Declarations that ecological problems can be understood as the sum of a series of discrete problems—too much fossil fuel use, too much pollution, too much militarism, too many people—reflect a view of the industrial world as machine, subject to tinkering and technological perfection, instead of as a deeply flawed entity. This worldview encourages a focus on those qualities and behaviors considered least essential to industrialism. Thus, for example, population growth is often considered, nearly reflexively, the *sine qua non* of environmental protection. The population of the poor South, the majority of the world's people, cannot continue, we are told, to increase, particularly if these people aspire to levels of production and consumption, pollution, and resource use now customary in the rich North. (The South's current share of global pollution is small compared with that of the North.)

The answer from the ecological commons is not to ignore the need to stabilize global population as part of a process of transformation, but to address the issue with a challenging realism. We must recognize that the rich nations cannot continue to exploit poor nations, cannot continue to demand crippling debt payments in hard currency earned from resource extraction and commodity cropping at "free" market prices to feed the industrial machine's insatiable appetite, cannot use the wars of the poor (for which they often bear direct responsibility) to justify a grand bazaar for weapons of mass destruction sold to competing elites. The population explosion is an artifact of the crisis of the world industrial system, not its cause. The South must build its own sustainable lifeways, in partnership with the North, acting as much in the role of teacher as in that of acolyte. The problems of the poor are not essentially the problems of an abstract "underdevelopment," but reflect the destructive impact and failures of industrialization and its global system.

The struggle for the creation of an ecological commons is the struggle for the building of an ecological democracy—community by community, neighborhood by neighborhood, region by region. It represents the struggle and work of fundamental social transformation from below. The commons is not just a vague atmosphere or vast ocean considered at a distance. The commons is intricately linked to people's lives, lifeways, and communities. The growth of the commons means a focus on the local, the personal, the common, as well as the relationship of the particular to the more general, more integrated embracing unities of an ecological civilization.

chapter nine

FROM INDUSTRIALISM TO ECOLOGICAL DEMOCRACY: TRANSITIONAL PATHS

THE KEY TO BUILDING AN ECOLOGICAL SOCIETY lies in the elaboration of a revitalized democracy. The core of this work is not political in the conventional sense, but involves a threefold task:

- To transform the existing market and planning system to one conditioned by ecological social choices and values.

- To nurture and coordinate the grand expansion of freedom and community stimulated by ecological transformation.

- To develop durable means of communication and decisionmaking to create and protect the ecological commons.

We must heal the old world while building the new. This means, in practice, that we begin with all the agonies and strengths

189

of a global industrialism in crisis. Utopian thought is a necessary spur to the human imagination, but transformation of the world system depends upon reality and necessity. This chapter presents a number of suggestions for concrete social and individual action in building an ecological democracy. All, of course, are interactive—the sum of these and many other steps needed to create an ecological society is more than the individual parts—and all are predicated upon dynamic change conditioned by a vigorous participatory process and not a dusty social blueprint.

The presentation is neither hierarchical nor exhaustive. These elements can point to likely policies, but it would be a mistake to adopt them as a guide to ecological transformation. Each case must be judged on its individual dynamics, not by abstract doctrine. This judging according to theory is the western economist's classic error.

For example, the relative successes and failures (in capitalist terms) of economic shock therapy in former communist states reflect not good or bad conceptions of markets, prices, or planning, but the historical, social, and institutional context of each state. Marshall Goldman notes of the failure of economic shock therapy to stimulate new production in Russia:

> The failure in the increase in prices to stimulate production was primarily a consequence of the institutional rigidities of the centrally planned economy. The absence of private trade and private wholesaling, manufacturing, and farming meant there was virtually no one who might be induced by the higher prices to produce more goods. The managers of state factories and monopolies would be paid their salaries whether or not they increased production; in fact they were probably better off with lower production and higher prices because black market or mafia operators would likely be able to pay them more under the counter. For that matter, a more effective and profitable operation would benefit the state, not the manager.[1]

The recent difficulties of the former communist states are relevant to our discussion in two ways. First, they represent the wrong approach, a desperate attempt to race down the track and leap aboard the capitalist train long after it has left the station. Most of these states are likely to find a future existence as low-wage producers analogous to Latin America in relation to the United States, especially if they continue to pursue the dreams of classic industrialism. Second, these difficulties show how local circumstances must determine approaches. The elements of ecological transformation discussed here are just that—elements, to be woven together as appropriate to local conditions. Moreover, while each can stand as a significant reform, their greatest value lies in the synergy of their simultaneous adoption.

These elements evoke possibility and change; they do not guarantee ecological transformation or even substantive reform. Each has the virtue (and handicap) that it can be undertaken from existing conditions; neither social nor political revolution is required before the transformation can be started. These venues for change are immediately addressed to industrialized nations; to an extent, they are also applicable elsewhere. Each begins with small steps. Each could spur human creativity, but each risks being blunted, resisted, and transformed. There is in this process a dynamic flux and balance between reform, co-optation, and transformation. Civilizations do not change with the ease of succeeding U.S. administrations, nor can they be purchased by consumers. Civilizations are the sum of the ways we live.

Selected Elements and
Venues for Ecological Transformation

These elements are a menu of possibilities, not a hierarchical list or a sequential action plan. Depending on local conditions, each can be a point of entry into the process of building an ecological democracy.

- Democratizing finance

- · Building community economies
- · Revaluating our children's future
- · Creating a social wage
- · Pursuing disarmament and demilitarization
- · Developing an industrial ecology
- · Dematerializing production
- · Developing a solar economy

Democratizing Finance

The argument for democratizing finance is not based upon any grand climactic crisis of industrial civilization. Rather, it reflects community interest in revitalization, catalyzed by the unsustainability of conventional industrial paths. In the hard-shelled world of finance and international relations, money is power. To democratize finance means to curtail the prerogatives of both the private and the public entities of largely unaccountable industrial powers that control the instrumentalities of finance. This effort involves reasoned community self-assertion and self-management.*

Bankers and financiers can destroy neighborhoods, cities, countries, and continents by withholding money. This withholding can involve refusal to loan money in a particular part of town (redlining), or it can involve capital "strikes," as occurred on the election of a British labor government or the socialists in France. If they are denied finance capital, whole communities, even

---

* A central problem of capitalist economics is that finance capital does not ease the swings of the business cycle. Finance is a *leading* indicator. When the stock and bond markets cough, when bankers contract credit, the economy catches a cold, and sometimes pneumonia, six weeks or six months later. The crowd nature of finance, and its current global electronic incarnation allows capital managers to follow the logic of a dice player on a once-in-a-lifetime winning streak and exaggerates the rhythms of expansion and collapse.

nations, find themselves in a state of enforced idleness, "unemployed"—not through lack of skill or imagination, but by a lack of money.

Capital supposedly flows in the prudent pursuit of greed—the maximum return for the minimum risk. This should mean that the best, most productive, least risky investments receive the most funds. (This argument is the central logic of capitalist microeconomics.) But in reality, repeated panics and collapses of speculative "bubbles" (whether in 18th- or 19th-century South Sea speculation, or tulip bulbs, or, in our time, shocks in real estate, oil futures, and currency speculation) suggest that the practice of finance is neither logical, nor democratic, nor in the common interest. Such speculation is neither labor nor investment. It is an attempt to make money very quickly through the passion of crowds.*

Prospects for the general democratization of finance may seem grim—global financial forces have never been stronger. But there is rather less reason for pessimism here than meets the eye when one considers the long-term power and influence of these structures. Even global finance is subject to the dynamics and politics of the global industrial system. The worth of financial assets, after all, reflects basic social choices. The value of these assets depends upon a willingness to keep agreements and to meet claims represented by financial instruments. Thus, the "political power" of central banks to influence financial speculation on a

---

* On a local level, a variety of experiments with local currencies and barter systems have provided available answers to ameliorate the lack of money provided by the overarching power of a financial system uninterested in community investment. Money, once a means of exchange that encouraged our efforts, has become the inhibitor of action, change, and community. These local experiments include such models as Ithaca (New York) Money ("Ithaca Hours"), where businesses and individuals exchange scrip for goods and services;[2] Local Economic Trading Systems (LETS) that allow people to exchange their work or goods for credit, with the balances kept track of by computer; and a number of local currency plans now being pursued in the northeast by Bob Swann of the E. M. Schumacher Society.[3]

global scale depends upon an underlying realization that, sooner or later, financial assets are rooted in industrial practice and the real social choices made by hundreds of thousands of disparate communities, large and small.

The dematerialization and speculation of global finance, the instability of the world's largest banks in the world's richest nations, and the swings of financial markets all reflect an underlying weakness in this system of value. The value of stock markets, currencies, real estate, loan portfolios, natural resources, the whole panoply, in fact, of industrial monetary valuation is threatened. The value of electronic financial assets, or resources such as Third World loans, is subject to grave dilution or even disappearance overnight—not only because of speculative excesses, but because of the crisis of industrial civilization.

Thus, for example, loans made to the South will never be fully repaid or written off—unless northern taxpayers are willing to come to the aid of the balance sheets of the banks of the North, and thereby allow the South to escape the unbearable and unending transfer of wealth to the North.

Or take the collapse of real estate in Japan. In recent years, Japanese banks have found themselves, like United States banks, with enormous portfolios of bad real estate loans—a development reflecting the global collapse of a speculative market, which reached its height in Japanese real estate. In 1992, Japanese banks held bad loans worth an estimated $300 billion. The twenty-one largest Japanese banks, including several of the world's largest banks, now have $162 billion in bad loans. Japanese housing finance companies, called *jusen,* have many billions in bad loans; the largest, Nihon Jutaku Kinyu, with $23 billion in assets, has only $145 million in reserves to cover billions of dollars of loans that will probably never be repaid.[4]

The financial problems engendered by the crisis of industrialism are local as well. Consider the U.S. savings and loan industry. This industry was formed in line with community values, to support home ownership and construction. Both investment policies and interest rates were regulated, and S&Ls benefited from tax credits on mortgage payments that strongly encouraged home purchases. In the 1970s, high inflation found savings and loans with a portfolio of low-interest, long-term mortgage loans and facing competition for deposits from new high-interest "financial products," such as money market accounts and junk bonds. The savings and loan industry, fearing decapitalization, turned to the Reaganite deregulators, who removed constraints on the investments they could make and on rates they could offer, and lessened the amount of regulatory oversight. The S&Ls then attracted huge deposits and invested imprudently. The bubble inevitably burst, leading to a bail out costing taxpayers hundreds of billions of dollars without any increased community control of the banking system.

Community-based banks represent not only an alternative to disastrous speculations. Development of community-based banking, and the eventual confederation of such banks, represents the closing of a financial circle between those who work, those who save, and those who invest, so that the interests of each are mutually supportive and balanced through an ongoing dialogue. The efficient role for banks is not to feed speculation, but to support community enterprises that will be the basis for ecological transformation. Certainly, the hundreds of billions of taxpayer dollars to be paid as bailouts for failed financial speculation in the United States speaks to the wisdom of community-based finance.

Democratizing finance means the growth of such forms as cooperative commercial banking, community development corporations and banks, credit unions, and cooperative savings banks. For a community economic system, money represents the ability of people to make agreements with each other—a means to facilitate action and not to forbid it.[5]

A paradigm is the *Caja Laboral Popular* (CLP) of the Mondragon cooperatives, which in 1991 had deposits of $3.5 billion, 206 branches, and equity of 10.04 percent of total assets (compared to the approximately 3 percent required in U.S. financial institutions).[6] As noted in Chapter Seven, the CLP began in 1959 when the new and rapidly growing Mondragon cooperative system found it difficult, as most cooperatives do, to obtain conventional financing. The bank is a "second degree" cooperative governed both by its owner members and by the member cooperatives of the Mondragon Cooperative Corporation. Each co-op signs a detailed Contract of Association with the CLP. The bank includes an *empresarial* (entrepreneurial) division[7] that provides sophisticated business consulting and planning services to existing co-ops, and helps plan and start new ones.

The bank's deposits come first from the associated cooperatives, but the financial bases of the system are individual capital accounts and owner member shares of co-op profits that the bank retains. The CLP also attracts many thousands of small savers and makes loans not just to the co-ops (it is limited by law to 40 percent to any entity), but to a large number of individuals as "household" or consumer loans, as well as making other commercial loans.

The CLP and the co-ops share some hard budget constraints. The bank can provide start-up loans and assist co-ops in economic difficulty, but such aid is subject to careful monitoring and vigorous discussion. The assistance comes only in return for sacrifices and responsible effort. The diverse interest of the bank's owner members and over 100 associated industrial cooperatives prevent risks that would endanger the system, and help keep activities focused on productive community actions.

Other examples of successful democratization of capital are worker equity investment funds, such as the Quebec Solidarity Fund and the Manitoba Crocus Fund, established on a provincial level in Canada. These funds receive small investments from individuals (who receive both national and provincial tax credits), and invest funds to finance employee-owned companies and to promote community economic development. In the United States, work on setting up such funds is proceeding under the guidance of the Industrial Cooperative Association of Boston.

One successful grassroots-based financial institution is the New Hampshire Community Loan Fund, organized in 1983 by Julie Eades, an activist with a business degree from the University of New Hampshire; Elliot Barry, a Legal Assistance lawyer; and Michael Swack, a community development professor and practitioner. In 1994, the loan fund had $3.5 million in loan capital, mostly obtained from individual and institutional investors willing to accept below-market rates of return. In ten years of operation, the rapidly growing loan fund had secured or leveraged $29 million worth of housing and had created 108 jobs.*

The financial debacle of the 1980s and early 1990s demonstrated the literal and figurative bankruptcy of conventional finance. Ultimately, finance is indivisible from the growth of a labor-managed community economics whose development is part and parcel of the democratization of finance.

Building Community Economies

A community economy is a mixed economy. It may include a variety of forms: co-ops, individual businesses, partnerships, corporations, public or governmental organizations. The community is defined by a common social space and common interests; it is local, but can be nested with others to make larger communities. At any level, community is essential for the creation and nurturance of the ecological commons.

---

* Hundreds of billions of dollars now in U.S. pension funds are generally invested with little democratic control and with little thought given to the wisdom of the investment beyond financial return. Here, democratization means providing policy and regulation to encourage ecological investments and support for the community. This could be helped by regulatory provisions, for example, providing a lower discount rate for institutions making such beneficial investments, favorable tax treatment, etc..

Community economics involves an integrated market and planning system informed by democratic and ecological values. It rests upon a civil society that acts to elaborate the social sector of life and contract the monetized sector. It strengthens grassroot social bonds and self-organization though mutual aid and the growth of democratic associations in daycare, education, home building and repair, food growing, fire and police protection, recreation, elder care transportation, community workshops, *et al.* As industrial and monetary values give way to these ecological and human values, ownership and control of business and governmental organizations are returned to communities and their members. Each community institution has power over matters that most directly affect it. Thus, community economics is based not only on rights of property, or on a narrow conception of citizenship, but on justice and unalienable human rights—in the true Jeffersonian sense of life, liberty, and the pursuit of happiness.

At bottom, the difficult tasks are not those that involve finding creative norms, describing ways of efficient operation, or eliminating negative externalities. Building a community economy—replacing absentee ownership and managerial government with direct ownership and participatory democracy— is essentially a political and social challenge, not a technical matter. Facing what seems to be a global industrial juggernaut at first appears as daunting as attempting to move heaven and earth. But the most difficult step is the first.

As Jaroslav Vanek has demonstrated in *The General Theory of Labor-Managed Market Economies*[8] and cooperative systems have shown in practice, direct community ownership is both efficient and durable. Participants (owner workers) are not only at risk financially, but they have tied their lives and communities to the well-being of the enterprise. This dynamic discourages failures, flattens the peaks and valleys of the business cycle, and responds effectively to social pain. The Mondragon system has effectively banished the disastrous effects of unemployment, even in the midst of an industrial capitalist universe, through the actions of a diverse cooperative group and, in combination with the co-op bank, by pursuing policies of transferring employees between firms, retraining, re-skilling, and retooling as needed.

In a community economic system, neither individual firm nor community is simply left adrift in a capitalist market sea. In a capitalist market system, the primary economic actor is the firm. Government efforts on a national level stimulate or retard economic activity through monetary and fiscal policy, and on a national and local level attempt to create a favorable business climate. In a community economic system, the economic actors are the firm, groups of firms, communities, and groups of communities. The market and planning system here has many more opportunities and responsibilities to equilibrate and ameliorate the effects of market swings before dramatic changes in national monetary and fiscal policy are needed.*

The ownership structure of such systems will clearly vary from place to place. The models developed at Mondragon, Seikatsu, and Co-op Atlantic are variations upon cooperative themes, but they are far from the only cooperative forms. Obviously, exploitative wage labor is inconsistent with community economics and ecological values. But neither corporate forms, as such, nor wage labor should be prohibited; rather, their nature, size, and conduct should be transformed. No one, for instance, should be forced to be a member of a co-op or any other type of firm. Wage differentials can be limited by law, custom, or tax and fiscal poli-

---

* Labor-managed community economics does not mean endless subsidies for the inefficient. Such an economy responds to market signals, but the response is conditioned by explicit social values. As economist David Ellerman suggests, the democratic cooperative firm represents, in one sense, the expansion and social generalization of the movement of managerial capitalism to make companies private through leveraged buyouts (i.e., use of debt by company managers to buy stock).[9] Cooperatives both internalize ownership within the firm and root its operation within the community that conditions its existence.

cies, but the important element is that the lowest paid worker earns enough to lead a decent life.

A community economic system would be able to periodically review corporate charters of private corporations (including cooperatives) and revoke those whose actions were harmful. Thus, a corporate entity that violated its charter and the community interest would not simply be fined or, at worst, forced into bankruptcy. Rather, its assets would be sold to ameliorate the effects of its misconduct, with the remainder divided among stockholders/owners.[10] As part of the community system, provision should be made to convert existing corporations to democratic cooperative ownership. The transition process should require first majority national, and then majority community, ownership of transnationals. Divisions of large firms should be spun off into viable community-based enterprises. Business and financial institutions, too, shall become community-based firms, not by nationalization or expropriation, but as part of transformation.

It is important to note that cooperative or community conversion is not simply a matter for bankers, lawyers, and brokers. A good current example is provided by Shenago Steel in Weston, Pennsylvania. After more than a year of negotiation with United Steelworkers Local 1032, the foundry's owners filed for bankruptcy and announced plans to liquidate. Union members began a forty-day-long occupation of the plant and, following much struggle and deliberation, won the right to purchase the facility in November 1993. Funds were raised with community support of the Steel Valley Authority and the A New Beginning Fund, which was started by a local pastor, the Reverend Art Fuller, and received donations, no-interest, and low-interest loans. The new worker-owned foundry, Shenago Quality Products, was capitalized with $1.3 million to buy the plant and a comparable amount for working capital and improvements.[11]

A growing infrastructure of loan funds, development banks (such as South Shore Bank in Chicago), and allied organizations provide technical assistance, organizing, advocacy, and loan capital across the United States. Many of these are loosely organized into the Federation for Industrial Retention and Renewal, which includes both national and local groups, such as the Boston-based Industrial Cooperative Association, pioneers in bringing Mondragon-style co-ops to the United States, Midwest Center for Labor Research, and both local and national Jobs With Peace campaigns.

The advantages of democratic community economic institutions are shown in their tendency to avoid deleterious actions even without external regulations. Industrialism survives because it can socialize—that is, take from the public—its most burdensome costs. Because such practices are unsustainable, regulatory mechanisms must be put in place to constrain the individual enterprise on behalf of the system as a whole. For community-based enterprises, however, the public as active polity identifies with the firm, and the question of the real cost and real effects of economic activity is raised immediately. Effects of actions are perceived as community effects.

Self-managing community institutions thus tend to make social choices. For example, the Mondragon cooperators decided not to enter the petrochemical business to avoid the obvious social costs of such activities. In general, regulatory mechanisms that must be imposed upon the traditional industrial enterprise tend to be internalized in community-based entities. This does not mean that community co-ops and institutions will always make socially and ecologically wise choices; but they have the kind of superiority to the conventional corporation that strategic nonviolence has over violent action: there may be death or violence in a nonviolent struggle, but, as Barbara Deming has pointed out in *Revolution and Equilibrium*, casualties and destruction will likely be far less than in war.[12] Such community-based institutions do not by nature view the abuse of power as an expression of efficiency. This way of thinking is not a matter of moral virtue, but of democratic control: abuse of power threatens not only broad community interests, but the well-being of individual members who are able to defend the integrity of community and commons.

It is, of course, essential for community economies to include supportive and democratic financial, educational, and social entities. Since self-management means the growth of civil society, and the contraction of state and private power, over the long term there will be a tendency to locate holders of capital within the firm and within the community. The model is of owner workers and community savers. As firms are reorganized into cooperative and decentralized institutions, equity markets (e.g., stock markets) will have less and less significance, and equities will gradually be replaced by bonds and other instruments that do not involve ownership. Creative loan instruments can be developed that would index returns to value added by the firm, thus taking into account both economic activity and inflation.

Following much hard work, the transformative potential of building community economies is that communities and community institutions will cohere and confederate in a cascading fashion in logical and larger groups of associations regionally and bio-regionally—by state, by nation, by global region, by planet. Free association of community-based groupings within a broad political framework will begin to take place alongside the diminished activities of the nation state.

Community Economics and Hard Choices

The pursuit of equilibrium means a search for a balance between rights and responsibilities in terms of common values. For example, a major question in any system is what to do about a failing enterprise—that is, an enterprise not just losing money, but using more of the social product than it produces and unable to survive without a subsidy from the larger community.

In industrial society, these questions do not always get the airing they warrant. For example, in the 1980s, there was much discussion over a federal loan guarantee for the Chrysler Corporation that both saved the company from bankruptcy, and preserved tens of thousands of jobs and the well-being of many communities. However, there was little discussion about an infusion of billions of tax dollars to bail out the Continental Bank of Illinois, a major commercial bank, when it faced insolvency, or about the complete bail out of hundreds of failed savings and loans at a cost of hundreds of billions of dollars (although some expressed amazement at the cost).

Similarly, in the former communist states of Europe there is great concern over the future of enormous state-owned industries—industries that are the mainstays of their countries' economies, but that are also often inefficient and so not competitive in a global market. In 1992, managers of state enterprises in Russia organized a political group called Renovation to advance their interests and warn, with justification, that rapid privatization or an abrupt end to subsidies would lead to economic collapse. But for many of these state firm managers the goal is clearly more the maintenance of a subsidized status quo, whether as "public" or "private" entities, from which they can profit handsomely, than a serious attempt to gradually transform their firms into efficient entities. In a quite different setting, a consultant studying cooperative conversion of state-owned firms in Kenya suggested that many of these enterprises cannot become viable without major structural changes that would eventually allow them to be competitive without subsidies.

Of course, for community economics the question of a so-called viable or competitive firm must include such issues as fair competition, based on adherence to universal social norms for wages, working conditions, environmental protection, and human rights, as well as fair terms of trade broadly defined. These terms address not only subsidies, but issues of equity, justice, and power. To a limited extent, such policies have sometimes been pursued by capitalist social democracy. *Within* the EC, the common basis for trade and unity is a harmonizing *upward* of the standards of poorer countries to approach those of the richer. To this has been added the attempt to generally adopt a much disputed social compact to define rights and responsibilities. If there is justice and fairness, it makes sense, not only from a narrow matter of capitalist market necessity, to soberly examine questions about subsidies.

An ecological society is not run on sentiment. It requires hard decisions on such questions based on the balanced interests of the particular and the general. This is a reflection of the nature and strength of community economies. For example, Mondragon has a comprehensive system of monitoring and planning designed to help member co-ops avoid financial difficulty. When problems do appear, co-op members are expected to take appropriate steps, including changing plans, products, and management; making additional financial contributions; and retooling. The co-op system provides assistance and support: workers may be temporarily transferred to other co-ops during cyclical downturns or during retooling; the co-op bank may make deferred payment, low- or no-interest loans; management experts may be sent to help the co-op. All these steps and decisions are taken as part of a continuing dialogue among cooperators within a co-op, between the co-op and the co-op group, and between the co-op and the co-op bank and its business division.

Some problems prove to be structural and not amenable to simple correction. For example, there may be overcapacity locally and/or globally in a specialized machine tool line, so that a realistic assessment of the market makes it clear the co-op cannot reach an adequate level of sales. But the unfortunate firm and its allies do not then use their power to convince co-op management or the government to transfer resources to their firms. Rather, Mondragon's pursuit of equilibrium means recognizing the facts through dialogue and negotiations that are often quite strenuous. This dialogue can lead to plans to make the co-op smaller and to permanently transfer some cooperators to other co-ops, or to combine it with another related co-op.

Actions in the ecological commons are not limited to protecting financial well-being, but must consider what is produced, how it is produced, why it is produced. Thus, the Mondragon cooperatives consider all plans in terms of both environmental and social impacts, and also consult interested unions and community groups on many key decisions.

Revaluating our Children's Future

An ecological commons rests upon a sense of continuity and value that strengthens and protects, instead of destroying, the social basis for an ecological society. Ultimately, this sense of value involves a redefinition of accounting from a tally of palpable results to a system in which things are valued in terms of the community. For example, the GNP could become a real index of social, economic, and environmental health. Pollution, pollution abatement, military production, and medical treatment for industrially induced disease—all now constituents of the GNP—do not contribute to our well-being, but have a negative, at best neutral, effect on society and should be so counted. The accounting system should also reflect charges for the use of nonrenewable resources (instead of the depletion credits now in use), and subtract the negative effects of air and water pollution, wildlands and wetlands destruction, etc.

Present accounting methods do not take these issues into consideration. For instance, one conventional measure of investments considers net present value of future income. The total value of all projected income from an investment is turned into a fixed amount in hand today needed to generate the future income. In other words, the investor asks, how much would I have to invest today at an acceptable risk to generate a given income over a given period of time? For example, compare two $5,000 investments in electric generators, one wind-powered, the other using an oil-fired motor. The latter is capable of producing more electricity though it costs more to operate. Projected net income of the wind-powered machine is $1,000 per year or $10,000 for a ten-year period, a net gain to the investor of $5,000. An investor who wanted to have $5,000 in ten years, and could earn 10 percent interest, would need $1,930—in other words, $1,930 growing at 10 percent a year compounded comes to just about $5,000. Thus, the present value of the cash flow from the wind machine investment would be $1,930. However, the oil generator could bring in $1,100 net per year, or a gain of $6,000 for ten years. The present value of the oil generator cash flow would be $2,317; under current standards, the oil-fired machine is clearly a "better" investment.[13]

In fact, this "better" investment uses a nonrenewable resource and pollutes, but this true cost is externalized by conventional accounting methods, which show only cash in hand. Ecological accounting will not discount the future earnings of nondepleting, nonpolluting production at the same rate as polluting alternatives, and will levy a charge against the oil burner.

Similarly, current accounting practices make it "profitable" to clear cut a stand of timber, dig a giant pit on that site to bury leaking toxic waste, build a waste-treatment plant to process the leachate from the dump, and erect a new hospital to treat the neurological diseases of those damaged by the poisoned water. Present accounting methods make this string of disasters more desirable than managing the woodlot for sustainable yield; they cannot consider the value of protecting and maintaining a wild place or a wilderness system in which forestry, if permitted, is conditioned by ecological concerns. Ecological accounting would support community economics: a community that depends upon agriculture and forestry would hardly find it worthwhile to devastate the land for short-term profits.

A number of measures that would account for the social and environmental effects of economic activity have been offered, such as the Index of Sustainable Economic Welfare by economist Herman Daly and philosopher John Cobb.[14] Their discussions provide a good example of the fact that accounting systems—"conventional" or "sustainable"—have everything to do with politics and value, and little to do with the so-called laws of economics. Beyond charges for environmental destruction and depletion, Daly and Cobb decide, for example, that national advertising expenses are merely a spur to consumption and brand loyalty, and should be subtracted from income, while local advertising provides useful information and should be a positive contribution.

Corporations, of course, are concerned not with such fine distinctions, but with profits and the value of company stock. In recent years, their focus has been increasingly short term. Thus, when a company that is using capital to make prudent, far-reaching investments shows a decline in profits for even one quarter, this decline is viewed as alarming; moreover, a two-quarter decline is a crisis, and a drop in annual profit signifies a disaster likely to threaten the job of the company CEO.

Current accounting methods, by rewarding destructive practices and discounting the future, betray our children and our children's children. The real issue is not foregoing current income for some future generation. The real choice is between feeding the appetite of a destructive industrial machine and maintaining the economic, social, and political basis for present and future dignity and prosperity.

Creating a Social Wage

The social wage represents both a human rights policy and an important step toward transforming production and consumption to diverse and freely chosen human ends. The social wage reflects the understanding that less is sometimes more—less money and less work, more freedom and more time for family, art, and pleasure.

What is singular about the social wage is that its root principle—a mechanism for the provision of some income for all—has unusually broad ideological support, from capitalist avatar Milton Friedman to French radical social theorist André Gorz, to U.S. social theorists Paul and Percival Goodman.[15] Under various names—for example, as "guaranteed annual income" or "basic income"—the social wage is popular, at least in theory, with European social democrats, Republican and Democratic opponents of the welfare system, and advocates of justice and children's rights.

In the context of building an ecological democracy, the social wage means income in exchange for socially useful work (from those who can work). The social wage, acting in concert with dynamic social and economic community associations, could be, in part, a bridge between our everyday reality and new social/political/economic arrangements.* The social wage as a full-blown national system may prove not to be necessary for dynamic community economies, but its elements—income in return for work, but separate from industrial wage labor; facilitating the efforts of community groups; replacement of some of the income transfer functions of existing social services in the context of democratic community development—deserve our attention.

A variety of designs have been proposed for social income plans. Friedman suggests a simple negative tax (without any work requirement) to supplement the income of all those who fall below a certain level. For example, if that level is $10,000 per year and you earn less, the government would make up the difference as a redeemable tax credit paid to you. Following this logic, the U.S.

---

*Social change must be rooted in practice: too often, a vision not only gloriously assumes that the status quo can be overthrown, but also expects to sweep aside the social-historical roots and deep structures that represent the actual material at hand for constructing our ecological societies. The word "utopian" is used as an epithet not so much to dismiss new social visions, but because those visions do not contain a reasonable and demonstrable connection to everyday reality. (The question of what is both reasonable and demonstrable is, of course, open to strenuous debate.)

Commission on Children in 1991 recommended a $1,000 tax credit per child, and the Clinton administration expanded the earned income credit to include working families of modest means. Such plans have collateral benefits: they help limit social service bureaucracies and income transfer functions by providing funds directly, and they let people choose how to spend those funds.

Recent variants suggest eliminating welfare by providing all able-bodied welfare recipients with a minimum or subminimum wage municipal job. While such employment would not remove families from poverty, it would supposedly remove them from the shame of welfare dependency and launch them upon a trajectory of upward mobility. More punitive plans, such as Massachusetts governor William Weld's 1995 welfare "reform," terminate benefits after two years, job or not (on the theory, I suppose, that destitution must build character). Such schemes seldom begin to make sufficient provision for daycare, job training, and other forms of education that could assist the poor to escape from poverty and dependency. Revenge against the poor and punishment of poor young women with children (so-called welfare mothers, a despised group) seem to be driving motivations for such policies.

The social wage as an element of building an ecological society is also predicated upon the pursuit of work; but this is socially useful work and is considered part of the general responsibility of citizenship, not a punishment for poverty or unemployment. For example, in his book *Paths to Paradise: On the Liberation from Work*,[16] Gorz proposes that each person should receive a share of the social product in exchange for a set amount of productive labor. You may be required, for instance, to work 1,000 hours per year to qualify for the social wage. Such socially defined work could and should include efforts now typically unpaid or underpaid, such as childcare, hospice work, and education. The social wage thus reflects society's choices of how to value the efforts of its members without monetizing them in a labor market. Communities can define socially useful labor in the context of a broad mandate that embraces a mixture of responsibilities and rights for all community members. Such responsibilities are rooted in what Mahatma Gandhi called the need for all to perform bread work.

The social wage could gradually become an organizing principle for society—not compulsory, not a social draft, but part of a general pattern of life and work integrated with education as a dynamic and ongoing experience. This is a radical departure from both the notion of a comprehensive welfare state and the myth of individuals finding fulfillment as a result of the actions of the market. Thus, the social wage can help communities as well as individuals move away from the industrial pursuit of production and consumption: it is predicated upon recognizing the good, on defining happiness and well-being in terms other than the relentless pursuit of income and objects.

How would we institute a social wage system? How would it function? These are interesting questions. The idea is not to make everyone an employee of the state. The social wage is not the consummate expression of social democracy. Rather, it should be integrated into the planning/market structure that shapes the ecological commons. Community members have the opportunity to decide what they value and support. A social wage is predicated upon optimization, not maximization—upon expanding the realms of personal freedom, family, and community. The social wage is meant, as Gorz suggests, to allow people both to satisfy basic and reasonable human needs *and* to have very substantial amounts of time and energy left for self-directed and community-focused pursuits—in short, to supplant the industrial demand for more with the ecological satisfaction of enough.

The social wage would be designed to provide all people with modest but decent food, clothing, shelter, medical care, education, recreation, etc. For example, in complying with a 1,000 hours per year work requirement (or 5,000 hours per five years or 20,000 hours per lifetime), a person would receive a bundle of social benefits and entitlements, not just cash. These benefits would include affordable housing for rental or purchase (home building would be socially useful labor) and affordable food (another socially useful form of labor). People could, of course, work more to earn more, or work less and receive a smaller share of the social wage, or choose not to participate—democracy requires the right of exit.*

What kind of work would qualify for the social wage? Gorz envisions a tripartite division: a "macro-social work sector" organized across society as a whole to meet basic needs; a micro-social community-based work sector, involving voluntary participation that could also perform some of the macro-social tasks; and the autonomous activity of individuals, families, and small groups. In this scheme, every local community must decide whether, and to what extent, to pursue self-sufficiency by substituting micro-social activity for some part of macro-social work. According to Gorz, complete self-sufficiency (a goal suggested by some in the ecology and self-management movement) is not especially desirable even if it were possible. Gorz notes that a community that can survive only in tight integration is not a place where individual liberties will flourish; for these liberties can exist only if there can be multiple solutions to the same problem—solutions open to individual and collective arbitration—and only if individuals are free to choose when and how they participate in community activity. The to-and-fro between optional, micro-social activity and autono-

---

* Social wage ideas are reflected, in some sense, by proposals for reduced work hours, such as the thirty-hour work week negotiated by some German industrial unions. These are predicated upon the idea of full employment and full pay through job sharing, as contrasted with the practice among U.S. corporations of increasing overtime for existing workers and accepting high unemployment to avoid pension and fringe benefit costs. Indeed, the idea of any sort of social wage seems much more visionary in the United States, with its cult of the private realm and of competition, than in Germany and Japan, with their relatively more communitarian and corporatist capitalist systems. (Much is made of the cooperative and participatory nature of capitalism in these countries, but little is said of their formal corporatist nature. In Germany, for example, labor union representatives participate in managerial decisionmaking, advancing their understanding of workers' interests.)

mous individual activity makes for balanced lives; complexity and variety, connections and overlaps keep open spaces for initiative and imagination. These are what make life worth living.[17]

The nature of a social wage system would evolve with the ecological society. Obviously, a negative income tax is relatively easy to implement, as it is essentially a cash grant. Such an approach would supplement industrial demand; but the social wage is meant less as a stiffener of demand than as an organizing principle to focus the energy of communities away from maximizing production and consumption.

Thus, an ecological social wage is not merely a measure to bolster the individual as free agent or an exercise in social democratic regulation. It represents a recognition that both socialism and liberalism have failed in their industrial manifestations. In building an ecological commons, the social wage strengthens individual freedom by allowing the individual to move away from the world of industrial production and consumption as an all-absorbing focus for life. At the same time, the social wage encourages—but does not require—individuals to freely associate in voluntary community institutions. The failure of socialism and liberalism does not mean the only option is to become a survivalist, armed with an M-16 rifle and guarding a cache of food in a basement bomb shelter.

Pursuing Disarmament and Demilitarization

We cannot build a sustainable and peaceful world by squandering a huge portion of our social surplus upon ever more destructive weapons and upon the cost of past, present, and future wars. Militarism is an insane luxury that the world can neither afford nor sustain.

Military expenditures represent self-fulfilling prophecies: expenditures on weapons impoverish nations and this impoverishment leads nations into wars, of which they have become all too capable. In the United States, the military Keynesianism of the Cold War era has left the country with an imperative to continue a redefined arms race even though the Soviet Union has disappeared. The U.S. post-Cold War "defense" budget is now about half of total world military spending.

Militarization serves industrialism by providing state mediation of economic activity focused on mobilizing vast complexes for military production, research, and bureaucratic control. Clearly, this is not simply a modern phenomena. Military organization was the model for the megamachine of ancient empires. Conservative philosopher Robert Nisbet writes, "Capitalism, nationalism, the territorialization of power, as well as its centralization, large-scale organization, mass society, technology; all of these make their first appearance in the modern West in circumstances strongly characterized by war and the military."[18] Thus, industrialism has always been characterized by an intensification of militarization. Its most grotesque incarnation was the nuclear militarism of the United States and the Soviet Union, which E. P. Thompson called "exterminism," a race toward mutual annihilation and impoverishment by opponents—and partners.

Militarism also serves as a venue for domestic control and repression. Especially in the poor nations, elites control armed forces lavishly supplied by the industrialized world with advanced weaponry and "training" most often used against domestic opponents, who typically represent movements for social equity. The military variously serves to keep (often unelected) presidents in power, landless or heavily indebted peasants in their place, low-waged, unorganized workers at factory jobs, or slum dwellers in their hovels. (Domestic repression and maintenance of existing power relationships, of course, are not only functions of the military in the poor nations, as seen in the use of the military to quell the Los Angeles riots of 1992.)

The focus for arms races has shifted from East-West to North-South and South-South axes. The Persian Gulf War unleashed a tidal wave of arms purchases, as governments in the region spent tens of billions of dollars to purchase weapons from the victorious allies. Military sales are a First World way to milk "hard currency," i.e., dollars, from the South.

Militarization is also used to plan, incite, and fight wars with other states, both for imperial advantage and for the ever popular purpose of creating a distraction at home (U.S. aggression in Grenada and Panama are good examples of actions serving both purposes). But the classic war of aggression of nation state against nation state seems less popular at this time; international actions now tend to involve the great powers enforcing the discipline of empire or conducting neocolonial wars through clients—the "low intensity conflict" program refined by the United States in Nicaragua, El Salvador, and Guatemala.*

These uses of militarism obviously have no place in an ecological democracy. On the contrary, demilitarization and disarmament are essential to maintaining an ecological commons as an expression of the values of freedom and community, unity and diversity. The two go along with the creation of ecological societies: they presuppose the transformation of power relationships from oppression and inequality to democracy and justice.

As we have seen, an ecological democracy means limiting the power of the state and strengthening that of communities. This shift includes confining the military to defense (problematic but possible); developing effective, nonviolent means of civilian resis-

---

* Most of the killing in recent years has taken place in civil wars and revolutionary struggles, often exacerbated by ethnic, cultural, and religious difference and magnified by the centrifugal forces tearing apart the nation state. In the former Yugoslavia, for instance, the international recognition of the territorial independence of Croatia, Bosnia, and Serbia transformed a civil and ethnically rooted conflict, driven by cynical designs of the powerful and ambitious, into a case of international aggression—within the supposedly privileged sanctuary of Europe. The NATO powers did not consider stopping genocide in Bosnia to be of vital interest. Leviathan has proven to be the bringer not of peace, but of repression and murder. As the slaughters of two world wars have made clear, Europe itself is no more immune to war and mass killing than the rest of the world under the global industrial system.

tance and defense, as in the Kapp Putsch in Germany in 1920 or the Velvet Revolution in Prague in 1989; and reducing national military forces to community-based and -controlled police.[19]

Some people have begun looking to the United Nations as a possible focal point for both peace-keeping and demilitarization. There is now a growing call for strengthening "the blue helmets" (UN military forces) to the point where they can play a role beyond monitoring cease-fires or patrolling borders. Those who make this argument often point to the UN role in the Gulf War. But this was a special case. Clearly, UN support of the Gulf War against Iraq was based on the consensus of the United States and its allies, and the agreement of other regional powers to swiftly use overwhelming military force (as opposed to continuing sanctions and support for internal Iraqi opposition). With control of oil at stake, the United Nations had little difficulty giving its imprimatur to the use of allied military forces to punish Iraqi aggression.

But the development of a permanent and potent military force under UN command based on UN Charter Article 43 is another matter, and is clearly an uncomfortable prospect for member nation states, forever protective of their prerogative to oppress and murder as necessary, and to avoid "interference" in their internal affairs. Such an enhanced UN force could obviously be employed to more actively protect refugees, enforce cease-fires, assist in the resupply of starving cities, intervene to stop genocide (as in Rwanda), and oppose international aggression particularly in its early stages (as in Croatia and Bosnia). But establishing such a force would mean more than just overcoming member states' reservations; the logic of such a force in a heavily armed world is extremely problematic. By participating in combat, UN forces would find themselves allied with one side, under attack, and likely to require help. Thus, absent a substantial military force, a UN army (which seems a contradiction for a peace-keeping organization) could trigger further military action. In a world moving toward demilitarization, such a force could be useful; but when hundreds of billions of dollars worth of new arms are sold every year, the UN military is too small to play a useful role, except in limited and specialized cases (and then only with the support of the major military powers).

In short, without movement toward cooperative security, a large, potent UN force that was more than just an instrument for big-power interests would be an artifact of globalization and integration, an expression of the need to enforce international discipline in an industrial order in cases beyond the reach of any single power or power grouping. Such actions would resemble the dynamics of the recent UN/U.S. actions against Iraq (with its imperial context) and in Somalia (with its initial humanistic context). Disarmament and demilitarization cannot, then, be won by a UN army, or any other army, but must be achieved by the pursuit of peace. To quote A. J. Muste: "There is no way to peace. Peace is the way."

Randall Forsberg, founder and director of the Institute for Defense and Disarmament Studies and drafter of the nuclear freeze proposal, suggests a slightly different approach to demilitarization. She now advocates a "cooperative security" plan that calls for a gradual transformation to a world relying on mutual security, limited military force, and ultimately a UN-controlled peace-keeping force sufficient to intervene effectively where necessary to prevent aggression. Forsberg's plan is based on the carefully negotiated reduction of military forces; the conversion of the military industry to civilian purposes; the development of military forces intended for defense; the growth of community-based nonviolent defense; and nuclear disarmament that moves from today's enormous arsenals to a period of minimal nuclear deterrents, and finally to nuclear abolition. Forsberg writes:

> In the long run, a cooperative approach should lead to a world in which "great powers" in the traditional military sense no longer exist. In that future world, peace and security would be provided by (1) multilateral ground, air and naval forces earmarked for military intervention or "peacemaking" under UN auspices, comprising fewer than, say, 500,000 troops in

all; and (2) national armed forces for territorial defense and domestic security, limiting all nations to border guards, coast guards, air defense forces, and a national guard or militia, comprising fewer than, say, 50,000 troops in all. Most people, if not all parts of the world, would support the principle of non-violence, both in international relations and in struggles to rectify injustices, secure civil liberties, or bring about social changes with or among states.[20]

Forsberg discusses the dynamics of a cooperative security plan within the context of the existing state system, suffused as it is with the self-interest of nations. Unfortunately, the experience of the last few years may suggest for elites the need for more and not less military force to defend themselves against their neighbors, and against the imposition of power by the United States and its allies. It is certainly in the interest of nations and the world's peoples to adopt policies of cooperative security. From the standpoint of national elites, however, threatened from without and from within, it is not at all apparent that demilitarization and disarmament are either desirable or possible.

This is not to slight the forces at work against militarism. In the United States, for example, pressing social problems place a powerful claim upon resources now being squandered upon military expenditures and create social forces that should find the pursuit of cooperative security vastly preferable to the traditional pursuit of military force. The nations of the world, individually and collectively, need to face the reality that conflict leads only to a perpetuation of a world of winners and losers, while cooperation creates the best outcome for all. Industrialized and newly industrialized states need to face not only the folly of continuing to divert resources to the military, but the folly of an export-driven arms industry selling to the highest bidder. This is true for all nations in the arms business—not just the United States, but the Czech Republic, Brazil, North Korea, China, France, Russia, Israel, Britain, Germany, Japan, *et al.* The economics that drive militarism must be confronted as well as the geopolitics.

State interest by itself, then, is insufficient to curb the excesses of militarism and the arms race, let alone transform the world's war system. What is essential is not debates over policy, but transformation from the grassroots: hundreds of billions of dollars of annual military expenditures should be used to help in the building of ecological democracies. Disarmament and demilitarization will not come about through diplomacy by elites, but through the practices of grassroots democracy.

Despite a fair amount of rhetoric, little real progress has been made in conversion of or worker retraining at military and military-related facilities. For example, although the Portsmouth Naval Shipyard in Kittery, Maine is experiencing severe cutbacks and is threatened with closing, neither the Navy, the U.S. government, the states of Maine or New Hampshire,[21] nor local or national unions have shown much interest in pursuing a serious conversion study. (Local workers have reason to be skeptical of retraining plans. A New Hampshire plan found places for only about seventy of the 600 workers laid off from the shipyard, and many of those at lower-wage, lower-skilled jobs. "Retraining" often means assistance in applying for jobs that no longer exist.)

Nor can questions of demilitarization and disarmament be resolved by market forces. The "market" for weapons depends on political decisions. An arms manufacturer, whether a "private" U.S. corporation or a "public" firm like the Soviet (now Russian) Design Bureau, generally has one major client, its own government, for which it produces ever more sophisticated hardware. Thus, the market is essentially an artificial political creation. Such a system requires political action to change it. For example, military conversion efforts need to become part of the matrix of local community economic development and change. It is not sufficient for the transnational corporations—major military contractors—to merely transform their order books, with federal assistance, from nuclear submarines to high-speed rail, even if this is possible. Conversion must consider not merely what is made, but how it is made—by whom and under what conditions.[22] However, both government and industry resolutely resist addressing those questions. Conversion represents a threat not merely to the military-industrial complex, but to the power relationships of industrialism in general; thus, conversion is important not just for demilitarization, but for social reconstruction. Demilitarization and conversion must be won not by the biggest batallions, but by the grassroots forces of community and peacemaking.

Developing an Industrial Ecology

Industrial ecology refers to the practice of production and consumption within the ecological commons. It combines three basic and interrelated aspects:

- The elimination of products and production processes that are destructive, poisonous, and unsustainable, and the replacement of them with sustainable and beneficial processes and products.

- The ongoing pursuit of efficiency, and the elimination of waste in resource and energy use.

- The development of production and consumption patterns based on reuse and recycling, where "waste" products are reclaimed and used as inputs for further productive processes.

Industrial ecology in the broad sense is the applied practice of ecological transformation; it will require looking at the components of resource and waste streams to find opportunities for conservation, and the elimination of toxic processes. Toxic plastics offer a good example. Polyvinyl chloride plastics (PVCs) are produced in enormous quantities (5.4 million tons a year currently in the United States, up from four million tons in 1981, then about one-sixth of total U.S. plastic production),[23] and are used in everything from shampoo bottles and waterproof clothing to water pipes and car parts. Vinyl chloride is made from natural gas or petroleum distillate, and is highly carcinogenic and toxic—a clear danger to workers, the general public, and the biosphere as it is released as a result of PVC production.

PVC products may be recycled (in 1989, only about 1 percent were), but most are buried or burned. Burning PVC releases hydrochloric acid, which requires "scrubbers"—devices in the smokestack that absorb the chemical—to prevent acid rain, plus a dump to dispose of the toxic sludge produced in the scrubbing process. Burning PVC also creates dioxins—a horrifically toxic material—at various levels depending on combustion temperature and conditions. Since so-called mass burn incineration is becoming a major means of treating all solid waste, the use of these plastics is an ecological disaster that will not be mitigated if the percentage recycled goes up five or ten or even fifty times.

An industrial ecological solution would be to replace PVC with substitute materials, such as glass, metal, and coated papers and fabrics, as well as less toxic and more easily recyclable plastics. The central question is not how to make PVC use more "efficient," but how to transform the nature and use of products PVC is now used to supply. PVC as a staple of the industrial system should be eliminated. There is no way to successfully mitigate its impact.[24]

As this example shows, industrial ecology is not simply a matter of a consumer recycling society on a grand scale. Indeed, production and consumption patterns, not just amounts of waste generated, are the real problem. While U.S. residents per capita consume more than their body weight in resources per day (presumably including fossil fuels, metals, water, wood, and agricultural products), this consumption yields only three and a half pounds of consumer "garbage."[25] Thus, elegant technical fixes to make this process "more efficient," while continuing maximal production and consumption, will merely slow, not stop—more importantly, not reverse—the rate of ecological and social destruction.

Another example is electrical power. Electric resistance heat produced by fossil fuel power plants is only 29 percent efficient in terms of energy input: on average, 11,600 BTUs of fuel must be burnt to produce one kilowatt hour (3,414 BTUs) delivered to a home. These plants burn fuel to produce steam to generate electric power; waste is a result of heat loss during combustion, inefficient boilers, and substantial generation and transmission inefficiencies inherent in central plant systems. (Note that this account does not include the enormous waste involved in the global costs of producing and transporting the fossil fuel.)

Both theory and practice have made it clear that very large improvements in efficiency are possible (within a fossil fuel world) through cogeneration, i.e., using the waste heat from the power plants to provide steam and/or hot water for district heating and/or cooling to city-sized areas. This is an old idea. For example, in Manhattan, the electric company, Consolidated Edison, has for many decades supplied cogenerated steam to heat many city buildings. Moreover, a great deal can be done to improve existing cogeneration designs. The most efficient systems can use low-temperature hot water to provide heating; reclaimed steam can also provide cooling through the use of steam absorption cycle devices. Cogeneration can be based upon networks of dispersed generating units for optimal efficiency. End use devices can also be made more efficient (for example, solar-assisted water-to-air heat pumps, reclaiming waste heat at every step). Combined with generation and distribution efficiencies, the potential for aggregate national and global savings is enormous.

Better even than such improvements would be a system based on dispersed photovoltaic arrays and wind generators networked to provide power to buildings designed for passive solar space heating and cooling. The underlying issue here is not merely making existing systems more efficient, but transforming them, for example, from fossil fuels and nuclear power to sustainable resource use. This transformation means a willingness to examine the political dynamics that allow the enormous costs, monetized and real, of existing energy systems to be ignored, hidden, or socialized.

What is true of energy is true of almost all other aspects of industrial society. In examining not only how things are made, but why, and not only how they are used, but why, industrial ecology is not merely bureaucratic regulation, but involves the active participation and judgment of people throughout society. Industrial ecology must mean the development of truly appropriate technologies—"appropriate" in terms of social purpose and use, not some abstract technical standard.

In sum, the industrial ecological process requires, first, an understanding of the complexities and real costs of existing processes; second, a conversion to ecological and sustainable products and use patterns; and third, screening new materials and processes before they are widely used. Each of these steps should be taken by communities at appropriate levels.

In industrialized nations, products should be made to bear their true costs in the market (the real cost of gasoline is about $10 per gallon—or much more if one includes such externalities as the cost of a war machine to control the Persian Gulf, or the fossil fuel contribution to global warming and species extinction). A true least-cost society that attempts to internalize all costs could in some areas approach an ecological one; but costing is essentially political and never "objective" or value neutral. Any costing system is based on assumptions about the value of what cannot be monetized—e.g., the cost of human life, species extinction, habitat destruction—and on estimates that are always conditioned by self-interest. A real industrial ecology represents not a super-technical fix by engineers and accountants, but an applied adjustment to the democratic processes of building the ecological commons.

Sustainability ultimately equals sufficiency—that is, in principle, sustainability on a finite planet must mean an end to the growth of industrial production and consumption. This idea means not redistribution of fixed assets, but transformation of material production and trade to the dematerialized. It means the sufficiency of the closing circles of industrial ecology; policies that embrace sufficiency, such as the social wage; maintenance of the commons as community domains to be used and protected. In all these cases, sufficiency and sustainability converge. And in an ecological society, sufficiency is defined not by technocracy, but by democracy.

Dematerializing Production

While the dematerialization of productive processes that has accompanied globalization is, in many ways, related to the necessity to maintain profit levels, it also reflects the shift away from unsustainable production to practices that are more harmonious ecologically. It has become a commonplace in the business press to note that information as product—in the form of computer software, computer books, computer data banks—uses very little material, and is largely not constrained by the environmental and resource considerations that afflict classic industrial activity. The exhaustion of cheap resources, the pollution of air and water, and the poor health of workers provide real and escalating barriers to industrial production. These are fetters upon globalization, which is inspired, in part, by the need to gain access to newer and relatively unpolluted regions to despoil.

There have been three basic responses to such environmental constraints. The first response is to reject them in the interest of short-term growth. Industrial firms facing increasing resource costs and declining profits—with production steady, declining, or advancing only fitfully—will attempt to remove regulations or seek more profitable venues. Despite rhetoric about "freeing" productive forces and depictions of regulations as political gestures rather than reflections of real-world constraints, and despite the blather about the environmental wisdom of unfettered markets, deregulation, such as that pursued by the Republican Congress in 1995, is, in fact, rooted in a denial of the environmental consequences of industrial production, an attempt to strengthen the wall around so-called externalities.

A second response is the move toward financial speculation: a shift from developing productive assets to the pursuit of profits alone. Perhaps the most alienated financial product is the so-called junk bond, a debt instrument backed by projected future earnings rather than tangible assets. When these bonds are used in the paper transfer of ownership, they simply encumber the labor and production of the future without creating new productive assets (such creation is the historical justification for stock and bond markets.)

These takeovers, driven by a desire for quick profits from companies whose assets are supposedly undervalued, have predictable consequences: assets are liquidated to pay for the junk bonds. For example, the Maxxum Corporation used junk bonds to purchase Pacific Lumber—a company once known for its sustainable, if not necessarily ecological, forestry practices—and then clear cut redwood forests to pay for their debt. Enormous debt pyramids based upon endless growth inevitably collapse, as greed and reality collide and lead to grand bankruptcies—such as those of the Federated Department Store empire, the global real estate ventures of Olympia and York, and the investor-owned utility Public Service Company of New Hampshire (in which public resistance to its Seabrook nuclear plant was crucial). And as speculators go broke, financial institutions heavily invested in bad debt also fail.

The third response to environmental constraints, broadly speaking, is the growth of the service sector. This growth is not just a matter of improving services, but involves monetizing realms of life once considered part of community activity—such as childcare and elder care, schools, etc. Especially in the age of automation, service work tends to create a pyramidal hierarchy: on top is a small group of highly trained and highly paid managers, engineers, and technical workers; next, a larger group of well-paid skilled technicians and executives (information technology allows fewer people in this group to accomplish more); at the bottom, the expanding service proletariat—the word processors, form fillers, xeroxers, burger flippers, cleaners, sales clerks, attendants, guards—that performs jobs requiring moderate to low skill and offering low pay. This is the reality facing many downwardly mobile production workers, managers, and technicians.

These dynamics of dematerialization driving the response to environmental constraints are an essential part of the gains for the so-called information revolution. The informational sector represents the new area for growth: telecommunications (voice, fax, etc.); computer programs; data bases; cable and paid television programming; "information" from biogenetic research; computer networks; a capital-intensive global electronic web of hardware; computers themselves; and increasingly portable information devices (all often products with a lifespan of six months to a year before newer, more advanced models appear). However, beyond the manufacture of hardware (made for the most part in highly automated factories, or assembled by unskilled labor anywhere in the world), the information revolution is a job-destroying revolution. Software entrepreneurs may become billionaires, but reproducing software involves relatively little material input or labor. Indeed, as productive work increasingly becomes mental activity—programming, designing new machines, integrating computers—we face the possibility that not only workers in the North, but the people of the South as a whole may become increasingly irrelevant.

Thus, the state of the world today reflects the twinning of globalization and dematerialization. People are less and less necessary (or tolerable) for the ongoing conduct of industrialism. *

---

* As industrial greed runs into environmental limits, it seeks dominance most

This dematerialization is not the harbinger of a "postindustrial" information age, but a necessity for the survival of an afflicted order. As with most things industrial, it is accomplished upon the initiative of the strong and at the expense of the weak.

However, the tendency toward dematerialization can also be the basis for development of an ecological society, if basic choices are made that condition both production and consumption and, more importantly, the social relations around them. As Gorz noted in *Paths to Paradise*, separating labor from production is an invitation to social wage strategies—not just to the creation of a huge underclass and the division of society into information-rich and information-poor.

The sale of computer programs and the sale of access to data banks cannot be the basis for the continuation of a mass wage industrial society—*but* the orientation to dematerialize production *can* be a fine fit with the freedom and community to be pursued by an ecological democracy. What will be depends on the choices we make and the actions we take. The industrial path leads toward the perpetual strengthening and elaboration of hierarchical systems to defend an ever shrinking circle of global privilege. The ecological path leads toward democratization and the shared burdens and benefits of freedom and responsibility.

Developing a Solar Economy

Developing a solar economy means not only turning to reliance upon renewable resources, but transforming the social relations that support the industrial system.

---

energetically through financial speculation, enforcing debt service, and reducing commodity prices—in part, by encouraging economies based on commodity exports while the North turns to high value-added substitutes for those commodities, e.g., fiber optic cable for copper; ceramic for platinum in catalytic convertors; petroleum distillates for rubber, cotton, wool.

Solar (or renewable resource) technologies are not necessarily incompatible with continued industrial domination. Amory Lovins has long argued that such technologies would bring, or at least tend to bring, a social transformation toward decentralized, democratically controlled, and environmentally sensitive forms.[26]

But in fact, transnational corporations and governments could mass-produce solar water heaters and photovoltaic panels in sweatshop factories—indeed, renewable resources may become the only choice on a poisoned planet. Nor does "renewable resources" necessarily mean appropriate scale—renewable power can come from destructive, massive hydro dams and other mega-projects.

Solar technologies are most meaningful as part of a transformation toward an ecological way, not as a simple substitution for existing technologies. Industrial dreams of limitless resources and limitless production and consumption will not simply be redeemed by solar technologies. This question of technological possibility vs. technological determinism is often subtle. We tend to imagine that machines reflect some sort of value-free imperative, as if the internal combustion engine automatically gave us the private automobile culture. However, Marx wrote, "the way in which machinery is exploited is quite distinct from the machinery itself."[27] In an ecological democracy, all aspects of technology—its use, its control, its spread—and the specific manifestations of given technologies are thus subject to social control and democratic choice. Renewable resource technologies, then, provide possibilities, but not because of any social or technological imperative.

For example, Southern California smog has produced a vast regulatory structure, ranging from control of aerosol sprays and backyard barbecues to requirements for zero emission vehicles. Thus, the Chrysler Corporation has announced it will offer fifty electric-powered vans at $120,000 each; General Motors plans a mass-production electric vehicle, the Impact, for $25,000 and has a prototype 100 miles per gallon gasoline car called the Ultralight. Meanwhile, students at the New Hampshire Vocational Technical College in Concord are working on their third or fourth photovoltaic-powered automobile on a very modest budget. If they can win a solar car race from Hanover, New Hampshire to Boston, Massachusetts, I should imagine the world's largest industrial corporation should be able to match their ingenuity.

Building an ecological society does not mean simply retrofitting Los Angeles and the surrounding agricultural lands—with their enormous and parasitic consumption of water, electricity, and petrochemicals—as a means to continue meeting L.A.'s needs for transportation, fertilizers, herbicides, and pesticides in an attempt to justify a social order characterized by the horrific disparities between wealth and poverty, walled neighborhoods and a choking automobile culture. Los Angeles is to the southwestern United States what the United States is to the world—an unsustainable, vulgar corruption of the dream of plenty.

Solar and renewables provide an excellent path for the growth of a community-based economy—that is, the integrated use of capital provided by development banks, credit unions, pension funds, and governments; formal and informal educational activities; technical assistance at all levels; research partnerships; and innovative tax and government procurement policies. Industrial power is incapable of embracing this potential freedom of solar transformation. It is only willing to impose solar conversion on its own terms. Our opportunity is to develop the use of environmentally, socially, and economically superior solar power as a venue to help us seize the day.

In sum, these transitional paths are invitations for community action and enterprise. They are less a docket for policymakers than a framework to encourage the participation of people and their communities in the day-to-day work of building better lives, to construct and strengthen step-by-step an ecological democracy.

chapter ten
───────────

CONCLUSION

SPRING AGAIN RUSHES AT US in the Mink Hills. Ice
cracks, the drive is rutted by meltwater. Maple syrup buckets and
lines are hung. Gardens are planned, seedlings started. The juncos
that swarm around the feeder with the red squirrels, woodpile
mice, and chipmunks are fattening, not frantic. Four deer, still sleek
after a too-warm, near snowless winter, cross Newmarket Road
and watch from the woods.

It's mid-March, time for town meeting and school meeting,
the convivial and not-so-convivial assemblies of neighbors. We
hold in flinty New Hampshire hands the diamond of our democracy. It's endangered, sometimes denatured, often pecked at. But
it is a base of community truth, our lever to move a little bit of
reality on the basis of our considered will. Democracy is the
incarnation of our community intentions, the small voices that can
become the many-part chorus of multitudes.

When neighbors gather together in late winter, it's not a
revival pageant in mock Athenian spirit. It is a chance to make
sense not only of budgets and fire trucks, but of the meaning of
both great and subtle changes in the balance of nature and society.

When it really means something, we take action not simply in our votes of *yea* or *nay*, but in our lives.

If there is to be a resolution to the crises afflicting industrial civilization, if there is to be an ecological transformation, it will come not from the commands of the powerful, or the ministrations of experts, but from the countless ponderings of those in countless communities. By fits and starts, in the pleasures of early mornings and sun-dappled evenings, from long marches, hard work, and time spent in dirty jail cells, from politics and art, an ecological democracy is being born and will grow.

Endings and Beginnings

Fundamental social change is an impatient and wayward undertaking. An ecological democracy does not put off human concerns until after the revolution; rather, its revolution is, in part, the measured expression of human concern. A good society is created by people who have begun to remove not only the confining stringencies of dehumanizing work, but the more palpable human stringencies that bind our spirits. An ecological democracy empowers freedom with love and care, melding the pleasures of the senses and the mind with the pleasures and duties of the heart.

The logic of an ecological democracy is the logic of connection, of inclusion. It is an expansive, creative logic with the generative power of recombination and evolution, a logic that understands order as ever shifting arrangements. And it is the logic of family and community: the discontent of modernity is expressed in the acceleration of separation—of children from parents and parents from children, of the individual from community. But an ecological democracy finds ways to nurture the dialogue of family and community, the song of ourselves.

Life's secret is its ceaseless capacity for renewal. Birth represents not just a fated end, a passing shadow, but renewal and change. Life not only inhabits the planet, life shapes the planet; it creates, maintains, and conditions the biosphere—the atmosphere, the ocean, the soil, the rock.

For forty years, it appeared the world would end with a bang, as East and West accelerated toward apocalyptic nuclear destruction. But an epochal change reversed the tide—not as a result of the logic of leaders, but by great and overwhelmingly nonviolent risings from below.

When the U.S. Congress voted a moratorium on nuclear testing in 1992, it was only page forty-nine news in *The Boston Globe*. The *Globe* made no mention of those who risked or gave their lives, of the tens of thousands arrested in the United States for nonviolent opposition to nuclear testing, of the millions who had marched and demonstrated and lobbied. This was a movement begun in the United States by women in the 1950s concerned about strontium 90 in their children's teeth and bones, continued by ordinary people who found a personal imperative for action and a collective ability to act. It offers an example of the kind of movements that over time will help weave the social fabric of an ecological society.[1]

Individuals and groups of people have made, and are making, choices that manifestly alter the course of events, the tone and temper of our times. When the finger tightens on the nuclear trigger, when ecological catastrophe looms, we are called to act as individuals and as communities, to throw ourselves into the breach once more—not for conquest, not even just for survival, but for the sake of life itself.

Ecological democracy is the work of ordinary people, the daily politics of communities in motion. Heroes we have had and will have aplenty, but what matters is the inspired heroism of ordinary people who find themselves in extraordinary circumstances and choose to act. Media and myth personify movements in leaders, but leadership is more the product of the whirling flux of social movements than the creation of singular genius. To await a leader who will guide us to the ecological promised land is to engage in a fool's search. The process of earth saving is a path of community and love. Ecological democracy is the striking off of blinders and the sensuous embrace of a still vibrant world.

The Next 500 Years

For industrial modernity, epochs are measured in decades, not centuries, certainly not millennia. The Cold War that defined my life (I was born in 1946) is now an historical memory. What has happened in our lives transcends the conventional flow of events debated by historians; history is not merely a matter of media images, elite struggles for power, or reminiscences of generals, tyrants, and democrats. Our lives and our civilization are shaped by the grand accretion and combination of experience, relationships, constructions, common and rare acts of a living past, and the dazzling and sometimes terrifying welter of circumstances.

The end of the Cold War represents the climactic moment of the heroic period of industrial civilization, the decisive end of classic industrialism (while the so-called developing world struggles to attain an illusory condition whose moment has come and gone). This is a crisis not simply of capitalism or socialism, of management or coordination, of legitimacy or belief. The crisis is systemic and fundamental.

A new democracy rushes in not as nostalgia for a preindustrial world, but as harbinger of an emergent ecological civilization. To speak of a poisoned world, an afflicted world, is not to speak of a dead world. There is still the glory of spring returning, the epochal struggle of flower head and bracken fern to break through the still cool and muddy earth. Industrialism's poisons and appetite can be stopped, abated, transmuted by the lifeways of an ecological democracy. Industrialism is not life. Industrialism is not humanity.

Global integration has squeezed time as it is wringing the world dry of resources: the capitalist industrial long term becomes next quarter, next week, or even tomorrow. Time drives the frenetic pace of commerce, of trading and deal making, reducing life to "pure market" relationships. Similarly, those struggling against the machine see the need for immediate action on many fronts—to preserve the last bits of wilderness; to save not just old growth, rain forests, and fisheries, but cultures and lifeways being obliterated and absorbed into the undifferentiated mass of slum and wasteland culture.

The disorienting tenor of the times makes it difficult to adopt the long view. As instability and change accelerate, imperatives are more clearly expressed; hierarchies act less to order and more to manage in the midst of disintegration, to extract the last requisite tribute from the slums, the South, the wild. To gain perspective does not mean to stop our struggles and congratulate ourselves on the ultimate triumph of the ecological worldview.

Involvement is crucial for building an ecological democracy: democratic and ecological lifeways must not just be won—as in a victorious struggle for power—but lived.

The work of days and weeks, of this day and next week, must become the work of generations and of centuries. This cannot be the product of a master plan, whether contrived democratically or arising from a prophet or a college of prophets (no matter how prescient). The plan must be lived; means must gradually become ends through a process of democratic dialogue and equilibration.

The qualities needed for this struggle include the patience to persevere. We must recognize that we may be disappointed and beaten down by industrial power again and again, but that we will resist, persist, and ultimately prevail—not through force of arms, but through the gritty velvet of necessity, truth, and transformation. Industrial society must change; it is up to us to define the nature and outcome of the changes. I believe, without millennial claims, that we are living in one of those grand and unsettled moments when the social structures and excesses of the dominant order are bringing forth the beginnings of a new civilization. This is a time not just of fear and of menace, but of possibility and optimism.

The Future as History

To approach the future we need understand our own reticence about the past. History has a social basis far removed from grand events. History marks the evolution and legacy of lifeways, the personal and social heritage of human experience. Centuries of upheaval have meant destruction, transformation, dispossession, and struggle—an accelerating pace of building up and tearing down. Our most intimate and deeply felt memories as individuals and as peoples are often armored and cloistered. The history of the ecological democracy to come will be described not simply by changes in material culture and the development of appropriate technologies, but by a broader change in heart, mind, and worldview. This is not a matter of ideas, but of lifeways. Such personal and social transformation is the human concomitant for the flowering of freedom and community, the creation of an ecological commons, the greening of cities, the coherence of an ecological worldview.

An ecological democracy is shaped and conditioned by a sensuous circle of *values*, a moral ecology based on the individual and community awareness of the consequence and resonance of our acts, of the complex and inextricable links between individual and group, private and public, freedom and community.

The ecological future will be marked by the practice of personal and community renewal, so that the forming dualisms are not merely redefined, but quieted. Ecological civilization involves the re-creation of hierarchies into fluid and democratic arrangements, a transmutation from progress as the cult of change to ethical choice as the basis for action.

The history of an ecological civilization is an unfolding panorama of social forms and lifeways. Already, amidst the agonies and menace of industrialism, there is a turning toward the dawn. This is not a dance to the blind music of history, but the summation of our individual and collective acts, choices, and strivings that slowly, by fits and starts, can transform the megamachine into the free communities of an ecological democracy.

It is time for all of us to understand that we are at work in a common effort: not a movement struggling for power, but a movement for reconstruction, a movement creating, building, and nurturing what will come to be known as the community of communities, an ecological democracy.

THE DECLARATION OF INDEPENDENCE

IN CONGRESS, JULY 4, 1776.

The unanimous Declaration of the thirteen united States of America,

When in the Course of human events, it becomes necessary for one people to dissolve the political bands, which have connected them with another, and to assume among the powers of the earth, the separate and equal station to which the Laws of Nature and of Nature's God entitle them, a decent respect to the opinions of mankind requires that they should declare the causes which impel them to the separation.

We hold these truths to be self-evident, that all men are created equal, that they are endowed by their Creator with certain unalienable Rights, that among these are Life, Liberty and the pursuit of Happiness. That to secure these rights, Governments are instituted among Men, deriving their just powers from the consent of the governed. That whenever any Form of Government becomes destructive of these ends, it is the Right of the People to alter or to abolish it, and to institute new Government, laying its foundation on such principles and organizing its powers in such form, as to them shall seem most likely to effect their Safety and Happiness. Prudence, indeed, will dictate that Governments long established should not be changed for light and transient causes; and accordingly all experience hath shown, that mankind are more disposed to suffer, while evils are sufferable, than to right themselves by abolishing the forms to which they are accustomed. But when a long train of abuses and usurpations, pursuing invariably the same Object evinces a design to reduce them under absolute Despotism, it is their right, it is their duty, to throw off such Government, and to provide new Guards for their future security. Such has been the patient sufferance of these Colonies; and such is now the necessity which constrains them to alter their former Systems of Government. The history of the present King of Great Britain is a history of repeated injuries and usurpations, all having in direct object the establishment of an absolute Tyranny over these States. To prove this, let Facts be submitted to a candid world.

He has refused his Assent to Laws, the most wholesome and necessary for the public good.

He has forbidden his Governors to pass Laws of immediate and pressing importance, unless suspended in their operation till his Assent should be obtained; and when so suspended, he has utterly neglected to attend to them.

He has refused to pass other Laws for the accommodation of large districts of people, unless those people would relinquish the right of Representation in the Legislature, a right inestimable to them and formidable to tyrants only.

He has called together legislative bodies at places unusual, uncomfortable, and distant from the depository of their public Records, for the sole purpose of fatiguing them into compliance with his measures.

He has dissolved Representative Houses repeatedly, for opposing with manly firmness his invasions on the rights of the people.

He has refused for a lnog time, after such dissolutions, to cause others to be elected; whereby the Legislative powers, incapable of Annihilation, have returned to the People at large for their exercise; the State remaining in the meantime exposed to all the dangers of invasion from without, and convulsions within.

He has endeavoured to prevent the population of these States; for that purpose obstructing the Laws for Naturalization of Foreigners; refusing to pass others to encourage their migrations hither, and raising the conditions of new Appropriations of Lands.

He has obstructed the Administration of Justice, by refusing his Assent to Laws for establishing Judiciary powers.

He has made Judges dependent on his Will alone, for the tenure of their offices, and the amount and payment of their salaries.

He has erected a multitude of New Offices, and sent hither swarms of Officers to harrass our people, and eat out their substance.

He has kept among us, in times of peace, Standing Armies without the Consent of our legislatures.

He has affected to render the Military independent of and superior to the Civil power.

He has combined with others to subject us to a jurisdiction foreign to our constitution, and unacknowledged by our laws; giving his Assent to their Acts of pretended Legislation.

For quartering large bodies of armed troops among us:

For protecting them, by a mock Trial, from punishment for any Murders which they should commit on the Inhabitants of these States:

For cutting off our Trade with all parts of the world:

For imposing Taxes on us without our Consent:

For depriving us in many cases, of the benefits of Trial by Jury:

For transporting us beyond Seas to be tried for pretended offenses:

For abolishing the free System of English Laws in a neighbouring Province, establishing therein an Arbitrary government, and enlarging its Boundaries so as to render it at once an example and fit instrument for introducing the same absolute rule into these Colonies:

For taking away our Charters, abolishing our most valuable Laws, and altering fundamentally the Forms of our Governments:

For suspending our own Legislatures, and declaring themselves invested with power to legislate for us in all cases whatsoever.

He has abdicated Government here, by declaring us out of his Protection and waging war against us.

He has plundered our seas, ravaged our Coasts, burnt our towns, and destroyed the lives of our people.

He is at this time transporting large Armies of foreign Mercenaries to complete the works of death, desolation and tyranny, already begun with circumstances of Cruelty and perfidy scarcely paralleled in the most barbarous ages, and totally unworthy of the Head of a civilized nation.

He has constrained our fellow Citizens taken Captive on the high Seas to bear Arms against their Country, to become the executioners of their friends and Brethren, or to fall themselves by their Hands.

He has excited domestic insurrections amongst us, and has endeavoured to bring on the inhabitants of our frontiers, the merciless Indian Savages, whose known rule of warfare, is an undistinguished destruction of all ages, sexes and conditions.

In every stage of these Oppression, We have Petitioned for Redress in the most humble terms: Our repeated Petitions have been answered only by repeated injury. A Prince, whose character is thus marked by every act which may define a Tyrant, is unfit to be the ruler of a free people.

Nor have We been wanting in attentions to our British brethren. We have warned them from time to time of attempts by their legislature to extend an unwarrantable jurisdiction over us. We have reminded them of the circumstances of our emigration and settlement here. We have appealed to their native justice and magnanimity, and we have conjured them by the ties of our common kindred to disavow these usurpations, which would inevitably interrupt our connections and correspondence. They too have been deaf to the voice of justice and of consanguinity. We must, therefore, acquiesce in the necessity, which denounces our Separation, and hold them, as we hold the rest of mankind, Enemies in War, in Peace Friends.

We, therefore, the Representatives of the united States of America, in General Congress, Assembled, appealing to the Supreme Judge of the world for the rectitude of our intentions do, in the Name, and by Authority of the good People of these Colonies, solemnly publish and declare, That these United Colonies are, and of Right ought to be Free and Independent States; that they are Absolved from all Allegiance to the British Crown, and that all political connection between them and the State of Great Britain, is and ought to be totally dissolved; and that as Free and Independent States, they have full Power to levy War, conclude Peace, contract Alliances, establish Commerce, and to do all other Acts and Things which Independent States may of right do.

And for the support of this Declaration, with a firm reliance on the protection of divine Providence, we mutually pledge to each other our Lives, our Fortunes, and our sacred Honor.

notes

CHAPTER ONE

1. Francis Fukuyama, *The End of History and the Last Man* (New York: Free Press, 1992).

2. Immanuel Wallerstein discusses the meanings of "civilization" in "The Renewed Concern with Civilization" in *Geopolitics and Geoculture: Essays on the Changing World-System* (Cambridge, England: Cambridge University Press, 1991), 235. For Wallerstein, "the modern world system is a capitalist world economy." *Geopolitics*, 162. I believe it is an error to ignore the consequences of its *industrial* nature.

3. Joseph Schumpeter, *Capitalism, Socialism, and Democracy*, 3rd ed. (New York: Harper & Row, 1980).

4. Vandana Shiva, "The Meaning of Global Reach," *Z Papers* (April-June 1993), 21-29.

5. Gene Sharp, *Social Power and Political Freedom* (Boston: Porter Sargent Publishers, 1980).

6. Wolfgang Sachs, ed., *The Development Dictionary: A Guide to Knowledge as Power* (Atlantic Highlands, N.J.: Zed Books, 1992).

7. Michael Jacobs, *The Green Economy: Environment, Sustainable Development, and the Politics of the Future* (London: Pluto Press, 1991), 76-77.

8. Clive Ponting, *A Green History of the World* (London: Sinclair-Stevenson, 1991), 403.

9. To get a good sense of the anti-environmental movement, see Ronald Bailey, ed., *The True State of the Planet* (New York: Free Press, 1995). This book was published in conjunction with the Competitive Enterprise Institute, a leader in the attempt by the Republican Congress in 1995 to pass so-called "takings" legislation that would protect polluters from environmental regulation. Its title is a response to the Worldwatch Institute's annual *State of the World* series, which they consider is infected with

environmental doom-and-gloom. For more nuanced support for industrial progress, see Gregg Easterbrook, "Here Comes the Sun," *The New
Yorker* (April 10, 1995), 38-43, for a capsule of his argument.

10. Edward O. Wilson, *The Diversity of Life* (Cambridge, Mass.:
Harvard University Press, 1992), 280.

11. Andrew Blaustein and David Wake, "The Puzzle of Declining
Amphibian Populations," *Scientific American* (April 1995), 52-57. The article includes citations in the scientific literature for the technically inclined.

CHAPTER TWO

1. Jean Baudrillard, *The Mirror of Production*, trans. Mark Porter (St.
Louis: Telos Press, 1971).

2. Lewis Mumford, *The Myth of the Machine: Technics and Human
Development* (New York: Harcourt, Brace Jovanovich, 1967), 212. Mumford
describes the ancient megamachine at length. See especially Chapter Nine,
"The Design of the Megamachine."

3. Details of notable developments in industrialization are from the
classic by Sigfried Giedion, *Mechanization Takes Command: A Contribution
to Anonymous History* (New York: Oxford University Press, 1948).

4. Industrial technological horizons are often considered of epochal
import. For example, by Alvin Toffler and his intellectually muddled and
politically rapacious disciple Newt Gingrich, *The Third Wave* (New York:
William Morrow, 1980).

5. Jacques Ellul, *The Technological Society*, trans. John Wilkinson (New
York: A. A. Knopf, 1964).

6. Arthur Green, *Seek My Face, Speak My Name: A Contemporary Jewish
Theology* (Northvale, N.J.: Jason Aronson, 1992), 101-2. This is a book I find
suffused with both a mystical and an ecological consciousness.

7. Immanuel Kant, "What Is Enlightenment?" trans. Peter Gay in
The Enlightenment: A Comprehensive Anthology, ed. Peter Gay (New York:
Simon & Schuster, 1973), 385-86.

8. Antoine-Nicolas de Condorcet, "Sketch for a Historical Picture of the
Progress of the Human Mind," trans. June Barraclough in The Enlightenment,
804-5.

9. These themes are explored in depth by Gene Sharp in *Social Power
and Political Freedom*, (Boston: Porter Sargent Publishers, 1980).

10. Roland Barthes suggests that using myth in the service of order
is "eternalizing" (and, in so doing, removes matters from being contested).
Barthes is a trail-blazing thinker who moved from leftist analysis to
semiotics. In "Myth Today" (written in 1956), Barthes adopts what for the

time was a quite radical and startling analysis. "Myth Today" in *A Barthes Reader*, ed. Susan Sontag (New York: Hill and Wang, 1982), 138.

11. Sigmund Freud, *Civilization and Its Discontents*, trans. and ed. James Strachey (New York: W. W. Norton, 1962), 15.

12. The contrast between industrialism's recourse to a manipulation of means and ends as opposed to its ostensible reliance upon a mechanistic, value-free cause-and-effect was suggested by psychologist Terry Kimper. Means become ends and ends means, not as part of an open and ethical covenant, but as an ever shifting manipulative process.

CHAPTER THREE

1. Conference Board study cited in *Z Magazine* (November 1993), 10-11.

2. *Disclosure Worldscope Company Profiles* (Bridgeport, Conn.: WDP, 1991).

3. The World Bank, *World Development Report* (New York: Oxford University Press, 1993), 199.

4. Thus, for example, in my town of Warner, New Hampshire, population 2,000, citizens held a vigorous debate over the wisdom of allowing a McDonald's franchise restaurant to open near a highway exit. Local control over water, sewer, traffic, and zoning could have been used to prevent the opening of this restaurant, but the battle was lost after opponents began to fight more with other townspeople than with the corporation, which did its best to identify itself with Americanism. Other nearby towns, particularly those with more wealth and/or lower tax rates, have successfully resisted McDonald's.

5. Brian Dumaine, "Is Big Still Good?" *Fortune* (April 20, 1992), 50.

6. Ibid. I assume that the magazine's editors, if not the article's writer, only intend to take the *perestroika* analogy for corporate America part way and not to its conclusion in the former Soviet Union.

7. Floris A. Malgers, "Inside Unilever: The Evolving Transnational Company," *Harvard Business Review* (September-October, 1992), 46-52.

8. *The Economist* (September 23-29, 1993), front cover.

9. Jane Jacobs, *Cities and the Wealth of Nations: Principles of Economic Life* (New York: Random House, 1984).

10. See, for example, James M. Sheehan, "The Greening of Eastern Europe," *Global Affairs* (Spring 1992), 158. This article offers an interesting critique of conventional policies of the World Bank and the Agency for International Development, and of typical environmental regulations.

11. R. D. Hayes, "Liquidating Libkovice: What Happens to a Village in Bohemia when Capitalists in Search of Coal Arrive?" *Los Angeles Times Magazine* (August 2, 1992), 23.

CHAPTER FOUR

1. See Alvin Gouldner, *The Two Marxisms: Contradictions and Anomalies in the Development of Theory* (New York: Seabury Press, 1980).

2. The tenor of the times is reflected on the cover of the paperback for Francis Fukuyama's *The End of History and the Last Man*, published by the Free Press in 1992 at the climax, as it turned out, of the Reagan-Bush years. The cover announces the book was the "Winner of *The Los Angeles Times* Book Prize" and is adorned with excerpts from a review by George Gilder from *The Washington Post Book World*: "Awesome...A landmark work... profoundly realistic...Supremely timely and cogent...The first book to fully fathom the depth and range of the changes now sweeping through the world."

3. Francis Fukuyama, *The End of History and the Last Man* (New York: Free Press, 1992), 81.

4. See, for example, Wilhelm Röpke, *A Humane Economy: The Social Framework of the Free Market*, trans. Elizabeth Henderson (Chicago: Henry Regnery Co., 1960), 3. "If it is liberal to entrust economic order not to planning, coercion, and penalties, but to the spontaneous and free cooperation of people through the market, price, and competition, and at the same time to regard private property as the pillar of this free order, then I speak as a liberal when I reject socialism."

5. Jean Chesneaux, *Brave Modern World: The Prospects for Survival* (New York: Thames and Hudson, 1992), 79.

6. For a biological example (I make no claims by analogy for the behavior of more complex species), consider the ability of bacteria of different species to exchange on a cellular level genetic material that provides resistance to antibiotics by strengthening cell walls. This ability certainly should, or could, be a revelation, as it not only challenges the accepted view of the speciation of bacteria, but shakes the pillars of the neo-Darwinian synthesis. Darwinism, rooted in a supreme confidence in the importance of random genetic variation, "survival of the fittest," and transmission by the winners of biological traits to offspring, is certainly not applicable to this cooperative and adaptive behavior of supposedly different species. The strength of Darwinism is rooted not simply in its anointed position as settled scientific doctrine, but in its ideological consonance with a capitalist worldview.

7. Benito Mussolini, "The Doctrine of Fascism," from *Encyclopedia Italiana*, Vol. XIV, in *Readings on Fascism and National Socialism* (Athens, Ohio: Swallow Press, 1984), 7.

8. Edward Goldsmith, *The Way: An Ecological World-View* (Boston: Shambala, 1993); Fritjof Capra, *The Turning Point: Science, Society, and the Rising Culture* (New York: Simon & Schuster, 1982); Morris Berman, *The Reenchantment of the World* (Ithaca, N.Y.: Cornell University Press, 1981); Arne Naess, *Ecology, Community, and Lifestyle: Outline of an Ecosophy* (Cambridge, England: Cambridge University Press, 1989); Henryk Skolimowski, *Eco-Philosophy: Designing New Tactics for Living* (Boston: M. Boyars, 1981).

CHAPTER FIVE

1. Behind lofty statements in favor of the common good, neoliberalism's motivation for reaching toward the chimerical goal of sustainable industrial development is expressed by an ad in "The Magazine of Environmental Management and Pollution Control," *Environment Today* (October 1993): the Gauntlett Group ("Environmental Engineering Specialists") offers a $895, three-day seminar on "Environmental Management Systems Total Quality Approach" and a $360 video. The headline is, "The Road to Sustainable Development: Profitability through Ecology."

2. William Clark, "Managing Planet Earth," *Scientific American* (September 1989), 47-54. The quotation is from page 54.

3. Pierre R. Crosson and Norman Rosenberg, "Strategies for Agriculture," *Scientific American* (September 1989), 128-35. The quotation is from page 135.

4. Michael Goldman, "Tragedy of the Commons or the Commoners' Tragedy: The State and Ecological Crisis in India," *Capitalism Nature Socialism* (December 1993), 66-67.

5. Environmental Protection Agency administrator Carol Browner argues that ecosystems protection requires deals such as the one she negotiated, as a Florida regulator, with the Disney Corporation, allowing further development near their existing facilities in exchange for large tracts of marsh and river land.

6. Quoted in Scott Alan Lewis, "Clinton's First Year: Environmental Disaster," *Peace and Democracy News* (Winter 1993/4), 33.

7. *Burlington* (Vermont) *Free Press* (January 16, 1994), 6A.

8. William Ruckelshaus, "Toward a Sustainable World," *Scientific American* (September 1989), 167.

9. Lester R. Brown, "Launching the Environmental Revolution," *State of the World: A Worldwatch Institute Report on Progress Toward a Sustainable Society* (New York: W. W. Norton, 1992), 174.

10. Ibid., 189.

11. Gro Harlem Brundtland, "How to Secure Our Common Future," *Scientific American* (September 1989), 190.

12. Michael Jacobs, *The Green Economy: Environment, Sustainable Development, and the Politics of the Future* (London: Pluto Press, 1991), 113.

13. The impact of annual exponential increases is quickly calculated by the law of 72. To calculate the amount of time it takes for a quantity to double under a set annual growth rate, divide 72 by the rate of increase, e.g., for 3% annual increase, $72/3 = 24$ years; for 6% annual increase, $72/6 = 12$ years.

14. Eric Hanson, "The Greatest Success Story Ever Told," *Toward Freedom* (October 1993), 21-22.

15. Mathematically, to determine the exponential growth of a Present Quantity (PQ) increasing at a fixed rate (r) annually over a given period of years (n): Future Quantity (FQ) = $PQ(1+r)n$. This is a familiar compound interest formula, but can be used to calculate increase of industrial output, population, or pollution. As the annual rate of change increases, for example, from 3 percent to 15 percent, the exponential function leads to enormous differences in a fifty-year time period. For example, at 3 percent annual growth a population of 1,000 would increase to 4,384 over fifty years, or four times the original population. At 15 percent growth, population would be 1,083,657, or 1,000 times the original. At 3 percent, it takes about twenty-five years for the population to double; at 15 percent, about five. Over fifty years, the power of exponential growth means that at 15 percent annual increase the growth would be about 2^{10} or over 1,000 times the original, compared to about 2^2 or just over four times the original. Of course, any of these curves—exponential, logistic, catastrophic—represent strictly deterministic and gravely oversimplified models of living systems.

16. Thomas Robert Malthus, "An Essay on the Principle of Population" in *Population, Evolution, and Birth Control: A Collage of Controversial Readings*, ed. Garrett Hardin (San Francisco: W. H. Freeman and Co., 1964).

17. Herman Daly, *Steady-State Economics: The Economics of Biophysical Equilibrium and Moral Growth*, 2nd ed. (Washington, D.C.: Island Press, 1991).

18. The logistic or s-shaped growth curve recognizes that, unlike the exponential, the rate of change of complex and interactive systems will change over time, for example, with the size of population. Pierre-François Verhulst and Raymond Pearl developed a classic logistic equation for the

rate of change in population growth over time: $dN/dT = rN(1-N/K)$. To determine the next year's (n+1) population of a Present Quantity (N) increasing at an intrinsic rate (r) annually (e.g., 1.15) with a maximum population carrying capacity (K): $Nn+1 = N + rNn(1-N/K)$. Mathematically, what this means is that the fixed annual increase (rN), that would yield an exponential growth as in Figure 5-1, is modified by the expression (1-N/K), that is (1 - current population/carrying capacity). As the population increases toward the carrying capacity, the expression (1-N/K) decreases, thus reducing the rate of population growth. This is why the logistic curve assumes its "s" shape, tending toward the maintenance of a stable population. And as the population decreases, the rate of population growth increases. The logistic equation is thus nonlinear; the rates of change differ from year to year. It is also iterative; the results of one year are used to determine the next year and thus based on feedback processes. Mathematically, for the logistic equation, as long as "r" is less than three, the population will eventually reach a single, stable population. This is the equation's attractor. (When "r" exceeds three, quite different and less stable dynamics appear that will be noted below in Figure 5-3 under the catastrophic.) Thus, all things being equal, the logistic suggests that systems that increase at modest rates tend toward reaching a stable quantity less than the environmental carrying capacity. Unfortunately, all things are not always equal. All sorts of destabilizing influences effect and dramatically alter the deterministic certainties of the logistic equations. The real world is a most complex system of relationships subject not only to determinist certitudes, but to the influences of chance and chaotic dynamics where small changes can cause a number of wildly different (albeit sometimes mathematically comprehensible) results. In the real world, carrying capacity can be degraded. It is not fated, as industrial supporters sometimes insist, that the capitalist industrial system is magically self-regulating, or that the earth will be able to withstand limitless industrial and population growth. For useful capsule accounts of logistic equations and chaos, see Robert Wesson, *Beyond Natural Selection* (Cambridge, Mass.: MIT Press, 1991), 30-35; and Michael Macrone, *Eureka: What Archimedes Really Meant* (New York: HarperCollins, 1994), 240-42.

19. Donella Meadows, Dennis Meadows, and Jørgen Randers, *Beyond the Limits: Confronting Global Collapse, Envisioning a Sustainable Future* (Post Mills, Vt.: Chelsea Green Publishing Co., 1992). This book was a follow-up to the earlier path-breaking study *The Limits to Growth: A Report for the Club of Rome's Project on the Predicament of Mankind* by the same authors and William L. Behren, III (New York: Universe Books, 1972).

20. Catastrophe is the straw that breaks the camel's back. Catastrophe is the behavior of ecological systems unable to withstand too much

abuse, or growth and change that is too fast, and becomes subject to what is described in *Beyond the Limits* as overshoot and collapse. The catastrophic recognizes not only that change can be nonlinear and subject to the influence of positive and negative feedback that amplifies affects; change is also subject to discontinuities. That is, sudden and dramatic changes that environmentally and mathematically are described as catastrophes. These typically fall in the realm of chaotic dynamics. The dynamics of chaos is mathematically subject to the influence of both periodic and strange attractors. Attractors have gained much attention in the scholarly and popular investigations of chaos, its mathematics, and applications. What's most striking is that chaotic dynamics can characterize a variety of equations, including the logistic, which represents under different conditions, as in Figure 5-2, the model for stability. When using the same logistic equation as in Figure 5-2: $N_{n+1} = rN_n (1-N/K)+N$, to determine the next year's (n+1) population of a Present Quantity (N) increasing at an intrinsic rate (r) annually with a maximum population carrying capacity (K), strange things start to occur when "r" is greater then three. The attractor is now split. Instead of approaching a single variable, the population alternates each year between two different amounts. This is called an attractor with a period of two. As "r" increases past 3.45, the attractor becomes four different values, then eight, and so on. This rapid fluctuation of population reflects the dynamics of rapidly growing populations as they approach carrying capacity. Finally, when "r" is greater than about 3.57 yearly, results are seemingly totally chaotic and are, in fact, under the mathematical influence of a strange attractor. This is a model for ecological collapse.

21. William and Paul Paddock in *Population, Evolution, and Birth Control: A Collage of Controversial Readings,* ed. Garrett Hardin (San Francisco: W. H. Freeman and Co., 1964).

22. *State of the World: A Worldwatch Institute Report on the Progress Toward a Sustainable Society* (New York: W. W. Norton, 1993).

23. Jeremy Leggett, "The Importance of Considering the Worst-Case Analysis in Global Warming" (distributed by Greenpeace, undated), unbound.

CHAPTER SIX

1. For example, Leni Riefenstahl begins her film, *Triumph of the Will,* with written text on the screen describing the choreographed 1934 Nazi Party Nuremberg rally as the redemptive fulfillment of German history. Susan Sontag in "Fascinating Fascism," an insightful consideration of Leni

Riefenstahl, notes that the film "has no commentary beyond the opening message because it doesn't need one, for *Triumph of the Will* represents an already achieved and radical transformation of reality: history become theater." Susan Sontag, *Under the Sign of Saturn* (New York: Farrar, Straus & Giroux, 1980), 83.

2. Tony Judt, "The New Old Nationalism," *The New York Review of Books* (May 26, 1994), 44.

3. And on a more pathetic note, Bill Clinton takes the death of Richard Nixon as an occasion for prolonged national mourning and much hagiography, instead of considering the enduring mark Nixon made on U.S. politics and the presidency.

4. Joshua Meyrowitz, *No Sense of Place: The Impact of Electronic Media on Social Behavior* (New York: Oxford University Press, 1985).

5. Karen Horney, *Neurosis and Human Growth: The Struggle Toward Self-Realization* (New York: W. W. Norton, 1950).

6. Wilhelm Reich, *The Mass Psychology of Fascism* (New York: Farrar, Straus & Giroux, 1970).

7. Albert Camus, *The Plague*, trans. Stuart Gilbert (New York: A. A. Knopf, 1948), 278.

8. Speech by Khalid Abdul Muhammed, November 1993, Keane College, New Jersey, quoted in the Wiesenthal Center's *Response* (Spring 1994), 2.

Jews were a rather insignificant minority in the antebellum South, accounting for less than 1 percent of slave ownership. A few Jews owned plantations and a few were active in confederate politics. In 1830, of 59,000 slaveholders owning twenty or more slaves, only twenty-three were Jewish and only seven Jews were among the 11,000 slaveholders owning fifty or more slaves. Of the South's master class, 99.9 percent was non-Jewish. See David Brion Davis, "Letter to the Editor," *New York Review of Books* (March 2, 1995), 45; and his article, "The Slave Trade and the Jews," *New York Review of Books* (November 22, 1993).

9. Aimé Césaire, *Discourse on Colonialism*, trans. Joan Pinkham (New York: Monthly Review Press, 1992).

10. Jean-Paul Sartre, *Anti-Semite and Jew*, trans. George J. Becker (New York: Schocken Books, 1948), 26-28.

11. Giovanni Gentile, *Genesis and Structure of Society*, trans. H. S. Harris (Urbana, Ill.: University of Illinois Press, 1960), 135.

12. Adolf Hitler, *Mein Kampf* (Munich: 1933), 556-57.

13. Lucy S. Dawidowicz, *The War Against the Jews, 1933-1945* (New York: Bantam, 1989), 336-39. We should remember, in this context, Jewish resistance in Warsaw in 1943. The Jews of Warsaw in radio messages cried out, "Storm heaven and earth," warning the world of their coming anni-

hilation and begging for assistance. On April 19, 1943, SS troops entered the ghetto to round up Jews for transport to death camps. The Jewish underground, the ŻOB (Jewish Combat Organization), with small arms and homemade incendiary bombs, began to fight back and drove the Nazis from the ghetto. Despite overwhelming German forces using artillery and flame throwers to totally destroy the ghetto, resistance continued until May 10, until the last Jews were killed or packed into railroad cars; seventy-five resistance fighters escaped through the sewers.

In 1994, as the murderous attack on Gorazde proceeded, a press release from the government of Slobodan Milosevic, ruling Serbia and Montenegro, referred to the Bosnian government and its army only as "the Muslims," calling on the United Nations "to immediately abandon the irresponsible and dangerous policy of joining the war on the side of the Muslims and to struggle against the war and for an unconditional, immediate and lasting cessation of fighting by peace, not by war."

As I write in 1994, the United Nations, NATO, the United States, and Russia are all deeply engaged in Bosnia. To permit continued aggression in the name of ethnic cleansing should be both politically and morally intolerable.

As a nonviolent peace activist, I cannot call for bombing or for other Americans to take up arms. I can advocate intensified political and diplomatic efforts; active grassroots support for the peace movements in Serbia, Croatia, and Bosnia; humanitarian assistance; and support for pacifist efforts in the war zone. This advocacy is our first responsibility and one that calls for personal acts.

But I also believe I cannot support endlessly denying those being slaughtered the right to self-defense. Sending guns to Bosnia (or elsewhere) in response to a desperate call and the reality of murder is not a recipe for peace or saving lives, or a substitute for political or personal action. But, unlike in Warsaw fifty-one years ago, it is an action clearly within the power of NATO and the United States.

If *all* political and conciliatory means are indeed exhausted, and if aggression and murder continue, the arms embargo against the Bosnian government should be lifted and people given a chance to defend themselves from annihilation. I fear the consequences of that act; but the cries for help are all too clear.

14. Gama'a al-Islamiya and al-Jihad are two of the strongest Muslim groups in Imbaba. The Muslim Brotherhood is the pioneering Islamist group, with strong intellectual and political, as well as religious, influence in the Islamic world. Mary Anne Weaver, "The Novelist and the Sheikh," *The New Yorker* (January 30, 1995), 60-61.

15. Similar anti-feminist and anti-egalitarian themes appear in Nazi ideology. According to Nazi Gottfried Feder, "The insane dogma of equality led as surely to the emancipation of Jews as to the emancipation of women." Quoted in "Patron Saints" by Jean McNicol, *London Review of Books* (May 12, 1994), 7.

16. I write of the collective energy and personal power of social movements from experience. In 1976, when I first became involved with the Clamshell Alliance and the struggle against the Seabrook nuclear project in New Hampshire, standing to make a few remarks in the local library made me very nervous. Walking onto the nuclear plant site in April 1977 with 2,500 other Clams, and then spending thirteen days as a prisoner in a National Guard Armory, one of 1,414 arrested, changed my life. It opened the gate to friendship and struggle, to victories and disappointments, to a willingness to question myself and our movement. My passage was, in part, the result of facing moments of considerable personal fear.

CHAPTER SEVEN

1. For Alan Thein Durning and Adam Michnik's views, see Jean L. Cohen and Andrew Arato, *Civil Society and Political Theory* (Cambridge, Mass.: MIT Press, 1992); Adam Michnik, "Higher Evolution," in *Letter From Prison* (Berkeley: University of California Press, 1985).

2. Consensus, it is interesting to note, is also the decision making process used by the Mayan-Indian-based Zapatista liberation forces today in Mexico. See Alma Guillermoprieto, "The Indian Wars," *New York Review of Books* (March 2, 1995).

3. For a brief, classic, and cogent statement of libertarian anarchism, see Peter Kropotkin's 1910 contribution on anarchism to the 11th edition of *Encyclopedia Britannica*, excerpted in Clifton Fadiman, ed., *Treasury of the Encyclopedia Britannica* (New York: Viking, 1992), 472-77. Kropotkin begins:

> Anarchism...the name given to a principle or theory of life and conduct under which society is conceived without government—harmony in such a society being obtained, not by submission to law, or by obedience to any authority, but by free agreements concluded between the various groups, territorial and professional, freely constituted for the sake of production and consumption, as also for the satisfaction of the infinite variety of needs and aspirations of a civilized being.

For a discussion of corporatism, see P. J. Katenstein, *Corporatism and Change: Austria, Switzerland and the Politics of Industry* (Ithaca, N.Y.: Cornell University Press, 1985).

Market libertarianism is aggressively on display in *Reason* magazine, a good point of entry for examining these ideas, as well as in publications of the Cato Institute in Washington, D.C.

For associative democracy, excellent books are Paul Hirst, *Associative Democracy: New Forms of Economic and Social Governance* (Amherst: University of Massachusetts Press, 1994) and John Mathews, *Age of Democracy: The Politics of Post-Fordism* (Melbourne: Oxford University Press Australia, 1989).

For guild socialism, see G.D.H. Coles's classic 1920 work *Guild Socialism Restated* (New Brunswick, N.J.: Transaction Books, 1980). With an introduction by R. Vernon.

For libertarian municipalism, see the writings of Murray Bookchin, in particular *The Limits of the City* (Montreal: Black Rose Books, 1986).

4. Mathews, *Age of Democracy* and Hirst, *Associative Democracy.*

5. Hirst, *Associative Democracy*, 26.

6. Hirst, *Associative Democracy*, 73.

7. A broad range of writings, from reformist to revolutionary, discuss the political, economic, and social aspects of ecology. The following are of interest:

Rudolf Bahro, *Building the Green Movement* (Philadelphia: New Society Publishers, 1986). Bahro, a German Green, warns of co-optation: "If Ecotopia is merely Utopia in the sense of a cheap castle in the air, then we have no future at all" (p. 174).

Murray Bookchin, *The Ecology of Freedom: The Emergence and Dissolution of Hierarchy* (Palo Alto, Calif.: Cheshire Books, 1982). Bookchin's magnum opus on social ecology.

Murray Bookchin, *The Limits of the City* (Montreal: Black Rose Books, 1986). Views on libertarian municipalism and a marketless ecological order.

Lester R. Brown, Christopher Flavin, and Sandra Postel, *Saving the Planet: How to Shape an Environmentally Sustainable Global Economy* (New York: W. W. Norton, 1991). The Worldwatch view of what must be done for sustainable progress.

Jean Chesneaux, *Brave Modern World: The Prospects for Survival* (New York: Thames and Hudson, 1992). A critique of the crisis of industrial modernity and a call for change.

Barry Commoner, *Making Peace with the Planet* (New York: Pantheon, 1990). Commoner's call for structural change in industrial business-as-usual.

Daniel Faber, *Environment Under Fire: Imperialism and the Ecological Crisis in Central America* (New York: Monthly Review Press, 1993). Faber is an editor of *Capitalism Nature Socialism*, which tends to focus on capitalist ecological destruction—based on what James O'Connor calls "the second contradiction of capitalism," the imperative for environmental destruction—and to underplay noncapitalist industrial dynamics.

Edward Goldsmith, *The Way: An Ecological World-View* (Boston: Shambala, 1993). Goldsmith begins to address specific political and economic aspects of an ecological worldview only in Chapter Fifty-six; nonetheless, a thoughtful vision.

Robert Goodland, ed., *Race to Save the Tropics: Ecology and Economics for a Sustainable Future* *(Washington, D.C.: Island Press, 1990). Tropical ecology by practitioners.*

Michael Jacobs, *The Green Economy: Environment, Sustainable Development, and the Politics of the Future* (London: Pluto Press, 1991). An economist's attempt at applied ecological economics.

Donella Meadows, Dennis Meadows, and Jørgen Randers, *Beyond the Limits: Confronting Global Collapse, Envisioning a Sustainable Future* (Post Mills, Vt.: Chelsea Green Publishing Co., 1992). World systems theory and the need for reform before it's too late.

Bruce Rich, *Mortgaging the Earth: The World Bank, Environmental Impoverishment, and Crisis of Development* (Boston: Beacon Press, 1994). The Bretton Woods Institutions and their inadequacies at their fiftieth anniversary.

Brian Tokar, *The Green Alternative: Creating an Ecological Future*, 2nd ed. (San Pedro, Calif.: R. & E. Miles, 1992). U.S. Green view from a veteran grassroots activist.

8. Bahro, *Building the Green Movement* , 171-72.

9. Bookchin, *The Ecology of Freedom*, 365.

10. Judy Elliott, "New Hampshire Recovery: An Inquiry into Recent Job Creation" (1994, RFD 8, Box 311, Concord, NH 03302).

11. Information on job loss from *The New York Times* (March 22, 1994).

12. Staughton Lynd proposes, "A Community Congress could be convened in every geographical region. Invitees would especially include entities trying to meet social needs on a self-help or non-profit basis." ("A Jobs Program for the '90s," *Social Policy* [Fall 1994], 22-35.) The aim would be to develop realistic plans for meeting real community needs, as Lynd begins to lay out for Youngstown, Ohio, addressing housing rehabilitation and construction, and daycare. Such conferences as an organizing and educational tool can demonstrate not only what has already been done, but what more can be reasonably accomplished.

13. My understanding of excess yielding a countervailing response is more Heraclitean than Marxian. That is, I explore these dialectical relationships not on the basis of inevitabilities, but as prospects and possibilities.

14. Wolfgang Sachs, ed., *The Development Dictionary: A Guide to Knowledge as Power* (Atlantic Highlands, N.J.: Zed Books, 1992). Among the works in this area that I have found useful are:

Vandana Shiva, "Resources" in *The Development Dictionary.*

Ashis Nandy, *Traditions, Tyranny and Utopias: Essays in the Politics of Awareness* (Delhi: Oxford University Press, 1987).

Ivan Illich, *Shadow Work* (Boston: M. Boyars, 1981).

Gustavo Esteva, "Development" in *The Development Dictionary.*

Carolyn Merchant, *Ecological Revolutions: Nature, Gender, and Science in New England* (Chapel Hill: University of North Carolina Press, 1989).

It is hard to draw any sharp line between the critique of industrial development, and Green and environmental thought. For example:

Clive Ponting, *A Green History of the World* (London: Sinclair-Stevenson, 1991).

"Whose Common Future," *The Ecologist: A Special Issue,* vol. 22, no. 4 (July-August 1992). A special issue on defending, reclaiming, and nurturing the global commons.

Elinor Ostrom, *Governing the Commons: The Evolution of Institutions for Collective Action* (New York: Cambridge University Press, 1990). An economist's view of principles that can inform sustainable lifeways.

15. Although Mondragon has received considerable attention, its significance as a means of addressing broad issues of social change beyond the Basque context is underappreciated. A number of books, dissertations, and articles deal with Mondragon before the 1990s, but little is available (and almost nothing in English) on more recent experience. The best source of current Mondragon co-op data, and general information on co-op plans and self-analysis, is found in the Mondragon co-op monthly glossy journal *T.U. Lankide* (T.U. means *Trabajo y Union*). See, for example, the issues: May 1993, "*Co-operativismo Una Fórmula de Adaptacion*"; July 1993, "*¿Cómo Nos Ven?*"; September 1993, "*IV Congreso*"; October 1993, "*El Futoro de las Co-operativas.*"

The Mondragon Cooperative Corporation Annual Report has useful information.

For a pre-1991 Mondragon bibliography, see William F. Whyte and Kathleen King Whyte, *Making Mondragon: The Growth and Dynamics of the Worker Cooperative Complex* (Ithaca, N.Y.: ILR Press, 1991) and my *We Build the Road As We Travel: Mondragon, A Cooperative Social System* (Philadelphia: New Society Publishers, 1991).

16. A translation of a 1993 paper, "The Effects of the Economic Crisis on the Mondragon Co-operative Corporation" by Baleren Bakaikoa of the University of the Basque Country in San Sebastian was made available at a summer 1993 International Conference on Co-operation at C. W. Post College on Long Island. Written from a Marxian perspective, this paper criticizes the current direction of co-op development as anti-democratic centralization and a weakening of co-op principles.

A more sympathetic perspective is presented in a spiral-bound July 1992 report by David Morris of the Institute for Local Self-Reliance, *The Mondragon Co-operative Corporation,* available on request (220 West King St., St. Paul, MN 55107; 602-228-1875). Morris reviews the Mondragon response to recession and globalization. He quotes Jesús Larrañaga, one of Mondragon's founders, that the co-op system in May 1992 "finds itself in a new competitive planetary scenario, where the validity of its socially oriented model will be tested."

A 1993 paper by Elizabeth Bowman and Bob Stone, "Worker Ownership on the Mondragon Model: Trap or Opportunity for Socialists?" to appear in *Beyond Communism and Capitalism: The Role of Markets in a New Socialism,* ed. Justin K. Schwartz (Atlantic Highlands, N.J.: Humanities Press) has a useful discussion of the broader applicability of the Mondragon model and interesting information, based on a 1992 visit, of co-op practices of hiring temporary waged workers.

Davydd J. Greenwood, *Industrial Democracy as Process: Participatory Action Research in the Fagor Co-operative Group of Mondragon* (Maastricht: Van Gorcum/Swedish Center For Working Life, 1991) has useful information, but not about the most recent developments.

17. Fagor, for example, in its Ulgor co-op (the name is an acronym of the first five cooperators) makes refrigerators and other white goods, and is in direct competition in the European market with transnationals, such as Siemens and Electrolux.

18. Bakaikoa, "The Effects of the Economic Crisis."

19. José Maria Mendizabal, *"Para Pensar El Futuro,"* *T.U. Lankide,* no. 373 (October 1993), 16-18.

20. See my *We Build the Road As We Travel* for a detailed discussion of *equilibrio.*

21. Information in English on Seikatsu is quite limited and most often found in brief, evocative articles. For example:

"Seikatsu: Live Autonomously, Build a Co-operative World," *Grassroots Economic Organizing Newsletter* (March-April 1994), 1-8; "Beyond the Consumer Society: Japan's Seikatsu's Club," *The Unesco Courier* (March 1992), 32-33; Barry Greer, "Greening The Red Sun," *Buzzworm* (January-February 1991), 20.

Kazumi Matsuoka of the University of Connecticut conducted research in Japan on Seikatsu in 1992. Some of her work was used in the *Grassroots Economic Organizing Newsletter*, which also included written answers to questions from Seikatsu members Kyoko Miyaji and Miho Takeuchi. Much of the Seikatsu material is in local newsletters that remain untranslated and generally unavailable in the United States. (Note that the 161 Seikatsu worker collectives is the same number—although they are different kinds of entities—as the 161 member co-ops of the Co-op Atlantic system.)

22. "Beyond the Consumer Society: Japan's Seikatsu's Club," *The Unesco Courier* (March 1992), 33.

23. It is worth noting that the most dynamic area of democratic cooperative activity in the United States is found in home health care co-ops, also predominantly female, following the model developed in the South Bronx by Cooperative Home Health Care and now used nationally by the Industrial Cooperative Association.

24. Information on Japanese consumer co-ops from Hiroshi Iwadare, "Consumer Co-operatives in the Spotlight," *Japan Quarterly* (October-December 1991), 429-35.

25. For information on the co-op movement as a whole in Atlantic Canada, see:

Moses Coady, *Masters of Their Own Destiny: The Story of the Antigonish Movement of Adult Education through Economic Cooperation* (Antigonish, N.S.: Formac Publishing Co., 1967).

Ida Delaney, *A Fieldworkers Account of the Antigonish Moment* (Hansport, N.S.: Lancelot Press, 1985).

Santo Dodaro and Leonard Pluta, "The Antigonish Moment as a Model of Regional Economic Development" in *Political Economy of Development in Atlantic Canada*, ed. M. A. Choudhuy (Sydney, N.S.: University College of Cape Breton Press, 1985).

26. The best available current writing on Co-op Atlantic, to my knowledge, is David Bedford and Sidney Pobihushchy, "Towards a People's Economy: The Co-op Atlantic Experience," *Interculture* (Summer 1993). *The Atlantic Co-Operator* is a useful local monthly available from Co-op Atlantic. Most information in the United States is partial, such as Terry Appleby, "Canadian Co-operatives: Economic Interdependence Breeds Economic Independence," *Co-op News* (November-December 1993), p. 1-4. Some analyses of the growth and mortality of co-ops in Atlantic Canada apply the statistical tools of population ecology to the cooperative sector. They have a few useful insights, but are of limited use. See, for example, Udo Staber, "Organizational Independence and Organizational Mortality in the Cooperative Sector: A Community Ecology

Perspective," *Human Relation* (November 1992), 1191-212. Staber notes that the weakness of the co-ops in Atlantic Canada is a reflection, in part, of not being a coherent community (p. 1209); this lack of community is precisely one of the problems that Co-op Atlantic is trying to overcome.

27. A rough United States parallel is community supported agriculture, where all members pay in installments a set annual fee to farmers (e.g., $300) to receive a weekly basket of fresh produce.

28. In contrast, Mondragon's Eroski retail co-op is worker-owned, with consumers playing an advisory role. In the United States, O & O Supermarkets in Philadelphia are an example of worker-owned and operated retail co-ops.

29. Adam Smith, *The Wealth of Nations*, ed. Edward Cannan (New York: Random House, Modern Library Edition, 1937), 490.

For a fascinating discussion of this question, see E. P. Thompson, *Customs in Common: Studies in Traditional English Popular Culture* (New York: The Free Press, 1993).

30. Quoted in Thompson, *Customs in Common,* 270.

CHAPTER EIGHT

1. See, of course, E. P. Thompson, *The Making of the English Working-Class* (New York: Vintage Books, 1966).

2. Garrett Hardin, "The Tragedy of the Commons" in *Population, Evolution, and Birth Control: A Collage of Controversial Essays* (San Francisco: W. H. Freeman and Co., 1964), 372.

3. Garrett Hardin, *Exploring New Ethics for Survival: The Voyage of the Spaceship Beagle* (Baltimore: Pelican Books, 1973), 172.

4. David Ellerman, formerly of the Industrial Cooperative Association and now of the World Bank, has written perceptively and compellingly on questions of property and rights. See, for example, his "Theory of Legal Structures: Worker Co-operatives," *Journal of Economic Issues* (September 1987), 861-91.

5. Elinor Ostrom, *Governing the Commons: The Evolution of Institution for Collective Action* (New York: Cambridge University Press, 1990), especially Chapter Three, 58-101. Appropriators are all those who use the commons; providers are those who help arrange for the commons' existence; producers are those who take steps to maintain the commons. Appropriators, providers, and producers may be the same people. For example, the appropriators in a fishing commons are all the fishers. Providers may include a foundation that supplies a computer used to coordinate the assignment of fishing areas and tally fish catches against

individual fishing quotas. Producers may maintain a common dock and fish-marketing facility.

6. From Ostrom, *Governing the Commons*, 31-32.

7. Fikret Berkes, "Fishermen and the Tragedy of the Commons," *Environmental Conservation*, 12 (1995), 199-206.

8. Frank Bryan and John McClaughry, *The Vermont Papers: Recreating Democracy on a Human Scale* (White River Junction, Vt.: Chelsea Green, 1992).

9. E. F. Schumacher, *Small is Beautiful: Economics As if People Mattered* (New York: Harper & Row, 1973).

10. This is the sense of E. P. Thompson when he wrote of the working class as not a category, but an expression of the reality of people's lives in particular situations.

11. Michael Albert and Robin Hahnel, *Looking Forward: Participatory Economics for the Twenty First Century* (Boston: South End Press, 1991) and Michael Albert, *The Political Economy of Participatory Economics* (Princeton, N.J.: Princeton University Press, 1991).

12. See, for example, the analysis by Alec Nove, *The Economics of Feasible Socialism* (London: G. Allen & Unwin, 1983).

13. See the *Review of Radical Political Economics* (Fall/Winter 1992) on the future of socialism led by Thomas Weisskopf's "Toward a Socialism for the Future, in the Wake of the Demise of the Socialism of the Past."

14. Pat Devine, *Democracy and Economic Planning: The Political Economy of a Self-Governing Society* (Boulder, Co.: Westview Press, 1988).

15. See, for example, Albert and Hahnel's response to their critics and to market socialism in "Why Participatory Planning?" in *Z Papers* (April-June 1994).

CHAPTER NINE

1. Marshall Goldman, "Needed: A Russian Economic Revolution," *Current History* (October 1992), 317.

2. For a broader discussion of local currencies, see Barbara Brandt, *Whole Life Economics* (Philadelphia: New Society Publishers, 1995), especially Chapter Sixteen. Information on Ithaca Hours from "Home Money Starter Kit" for $25 from Ithaca Money, Box 6578, Ithaca, NY 14851, 607-273-8025; also "How To Organize Your Own Neighborhood Exchange" for $2 from Anne Slipean, 21 Linwood St., Arlington, MA, 02174 and E. F. Schumacher Society, Box 76, RD3, Great Barrington, MA 01230, 413-528-1737.

3. In 1994, there were at least 486 LETS operating in Canada, the United States, Australia, and New Zealand. Background about LETS from Michael Liston, Landsman Community Savings, 375 John Johnson Ave., Courtenay BC VEN2T2 Canada, 604-338-0263.

4. Larry Holyoke and William Glasgall, "Crunch Time at Japan's Banks," *Business Week* (November 16, 1992), 56.

5. This idea was suggested to me by Terry Mollner of the Trusteeship Institute.

6. *Caja Laboral Popular, 1991 Annual Report* (printed on *Papel Ecologico*).

7. Now spun off as an independent co-op, LKS.

8. Jaroslav Vanek, *The General Theory of Labor-Managed Market Economies,* (Ithaca, N.Y.: Cornell University Press, 1970).

9. Conversation with David Ellerman.

10. Challenging the corporate charter of incorporation is perceptively considered by Richard Grossman and Frank Adams, *Taking Care of Business: Citizenship and the Charter of Incorporation* (Cambridge, Mass.: Charter, Inc., 1993), pamphlet.

11. Joe Bute, "Shenago Valley Foundry Saved" and Jacqueline Cromeans, "How Shenago Workers Got the Capital," *FIRR News* (Spring 1994).

12. Barbara Deming, *Revolution and Equilibrium* (New York: Grossman Publishers, 1971).

13. Present Value: PV = present value, FV = future value, N = number of years, I = interest. $PV = FV/(1+I)^N$. Example: $PV = \$5,000/(1.1)^{10} = \$1,930$ for wind machine; $PV = \$6,000/(1.1)^{10} = \$2,317$ for oil-fired generator.

14. Herman Daly and John Cobb, *For the Common Good: Redirecting the Economy Toward Community, the Environment, and a Sustainable Future* (Boston: Beacon Press, 1989; revised 1994).

15. Paul and Percival Goodman, *Communitas: Means of Livelihood and Ways of Life* (New York: Columbia University Press, 1990).

16. André Gorz, *Paths to Paradise: On the Liberation from Work* (Boston: South End Press, 1985).

17. Ibid., 63.

18. Robert Nisbet, *The Social Philosophers: Community and Conflict in Western Thought* (New York: Crowell, 1973), 53.

19. In Germany in 1920, in response to a right-wing takeover, the Kapp Putsch, supporters of democracy, launched a policy of noncooperation, a general strike, and a call to the military to abandon support for the uprising. The legal government's leaflet, "The Collapse of the Military Dictatorship," was handed to troops by strikers and dropped by plane

over Berlin. As support for the putsch waned, Kapp resigned and fled to Sweden. Troops mutinied against his successor and the putsch collapsed. See Gene Sharp, *The Politics of Nonviolent Action* (Boston: Porter Sargent, 1973).

20. Randall Forsberg, "Why Co-operative Security? Why Now?" *Peace and Democracy News* (Winter 1992/1993), 31.

21. New Hampshire is in a boundary dispute with Maine over ownership of the shipyard that is in Portsmouth harbor. Many shipyard workers are New Hampshire residents.

22. An interesting first step was taken in 1992 by the New London, Connecticut Listening Project of the War Resisters League to examine community attitudes about the future of the area's major employer, the General Dynamics nuclear submarine shipyard. The Listening Project concluded that there existed strong community support for economic revitalization and protection of this community and environment; concern about unemployment and the weakness of regional planning; general support for conversion of a military to a civilian economy; a general lack of information about economic conversion; a belief that economic decisions are not made by ordinary citizens; and a felt need for a shared vision and regional planning. The next stage of the program is organizing an educational agenda. Contact: Community Coalition for Economic Conversion, 1595 Norwich-New London Turnpike, Uncasville, CT 06382; call Joanne Sheehan, 203-887-6869.

23. Joel Bleifuss, "Have your PVC and Dioxin, too," *In These Times* (March 6, 1995), 12.

24. Information on PVC from Robert A. Frosch and Nicholas E. Gallopoulos, "Strategies for Manufacturing," *Scientific American* (September 1989), 144-52.

25. *Rocky Mountain Institute Newsletter* (Summer 1993), 5.

26. Amory Lovins early classic is *Soft Energy Paths: Toward a Durable Peace* (San Francisco: Friends of the Earth International, 1977). See also Amory Lovins *et al.*, *Least-Cost Energy: Solving the CO_2 Problem* (Snowmass, Co.: Rocky Mountain Institute, 1989).

27. Karl Marx and Friedrich Engels, *Collected Works*, vol. 38 (Lawrence and Wishart, 1982), 99. Quoted in Joe Weston, ed., *Red and Green* (London: Pluto Press, 1981).

CHAPTER TEN

1. The anti-nuclear testing movement would include, in the 1980s and early 1990s, a panoply of citizens' groups including: the religious

peacemakers of the Nevada Desert Experience; the Nuclear Weapons Freeze Campaign; the Coalition for a Comprehensive Test Ban; the Downwinders; Atomic Veterans; Nevada Citizens Alert; Greenpeace; and the American Peace Test (APT), a mass nonviolent action organization, which helped inspire the successful Soviet "Nevada Movement" that played a major role in ending Soviet testing in Kazakhstan. While the APT specialized in mass civil disobedience actions at the Nevada test site, it was just one of many groups engaged in "back country" actions. Scores of courageous people over the years, either alone or in small groups, walked into the Nevada desert or sailed into Pacific nuclear test sites and, by approaching ground zero, sought to stop—and sometimes did stop—nuclear tests.

INDEX

A

Abbey, Edward, 23

Accounting, conventional vs. ecological, 205-7

Adams, Frank, 57, 261

African National Congress, 138

Afrikaner Resistance Movement, 128

Age of Democracy: The Politics of Post-Fordism (Mathews), 141

Agency for International Development, 245

Agora, 77, 171

Albert, Michael, 185-86

Amphibians, decline of, 21

Anarchism, 140, 253

Anthropocentrism, 28

Anticipos, 154

Antigonish Movement, 158

Anti-nuclear movement, 146n, 231, 253, 262-63

Anti-Semite and Jew (Sartre), 128

Anti-Semites, 75n, 116, 128

Anti-Semitism, 120, 127, 128, 130

Appleby, Terry, 258

Arato, Andrew, 253

Aristotelian, 146

Association. *See* Ecological democracy

Associative Democracy: New Forms of Economic and Social Governance (Hirst), 141

Associative democracy. *See* Ecological democracy

Atlantic People Housing Ltd., 158

Authoritarianism, 113-36; and African Americans, 126-27; and empowerment, 133-35; and fascism, 120, 122, 132; and fundamentalism, 115, 116, 122, 131; and mass murder, 127-28; and the nation state, 129-30; and nationalism, 114-19; as order, 119-21; as psychological, 124n; redemptive, 114, 119, 122, 124-25; rise of, 11, 24, 71; and technique, 122-24, 127n; and theocracy, 130-32; and totalitarianism, 115, 119, 121-22; weakness of, 135-36. *See also* Nazis

ABOUT SOUTH END PRESS

South End Press is a nonprofit, collectively run book publisher with over 180 titles in print. Since our founding in 1977, we have tried to meet the needs of readers who are exploring, or are already committed to, the politics of radical social change.

Our goal is to publish books that encourage critical thinking and constructive action on the key political, cultural, social, economic, and ecological issues shaping life in the United States and in the world. In this way, we hope to give expression to a wide diversity of democratic social movements and to provide an alternative to the products of corporate publishing.

Through the Institute for Social and Cultural Change, South End Press works with other political media projects—Z Magazine; Speak Out!, a speakers bureau; and the Publishers Support Project—to expand access to information and critical analysis. If you would like a free catalog of South End Press books or information about our membership program, which offers two free books and a 40 percent discount on all titles, please write to us at: South End Press, 116 Saint Botolph Street, Boston, MA 02115.

OTHER TITLES OF INTEREST

Confronting Environmental Racism
By Robert D. Bullard, ed.

The New Resource Wars
By Al Gedicks

Defending the Earth
A Dialogue between Murray Bookchin and Dave Foreman
By Steve Chase, ed.

ABOUT THE AUTHOR

Roy Morrison is a longtime anti-nuclear and peace activist, and the author of *We Build the Road as We Travel: Mondragon, A Cooperative Social System*. He works as an energy consultant and is policy director of Energy America Education Fund, a safe energy political education group. He gives lectures and holds workshops on cooperatives and community economics, energy conservation, and the transition to an ecological democracy. He lives in Warner, New Hampshire with Jan Schaffer and their son Sam, age 2. Roy Morrison can be reached at PO Box 114, Warner, NH 03278.